THE GREEN TUNNEL

A Hiker's Appalachian Trail Diary

PATRICK BREDLAU

"The Green Tunnel: A Hiker's Appalachian Trail Diary," by Patrick Bredlau. ISBN 978-1-62137-799-3 (softcover); ISBN 978-1-62137-800-6 (eBook).

Published 2015 by Virtualbookworm.com Publishing Inc., P.O. Box 9949, College Station, TX 77842, US.

Manufactured in the United States of America.

TABLE OF CONTENTS

INTRODUCTION

The Appalachian Mountains meander through a substantial portion of the eastern United States, and extend from central Alabama in the south to New Brunswick, Canada, in the north. Benton MacKaye, a noted conservationist and outdoor enthusiast, promoted the idea of establishing the Appalachian Trail as a wilderness refuge that would offer an escape from city life and a retreat for World War I veterans. His proposed trail system called for an interconnected series of work, study, and farm camps to be situated throughout the Appalachian Mountains.

By 1922, the first miles of the new trail had already been completed in Bear Mountain State Park, overlooking New York City. With the help of countless volunteers and the Civilian Conservation Corps, the entire trail system was finally completed on August 14, 1937. The newly-created Appalachian Trail now ran all the way from Mt. Oglethorpe, Georgia, to Baxter Peak on Mt. Katahdin, Maine. Thirty years later, when the National Trails System Act was signed in October 1968, the Appalachian Trail officially received status as a national scenic trail.

In 1958, due to land development near Mt. Oglethorpe, the southern end of the Appalachian Trail was relocated to Springer Mountain, Georgia. Trail rerouting is an ongoing process. Every year changes are made to reduce the effects of erosion, provide greater access to the trail, and improve the quality of the wilderness experience. By 2014, the length of the trail had increased from 2,044 miles to 2,185 miles.

During my thru-hike, I routinely encountered trail detours caused by hurricane damage, pipeline construction, washed-out bridges, floods, and erosion. Even though the Appalachian Trail was never intended to be the most efficient route between two points, it does generally follow a north-south course.

The goal of the Appalachian Trail Conservancy (ATC) is to give the backpacker the best wilderness experience possible. By design, the Appalachian Trail avoids towns and cities and takes a circuitous route over and around the mountains, frequently changing direction to utilize federal and state lands and stay clear of private land.

All these factors work together to continually lengthen and alter the course of the trail. Today's Appalachian Trail meanders like a river through fourteen states. The chain of mountains in the entire range, measured north to south, is only 1,500 miles long. When traveling by road, the distance between Springer Mountain and Mt. Katahdin is 1,434 miles. By air, the distance is only 1,118 miles. And since the Appalachian Trail actually begins and ends on top of mountains, thru-hikers must hike an additional fourteen miles of rugged approach and exit trails in order to summit and descend both Springer Mountain and Mt. Katahdin.

Some paths chosen for the Appalachian Trail make sense to the designers, but they often confound me. This usually occurs when the trail follows a circuitous path through large expanses of undeveloped land, even though a shorter route is available. Sometimes, the path feels expressly designed to create a more strenuous trail experience. Hikers refer to sections such as these as pointless ups and downs, or PUDs.

The Appalachian Trail is the longest continuously marked trail in the world. Approximately 165,000 two-by-six inch white strips, called white blazes, are painted on rocks and trees. White blazed trails were developed to give the hiker a heightened sense of wilderness, even when civilization is close by. According to the Appalachian Mountain Club, on average, the A.T. crosses a road every four miles. Roads sometimes intersect the trail more often, and other times are spaced further apart. Occasionally the Trail skirts, or enters, towns and villages.

2000 MILERS

According to the ATC, an estimated two to three million people hike portions of the Appalachian Trail every year, but few attempt to hike the entire trail. Fewer still try to complete the A.T. in less than a year. Finishing the entire Appalachian Trail within twelve months is an enormous achievement, and is referred to as a thru-hike. In addition to the incredible length of the trail, the elevation changes required to scale the numerous mountain peaks have been compared by some to climbing Mount Everest sixteen times. A thru-hiker must contend with severe weather and difficult trail conditions while covering as many miles a day as possible and finding places to resupply food and water along the way. All these factors add extra miles to the journey, as much as three to five hundred unofficial miles.

A distinction is made between thru-hiking and section hiking. Section hikers cover large distances in a year, and may or may not hike every section of the Appalachian Trail over time. When a section hiker or thru-hiker successfully completes the entire Appalachian Trail, they qualify to become a "2000 Miler." The term was coined in the late 1970s to recognize the emergence of this particular type of long-distance hiker.

According to the ATC, more than 14,000 hikers have received the 2000 Miler award. For the last three years, approximately twenty-six percent of all hikers attempting to complete the entire Trail have applied for the 2000 Miler award. As of December 31, 2014, twenty-six percent, or 756 of the 2,864 attempted thru-hikers that year, submitted paperwork for the 2000 Miler award. I have, however, met successful thru-hikers who are not listed as 2000 Milers. One in particular chose not to fill out the paperwork because he was a fugitive. I didn't know this at the time, and only later became aware of his true identity when he was captured in the spring of 2015. Others are omitted because they are either unaware of the process, or are unwilling to put the effort into mailing a completed application back to the ATC.

Twenty-five percent of all 2000 Milers are women, and more than half of all successful thru-hikers are in their twenties. Five-year-old Christian "Buddy Backpacker" Thomas became the youngest 2000 Miler in 2014. In 2004, Lee "Easy One" Barry became the oldest successful thru-hiker at age eighty-one. Being able-bodied is not a requirement. People with disabilities hike the Trail and receive the 2000 Miler award. International hikers, visiting the States with six-month visas, often hike long sections of the Trail; some even become 2000 Milers.

TRAIL MAGIC

I learned about trail angels and trail magic while preparing for my thru-hike. So when I encountered trail magic for the first time, I was excited and thankful, but not surprised. What did surprise me, though, was its all-pervasiveness along the trail. At first I didn't understand the important role that trail magic played in the success of long-distance hiking. People who offer trail magic are called trail angels, and they become welcomed allies of every thru-hiker.

I don't know when or where the term originated, but it's an apt description. My wife compares trail angels to people who love to feed the birds. Trail angels offer countless acts of charity, and their generosity goes beyond anything I have ever experienced or witnessed in my life. They provide trail magic all along the trail, and frequently, in the most surprising places.

Trail magic usually appears in the form of food, water, housing, transportation, slackpacking shuttle service, information, and first aid. It always boosts a hiker's spirit and restores their faith in mankind. Trail angels sometimes go to great lengths in terms of time, effort, and money in order to provide large amounts of trail magic.

Trail magic is unpredictable. It may appear several times a day, then vanish for days and weeks at a time. I grew to approach road crossings with anticipation, like a child on Christmas Eve, dreaming of the tantalizing possibility of trail magic. Early in the hike, trail magic usually appeared in the form of food. As I moved north, trail magic morphed into caches of clean drinking water, thoughtfully placed in the long, dry stretches on the trail. Further north, trail magic showed up as free transportation. In Pennsylvania, one particular trail angel provided vital spiritual and moral support when I had hit bottom and was ready to give up hope.

FOREWORD

This Appalachian Trail thru-hike account is based on the daily journals I maintained during nine months of preparation and training in Illinois, and six months of northbound A. T. hiking.

I hiked northbound from Springer Mountain, Georgia, and covered fourteen states: Georgia, North Carolina, Tennessee, Virginia, West Virginia, Maryland, Pennsylvania, New Jersey, New York, Connecticut, Massachusetts, Vermont, New Hampshire, and Maine. Originally, I had hoped to complete the hike by September 5, 2014, but injuries forced me off the Trail for three weeks of recovery. Once healed, I headed back to the point where I had left the trail and continued hiking for more than two months. I summited Mt. Katahdin on September 29, 2014.

In the beginning, I used a trail plan to project daily hiking distances, and to pinpoint every stop and supply location. But the realities of the Trail, the weather, and physical conditions soon forced me to abandon this plan. I started using it instead as a rough guide to calculate a completion date that could assure summiting Mt. Katahdin while it was still accessible. Mt. Katahdin is located within Baxter State Park in Maine. The park officially closes every year on October 15th. Park rangers, however, constantly monitor Mt. Katahdin's weather and climbing conditions. When necessary, they close off the mountain to hikers, regardless of the date or time of year. Every northbound thru-hiker knows this by heart, and is driven by the call to summit Mt. Katahdin as soon as possible.

PREPARATION

The last time I backpacked was in 1996. It was a three-generation Father's Day trip with my 68-year-old father and 13-year-old son. We hiked for three days to the bottom of the Grand Canyon. Even though the climb out of the Canyon was rigorous, the experience left me dreaming of more backpacking adventure. Time passed. Over the next eighteen years, I jogged, exercised, occasionally camped, but never backpacked.

It wasn't until retiring in May 2013 that I started looking into repeating, or expanding on, the Grand Canyon backpacking trip. So, at age 59, after 38 years of working in a high travel, sedentary job as a federal bank examiner, I finally set my sights on hiking the Appalachian Trail. The A.T. had always interested me, even as a child. Here was my chance to hike it. I never thought about hiking the entire Trail. It was going to be a moderately difficult backpacking adventure.

The first thing I had to do was assess my physical condition. That spring, I hiked for a week in May near Boulder, Colorado. Out of shape and slightly overweight, I still hiked better than expected. During this trip I purchased my first new hiking gear, a set of Black Diamond trekking poles. I had never used trekking poles, so it took time to learn how to hike with them properly. When I returned home from Colorado, I began researching backpacking equipment and reading books about the Appalachian Trail.

The idea of completing the entire trail took hold while trying to decide which section of the Appalachian Trail to hike. I was retired now. Why not just go for it? During the summer months of 2013, I put together the first of what would be many trail plans using the newest edition of The A.T. Guide: a handbook for hiking the Appalachian Trail, written by David "Awol" Miller; and the Appalachian Trail Thru-Hikers Companion, published by the Appalachian Long Distance Hikers Association (ALDHA), also known as The Guide. With these guidebooks, I calculated how far I needed to hike each day and where and how to find food and water. My plan seemed reasonable. It would take 171 days to hike an average of 12.75 miles per day. The plan included "zero days" (trail lingo for resting days) and "nearo days" (more trail lingo for low mileage days). I finally settled on a start date of March 18, 2014, my 59th birthday.

By adding 171 days to this date, I discovered the completion date would be September 5, 2014. My wedding anniversary is September 8th. My wife and I had never been to Maine or, for that matter, the Northeast coast. We could celebrate my hiking victory, and then leisurely tour this part of the country together. My wife was looking forward to seeing the New England fall colors.

I intended to use my old backpacking and camping equipment, which was still in pretty good shape. Back when I purchased the gear, I couldn't afford ultra-light equipment, so I bought the best in my price range. It seemed reasonable at the time since I wasn't hiking very far, or for very long, and someone was usually close enough to help in an emergency.

But now, as I read about the latest advancements in ultralight backpacking gear, my old equipment looked heavy, obsolete, and inadequate for an Appalachian Trail thru-hike. New equipment however, would cost more than the few hundred dollars set aside in my initial budget. Fortunately, my financial situation is more secure now than when I was a younger man.

With my wife's blessing, I started spending an incredible amount of time talking with staff members at REI, my favorite outdoor recreation store. Several of them had hiked the Appalachian Trail and gave me good equipment advice. I visited Moosejaw, another sporting goods retailer, and spoke with their experienced staff. They steered me in the right direction, especially regarding Internet shopping. In the end, I spent nearly $1,700 on new equipment at REI, Moosejaw, and other specialty outfitters on the Internet. Some of the gear is amazingly ultralight.

The most expensive items were the Big Agnes Fly Creek UL2, an ultralight two-man tent with a ground footprint, and the Sierra Design Zissou twelve-degree sleeping bag. Instead of choosing a lighter weight one-man tent, I opted for a heavier two-man tent with extra living space, since it would be my home for nearly six months. Would I regret this decision? Time would tell. I returned brand new backpacks and boots regularly because of poor fit. Now, all my equipment was new, except for a summer sleeping bag.

It took about a year to purchase everything, mostly because of the time required to try out, return, and replace much of the gear. I began to wonder if I was fooling myself about pack weight. Could I really fit all the necessary food, water, fuel, and equipment in a 28-pound pack? Twenty years ago, long distance hikers were lucky to reduce their pack weight down to 45 pounds.

By late September 2013, I was hiking several days a week in the Cook County Forest Preserves, carrying a range of 25 to 50 pounds in my backpack. By the end of the month, I had hiked 32 miles and my little left toe was in pain. Despite the pain in my toe, hiking wasn't too difficult, so I began adding stair climbing to my training routine.

My favorite place to practice is the Swallow Cliff Stair Climb in Palos Hills, Illinois. Carved into the side of a steep hill and originally built as a ski jump and toboggan run, the stairway is comprised of 125 irregularly spaced, steep flagstone steps. Walking up and down the stair climb is murder! The change in elevation is only ninety feet, but you feel it in every step. The first day I carried a 38-pound pack and completed ten laps in an hour. Afterwards, I couldn't walk for three days, and was sore for a week. On my second attempt, a week later, I carried a five-pound pack and was able to complete fifteen laps. I was tired, but not too sore.

During training, nearly everyone asked the same four questions: "What about bears? Aren't you going to carry a gun, bear repellent, or big knife? Won't you be lonely?" And, "Why are you doing this?"

First, let's talk about bears. I discovered a list of bear attacks on the all-knowing website, Wikipedia. More people are killed by bears in major cities than on the Appalachian Trail. Those mangled city dwellers were attacked while doing things they shouldn't, like provoking bears in zoos or in captivity. I did find one instance of a bear attack near the Appalachian Trail at a campground in the Great Smoky Mountains National Park. Out west in the Rocky Mountains, people do get killed by bears, but it's still on a small scale.

My personal experience with bears has left me with this attitude: "Leave them alone, and they'll leave you alone." Black bears are small and prefer stealing your food, rather than fighting for it. You can drive them off by shouting. Besides, bears have a much easier time mooching food from roadside tourists. Like every careful backpacker, I planned to store my food inside a stuff bag lined with a plastic garbage bag. It would then be thrown over a tree limb or bear line with a rope while camping. I didn't plan on losing sleep over bears.

I decided not to carry a gun, bear repellent, or large knife. They're impractical, heavy, and illegal. Discharging a firearm could result in a lot of unwelcome trouble from law enforcement. Gun laws in the fourteen states and two national parks along the Appalachian Trail vary widely with differing requirements regarding firearm possession. I planned to bring a small pocket knife and use it for cutting and opening packages.

As for loneliness, thousands of hikers populate the Appalachian Trail during the spring, summer, and fall seasons. Most backpackers tend to congregate in the same places where shelter and water are located. I looked forward to the camaraderie of the trail and possibly forming new friendships, but realized there might be times when solitude would be preferable over company.

And the last question, "Why am I doing this?" I don't really know...yet. I've thought about it, but so far haven't found an answer. I hope to discover new insight about the deeper meaning of life, or my own purpose, but won't be surprised if, after hiking 2,185 miles, I am still no closer to a better understanding than when I started the journey. Stay tuned.

TRAINING LOG

OCTOBER 17, 2013

151 days before the hike. Today I completed one hundred miles of training. Last week, I hiked eight miles a day in less than three hours, on hilly terrain. This pace is much faster than I expect to hike in the Appalachian Mountains. I carried a 28-pound backpack, my target maximum pack weight. My little left toe still hurts. I may purchase a pair of expensive orthotic shoe inserts to help solve the problem.

While reading a forum on the Trailjournals.com website, I came across a discussion about Achilles tendon pain. The writer said that it can be caused by taking too long of a stride while walking. As an experiment, I shortened my stride, and most of the tendon pain diminished. The shorter stride doesn't slow me down, and seems to be more comfortable.

I'm still working on sock combinations in hopes of curing my toe pain. Liner socks prevent most blisters, but make my feet hot and sweaty. I'm going to try wool socks. So far, October is cold and rainy. As a result I'm testing the rain gear and cold weather clothing. The Frogg Togg rain gear is working out, and I don't get overheated in the 45-degree rainy weather. Clothing choice is still a challenge. A short-sleeved shirt and short pants work fine with rain gear, even in the low forties, but as soon as I stop hiking, I get chilled. When it comes to pack weight, clothing is heavy, sometimes too much. What to bring, get rid of, or switch?

As winter approaches, I'll continue to experiment with clothing combinations. I might replace the Dromedary hydration bag with a Platypus. The bag's drinking hose connection protrudes into my backpack, and it kinks and leaks if I'm not careful. Once while hiking, the hydration bag leaked an entire quart of water inside the pack. Everything was soaked. Worse, without any drinking water, I was parched by the end of the hike.

OCTOBER 18, 2013

Today was interesting, my first real day of cold weather training. I began hiking in the dark, using a new Black Diamond rechargeable headlamp, which works great. The temperature was about 29 degrees with a 24-degree wind chill factor. Hiking in cold weather clothes and carrying a 32-pound pack on fairly level ground soon had me overheated. I removed my gloves and peeled down to an outer shirt and tee shirt.

After an hour of hiking, it started to rain and snow, and the rain gear overheated me even more. I put on liner gloves and opted for a ball cap, because the fleece stocking cap was too warm. I need to find a middle ground on hats. Maybe I'm overestimating cold weather clothing needs.

After an hour of cold weather hiking, the hydration water bag tube was filled with ice slush. Freezing water in hydration bag tubes can be a problem. A tip posted on the Trail Journals hiker forum suggested blowing water back into the tube of the hydration bag after each drink. This worked just fine.

OCTOBER 22, 2013

I started an online hiking journal posted on Trailjournals.com today and began preparing menus. I've decided to go with an alcohol stove instead of a butane or propane canister stove. Many canister stoves weigh less than an alcohol stove, but their eight-ounce fuel canister weighs five ounces by itself, and thirteen ounces when full. Also, it's hard to use up all the fuel and you can't tell how much is left in the canister. Alcohol stoves are harder to use, potentially more dangerous, and slower to heat, but weigh less and are inexpensive to operate, with fewer failure points. Alcohol can also be used for first aid, as well as a campfire starter. Multitasking is critical when selecting hiking equipment.

While testing the alcohol stove in cold weather, the time it took to boil water was impacted by increased wind direction and low temperatures. Alcohol stoves normally take three or four times longer to boil water than canister stoves. This doesn't bother me, because I only plan to cook at the end of the day's hike. Recently I learned that a bottle of Heet can also be used as fuel for an alcohol stove. It's supposed to be cheaper, faster, and easier to ignite than alcohol, so I've decided to carry Heet.

I've started tracking the calories, weights, and susceptibility to hot and cold temperatures of various store-bought food items. I've decided to buy food along the trail instead of relying on mailed food drops. Food drop deliveries force you to stop at specific post office locations at set times. I want the freedom to change trail plans at will. Too often, I've heard about hikers waiting around for post offices to open, in order to pick up their packages.

NOVEMBER 20, 2013

119 days to go. I just read about Jennifer Pharr Davis. In 2011, she set a speed record for hiking the Appalachian Trail in 46 days, eleven hours, and twenty minutes. She averaged 47 miles per day and was supported along the way by her husband. Davis may not have carried a pack, but I appreciate the physical demands of her accomplishment. I was a track and field athlete at Indiana University, a Big Ten school. Even in my prime, I could never imagine hiking or running 47 miles in a day, let alone 47 consecutive days on rough terrain. Jennifer Pharr Davis has written several books and is a proven endurance champion on other long-distance trails. And only 28 years old when she set this record, more than half my age, the same age as my youngest child!

My feet and legs hurt most mornings, and this is only prehike training. Here, I am still able to eat well, sleep in a bed, and limit my exposure to rough weather within training hours. I hike on hilly terrain approximately eight hours a day, carrying a pack that weighs between 30 and 50 pounds. In October, I completed 79 training miles. In November, I'm up to 78 miles so far. My training pack is heavier than the one I plan to hike with on the Appalachian Trail. This is an adjustment for the minimal elevation changes found here in Illinois. During this winter season, I expect to push the limits of my equipment, clothing, and stamina before heading out on the A.T. in March.

I went to see a podiatrist for advice about the pain in my left little toe and Achilles tendon. He said the problems were caused by boots that were too tight. I switched to New Balance 1569, a wider and stiffer pair of new boots. He also fitted me for custom orthotic inserts.

I continue to practice outdoor cooking by using my alcohol stove to prepare Ramen noodles and Knorr packaged meals. The stove takes longer to cook in cold weather and will probably take even longer on the trail, where the water will be ice cold.

MID-DECEMBER TO MID-JANUARY

Training has been limited by bad weather, equipment problems, and injuries. In December, I was able to get in 60 training miles and several days of stair climbing. The snow isn't melting and is piling up. The forest preserve trails are turning to ice because of the high number of people using them. As a result, I've been walking on an indoor track lately, which makes me the center of attention. Everyone keeps asking me what the heck I am doing. Why am I carrying a backpack, and how much does it weigh? I meet a lot of nice people, but they think I'm a bit odd. The weather forecast is predicting extremely cold temperatures next week, a polar vortex. Looks like another week of zero outdoor training.

I am trying to find another option for replacing the hydration bag system. The bag is hard to fill in streams. Plus, I have to take off my pack, pull out the hydration bag, and physically examine it in order to find out how much water is left. The Sawyer Mini water filter system bags are also difficult to refill.

While shopping at the after-Christmas REI garage sale, I bought a Granite Gear Ultralight Crown V.C. 60 Liter backpack for only $47. I've already managed to hike with it on the ice trails. I love the pack. This will be my trail pack instead of the Deuter pack purchased in the fall. Although the Deuter is easier to load and carries more weight, the Granite Gear pack is much lighter. The weight savings are achieved at the expense of a support frame, but I still prefer the lighter weight. I'll just have to learn how to properly load the Granite Gear pack.

MID-JANUARY 2014

The New Balance boots are tough to break in and difficult to size. Cold weather is compounding the breaking in process and keeping the boots stiff. I've exchanged the boots twice already because they run small in size. Right now, I'm wearing a full size longer and wider than my normal shoe size. More toes continue to become injured because of the sizing problem and cold weather. I went to see my regular doctor today and he diagnosed the problem as cellulitis, a serious bacterial infection. He is treating me with penicillin. Although the doctor says I should be able to start my hike in March, I need to stop training for the next ten days. If there's such a thing as a good time to be injured with a serious infection, I guess now is the time. It hasn't stopped snowing since late December, and the temperatures remain frigid. Training has been limited to the Swallow Cliff stairs and the indoor walking track. Getting injured so close to my departure date is frustrating, but I'll use the next ten days to finish the planning details and research more food options.

JANUARY 20, 2014

Only 56 days before the hike. I'm writing this journal entry on my cell phone in an attempt to improve texting skills. January 3rd was the last time I accomplished any real training. The cellulitis is almost healed, and the doctor thinks I should be able to train again. It's surprising how well I have stayed in shape during this illness. The severe weather here in Chicago continues to make outdoor training difficult. All my gear is purchased except for a camera cell phone. I was going to buy a digital camera, but realized it is more cost effective to upgrade my cell phone. Using my cell phone to write and post journal entries is proving difficult, so I've decided to try talking into the phone instead of typing. This method is not perfect either. Too often, the words are misspelled, and the phrases and sentences that appear don't resemble anything I had in mind. As a result, my journal entries are confusing and poorly written. I'll do my best to edit the mistakes when I upload the entries to my trail journal.

More people have asked to hike with me for short periods on the trail. My son and I have worked out the dates, along with a longtime friend. I've decided my trail name will be Road Warrior. That's what I used to call myself after travelling 38 years for a living.

FEBRUARY 3, 2014

Forty-two days left. The cellulitis is gone and my feet are fine, except for a sore Achilles tendon. Not being active for so long has weakened me to some degree, but not seriously. It's time to get back to training. January's injuries and cold weather brought the monthly training figures down to just a few days of stair climbing and no more than 35 hiking miles. Most of the training takes place at a health club now, because the snow is too deep, and the temperatures too cold. A few days ago, I walked 11 miles in less than three hours on an indoor track. Today I finished seven miles in two hours. Both times, I carried a 31-pound backpack without difficulty. It may only be a level track, but it's all I have to work with at the moment.

Equipment is nearly complete, just tweaking little things like first aid and repair kits, clothing, etc. I'm still shopping for a cell phone. Without consumables like food, water, fuel, and camp shoes, the winter pack weight is nearly eighteen pounds. I still can't decide whether or not to bring camp shoes. The Granite Gear 60L Crown Vapor Current continues to impress me. I tested a pair of Vasque Breeze 2.0 boots, and returned them because the toe box was tight. After a long search, I finally purchased a pair of Merrell boots in my size and width, and plan to wear them on the Trail. The Frogg Togg rain suit is already in rags. The pant cuffs are shredded and the jacket ripped. Still, they're cheap, disposable clothing, so I will buy another set. Frogg Togg: five stars for weight; one star for durability.

FEBRUARY 16, 2014

Health is good, with cellulitis a thing of the past. Training is going well. In the last two weeks, I completed several ten- and fifteen-mile training days on the indoor track, carrying a 35-

pound pack. I'm in maintenance mode now, so I'll only hike a few daily miles. Yesterday I purchased a small hip belt for my pack. Even though a medium hip belt fits fine right now, I'll lose weight on the trail. I've rigged up the pack with the smaller belt and expect to shrink into it over time. I finally purchased a new phone, a Samsung Galaxy 4, and plan to use it as a camera and for posting journal entries. It will take a while to learn how to use it properly.

FEBRUARY 17, 2014

Another polar vortex! Training is called off today. I hope the weather warms up by mid-March when I start hiking in Georgia.

My base winter pack weight is sixteen pounds, nine ounces. With three days' worth of added consumables, the pack will weigh 25 pounds. I could cut more weight by removing items like toothpaste, but prefer keeping it. Besides, the tube will shrink over time. I am packing a few luxuries: a two-man tent; twelve and a half ounce camp shoes; a pillow; toilet paper; deodorant; a well-stocked emergency first aid kit; and an Appalachian Trail Passport. I'm still struggling with the decision to bring camp shoes.

I like my inflatable pillow; it's a Cocoon and weighs three and a half ounces. It should be more comfortable than sleeping on a wadded bundle of worn, sweaty clothes, and it will smell better, too. I'm not sure how much toilet paper to bring, so I'll start off with a whole roll of double-ply tissue. TP weighs more than I thought. I could shave off more pack weight by leaving the deodorant behind, but at the expense of hygiene. Summer pack weight is expected to be fifteen pounds. Sunscreen and bug spray will be purchased as needed.

All of these estimated weights are based on dry, clean equipment. Water and dirt will add a minimum of one to two extra pounds over the course of the hike. To save weight, I'm carrying the minimum amount of warm clothing, and anticipate being cold at times. I'm bringing one pair of pants, and letting the rain pants double as a second pair. If I find that I don't have enough warm clothes, I'll buy some along the Trail.

My wife thinks I should change my trail name to "Ready to go!" I keep saying this over and over again. I am so ready to go, and these last few days just seem to drag. I'm already planning to switch out my winter gear for summer gear in mid-May, just north of Damascus, when my son will hike with me for a week.

After reading some of the current hikers' journal entries, I'm happy with my decision to start hiking in mid-March. February weather on the Appalachian Trail is rough, and a surprising number of hikers have already called it quits within the first fifty miles, many with injuries. I wish them all the best, and hope they can try again. I'm starting to realize this adventure will be more difficult than I thought, regardless of my advance preparation. Expect to meet the unexpected at every step.

I recently talked to a thru-hiker who finished the A.T. a few years ago. He said the hike was going well until he was nearly at the end, next to Baxter State Park in Maine. His alcohol stove spilled, catching his clothes on fire. By the time he put out the fire, his arm and leg were burned, along with most of his trail clothes. The closest place to get medical attention was inside Baxter State Park, so he kept on hiking. Luckily, he was able to finish his thru-hike that year, burns and all. If I don't make it all the way, I'll be disappointed, but I especially don't want to be forced off the Trail before getting very far.

My stride measures between 24 and 30 inches. If a 24-inch stride covering 2,185.3 miles equals 5,769,192 steps, then a 30-inch stride would result in 4,615,354 steps. A big difference! This doesn't include the approach trail and exit trail distances, plus all the side trips to find water, food, fuel, and shelter, not to mention getting lost. This is going to be a lot of walking!

FEBRUARY 28, 2014

We'll drive to Amicalola Falls State Park in Georgia on March 16, check in at the Lodge, and then visit the Trail Fest taking place in nearby Dahlonega. On March 17, we plan to tour the state park and waterfalls, and scope out the approach trail to Springer Mountain, the southernmost terminus of the Appalachian Trail. On March 18, my 59th birthday, I'll start hiking after a hearty breakfast at the Amicalola Lodge.

Here in Chicago, winter is holding on. The current polar vortex was supposed to end today, but more snow is on the way. I can't wait to head south and see grass again. I uploaded a photograph of my gear yesterday on my trail journal and the deodorant generated a lot more response than expected. Thanks, everyone, for reading my journal! Deodorant on the trail may be a lost cause, but surely there will be times when I will want to use it.

My rationale for carrying deodorant is the same as for carrying extra clothes. I plan to use deodorant and change into clean, or as clean as possible, clothing when heading into towns or places where people are less appreciative of trail perfume. I hope it will serve to create a kinder and gentler first impression. Spare clothes can also be used to layer up against cold weather and provide an opportunity to change into dry clothes if you get wet. They can also be used as pajamas, if I need the extra warmth. Maybe bringing deodorant makes me more of a renegade than a road warrior. Should I change my trail name to Renegade? I searched the list and couldn't find anyone from the Class of 2014 with that trail name.

MARCH 7, 2014

During my training months, I hiked a total of 354 miles carrying a pack, and climbed 300 laps on the Swallow Cliff stairs. There is nothing more to gain from continued training. Besides, I might end up hurting myself. My starting base pack weight is slightly over 16 pounds. Once again, I removed the camp shoes from my gear. I'll buy a pair of flip flops during the hike if I feel the need to get out of my boots.

Too many hikers are already discussing injuries in their trail journals. I'll be heartbroken if I get hurt right away. One hiker wrote about injuring his leg at a hostel the night before he was to begin the Trail.

The Illinois State Museum Lockport Gallery has recently agreed to promote my Appalachian Trail hike as a charitable fundraiser. For many years, my wife and I have volunteered at this wonderful museum, and continue to do so. The Lockport Gallery is a branch of the Illinois State Museum that focuses exclusively on Illinois art and artists.

On Tuesday, March 11, 2014, the Lockport Gallery presented my upcoming Appalachian Trail hike at an event open to the public. The museum director also published an article about my hike, which is still available on Twitter, @ILStateMuseum. Please make a donation, and mention my name, by calling or sending an email through the website: museum.state.il.us/ismsites/Lockport.

Just realized the Sawyer Mini Water Filter doesn't fit the new design of the energy-saving cap on most plastic water bottles. After all the problems I had trying to use the Sawyer Mini with the hydration tubes and hydration bags, I decided to ditch the Sawyer water bags and carry a 24-ounce water bottle for unfiltered water. Filtered water would be poured directly into the hydration bag. Another water bottle, cut in half, will serve as a scoop for shallow streams, as needed.

Weather plays a big role in alcohol stove performance. In warm weather, the stove is easier to operate and boils water faster. In cold weather, it's tricky and slow. While testing my Esbit alcohol stove during winter, I found that cold weather makes the alcohol difficult to light. Once lit, it takes up to three minutes for the stove and alcohol to preheat sufficiently in order to operate properly. On a cold day, with temperatures ranging between 25 and 30 degrees, it took three minutes to heat up the stove, then ten more minutes to boil 16 ounces of cold water, a total of thirteen minutes. Altitude adds even more time to the cooking process. The Esbit cook set uses the cup as a lid. Placing aluminum foil over the top of the pot cut nearly two minutes off the cooking time. Even in the coldest conditions, only 1.1 to 1.3 ounces of fuel was needed to boil 16 ounces of water. I plan to carry no more than ten or twelve ounces of fuel, and store it in a water bottle with a different size and shape that doesn't fit my Sawyer Mini, in order to differentiate it from the one I'll use for drinking water.

I've switched to a non-scented antiperspirant deodorant. Thanks to everyone on the trailjournals.com trail forum for the safety advice. I should have realized the risks in carrying scented deodorant. After reading some posts about the prices at Mountain Crossing Outfitters at Neel Gap, I checked their website and found their prices to be less than, or comparable to, gear sold in Chicago, excepting for Walmart. No complaints, but hikers living in lower cost of living areas may think otherwise. FYI, alcohol costs 25 cents an ounce. Looking forward to warmer weather and hoping the polar vortices have ended. Snow is predicted next week.

Over the last few months, I've read several trail journals of hikers who plan to start the Appalachian Trail on the same day as me. After contacting several of them by email, I became friendly with a guy called Freedom. We have decided to meet up at the Amicalola Falls State Park and start out hiking together.

[Note for laughs]

My father met a guy in Indianapolis who claims to have hiked the entire Appalachian Trail with a rifle. Ha! Don't believe it. Common sense, trekking poles, and a pocket knife are more than enough protection.

MARCH 16, 2014

My wife and I left for Georgia on March 14th. On the way, we stopped over in Indianapolis for a kickoff party with family. We finally arrived at Amicalola Falls State Park in thick fog on Sunday, March 16th. After checking into the Lodge, we drove to Dahlonega to attend Trail Fest.

We arrived late and the festival was already packing up. We met a young woman whose trail name is Joe Cool. She had already been hiking on the Trail for a few days, but came back to Dahlonega for Trail Fest. Joe Cool is the first real hiker I've met.

The next day, we toured the state park and enjoyed the historic Amicalola Falls Lodge perched high above the falls. We couldn't see much of the falls that day because of continual fog. Amicalola Falls are the largest waterfalls east of the Mississippi River. The lobby of the Lodge buzzed, filled with excited and anxious hikers counting down the hours before they set out on the Trail.

I met Freedom, along with his wife and friends, who'd traveled with him to see him off at the Trailhead. Freedom was taller than me, and like many hikers starting out, a bit overweight. He was a member of a Christian motorcycle group and had retired from the food industry. Freedom said he hadn't completed as much training as he hoped.

I met other hikers at the Lodge who planned to head out on the Trail the same day as me. Before the evening was over, we had formed a solid group. We were all about the same age, in our late fifties to early sixties, and shared our thoughts on

21

equipment, hiking plans, and the adventure that lay ahead. We gathered together in the comfortable sitting area of the Lodge lobby, and our wives took group photographs of the five of us standing together in front of the huge stone fireplace.

Achin' was slightly older, taller, and heftier than the rest of us. He also carried the heaviest pack, weighing in at 39 pounds. Achin had never backpacked before, but had read more books about the A.T. than any of us. Chiggabite was also tall and sturdily built. He ran a hardware store and dreamed of completing an A.T. thru-hike. My Way was about my size, but wiry and fit, and embarking on his fourth thru-hike attempt. My Way was the ultralight winner, carrying next to nothing, and hiking in running shoes. He planned to hike at least twenty miles every day. Freedom and I considered leaving a day early, on the 17th, but the weather forecast looked unpromising.

MARCH 17, 2014

My Way set off on the trail early this morning. Again, the weather was foggy, with cold, increasing rain. Creeks were coffee-brown and swollen. I wasn't looking forward to drinking water out of those streams. Freedom and I studied the heavy, rain-soaked skies and decided to stick with the original plan, heading out tomorrow on March 18th.

The Dahlonega Trail Fest was rained out, so my wife and I drove around the Blood Mountain area, scoping out the sections of the trail I planned to cover in the next three days. We saw several hikers out in the fog and rain, trying to keep warm. I was filled with excitement, and even in these dreary conditions, I couldn't wait to start. After shopping for a few more food supplies, we headed back to enjoy our last night at the Lodge.

At the Lodge, some of the military personnel affiliated with the Wounded Warriors and Hiking for Heroes organizations were getting ready to climb up the approach trail to the top of Springer Mountain. These two hiking groups had been established to support wounded soldiers and veterans suffering from post-traumatic stress. Their goal is to help veterans hike off the war and follow in the footsteps of Earl V. Shaffer, the first thru-hiker who sought to hike off the effects of World War II, and uphold Benton MacKaye's vision of the Appalachian Trail as a refuge and retreat for war veterans.

By talking with them, I learned that many of the Wounded Warriors are assisted by a large support group who provide equipment, supplies, first aid, and transportation, when needed. My trail name, Road Warrior, was starting to sound like I could be a part of either one of these military groups. It would seem dishonest if people mistakenly associated me with them. I had never served in the military. So, I decided to shorten my trail name to simply RW. RW could now take on new meanings besides Road Warrior. It could be short for all sorts of things, like Right Way, Really Weird, Running Water, and so on.

Freedom and I registered as official thru-hikers at the Amicalola Falls State Park Visitor Center. I became Hiker 507, and Freedom was Hiker 508. We weighed our packs and took lots of pictures. At the very last minute, based on My Way's strong opinion that it's better to reduce weight than eat hot meals, I left my entire cook set and fuel container behind. And because of the heavy rain, I decided to switch out the Frogg Togg rain jacket with the more robust Marmot Precept, weighing an additional seven ounces. Now my pack weight, with a liter of water and two days of food, was 21 pounds. Freedom's pack weighed 31 pounds. We head out tomorrow!

During the evening I met Tic Toc, who had attempted to hike the entire Appalachian Trail several years ago. Tic Toc gave me one important piece of advice: Never quit on your worst day. This one piece of advice saved my hike.

THE HIKE

DAY 1 MARCH 18: SPRINGER MOUNTAIN TO HORSE GAP.
TODAY'S MILES: 10.5
TRIP MILES: 10.5

Freedom, Chiggabite, and I decided to bypass the approach trail near the Amicalola Falls Visitor Center. It adds an extra 8.8 miles of steep, rugged climbing before actually getting to the start of the Appalachian Trail. The southern end, or terminus, of the Appalachian Trail is located on top of Springer Mountain.

After a hearty breakfast in the Amicalola Lodge dining room, my wife drove Freedom and me up a winding mountain access road, and dropped us off at a parking lot situated 0.9 miles from the Springer Mountain summit. Chiggabite drove separately with his wife, so we didn't see him all day. Achin' decided to hike the full approach trail. He will most likely begin the official trail tomorrow.

Freedom and I hiked the 0.9-mile path to the top of Springer Mountain by following the white blazes painted on rocks and trees. A white blaze is a 2x6 inch strip of white paint spaced at intervals along the Trail. To walk the length of the Appalachian Trail, all a hiker needs to do is follow the white blazes. So far, the blazes have been easy to spot.

According to my trail plan, it would take 8.5 miles to reach Hawk Mountain Shelter today. The trail is harder than I thought and packed with people all day long. Either I was trying to get past them, or they were trying to get in front of me. In addition to all the hopeful thru-hikers, loads of college students were on the trail because of spring break.

I was amazed to see so many backpackers carrying weights of 40, 50, 60, and in one case, 75 pounds. This last hiker, a recently discharged soldier, said he thought 75 pounds was light. I couldn't imagine what must be inside his pack to make it so heavy. The temperature was about 41 degrees, and Freedom and I hiked in and out of the clouds all day. The Trail had steep climbs and the paths were muddy most of the time. Lots of large rhododendrons were growing alongside the trail. We met many fellow hikers, and enjoyed talking with them.

We made it to Hawk Mountain Shelter by 3:00 p.m., and the area around it was packed with tents. Thirty to fifty hikers had already set up camp for the night. While Freedom and I filled up with water, we decided to keep hiking because of the crowd. It was still early, and we were starting to worry that if we didn't do more miles today, we might not reach Woody Gap tomorrow, where my wife would be waiting for us in the parking lot.

A member of the Wounded Warrior support team recommended Horse Gap as a good tenting location, so Freedom and I hiked two more hard miles to get there. We put up our tents next to a forest service road, and ate dinner by 5:30 p.m. I had filled up with nearly four liters of water at Hawk Mountain Shelter because I knew there wouldn't be any water at Horse Gap. I needed enough for two meals before reaching the next water source. Freedom didn't carry as much water and ended up using most of his supply before the night was over.

Since I didn't bring a cook set, I ate dry food. Cinnamon raisin bagels, summer sausage, block cheese, trail mix, honey-nut protein bars, and candy bars were my food of choice because of their high calories, protein content, and durability. It isn't the lightest food to carry, but without the weight of a cook set, I didn't have to rely on dehydrated food. All my food could be eaten while hiking or on short breaks, and I didn't need to spend time preparing food.

Instead of hanging my food from a tree that night, I placed the food stuff bag inside the plastic trash bag doubling as a pack liner, and slept with it inside the tent. I did worry about bears, but not much. They were probably still hibernating. Our first day on the trail was over. We had hiked ten and a half official miles, but if you count the path up Springer Mountain from the parking lot, a total of eleven and a half miles.

DAY 2 MARCH 19: HORSE GAP TO WOODY GAP.
TODAY'S MILES: 10.5
TRIP MILES: 21.0

It started to rain around 2:00 a.m. and when we woke up about 7:00 a.m., it was dark, foggy, and raining. As the old A.T. saying goes: "No pain, no rain, no Maine!" Last night, the temperature got down to 38 degrees. The sleeping bag kept me very warm all night, and the tent stayed dry. The ground was hard, but excitement and a minimal Therma-rest sleeping pad were the only cushions I needed. Today's destination was Woody Gap, according to my trail plan, with a stopover in Suches, Georgia, to buy more food. We started hiking about 8:00 a.m., with wet tents in our packs, and headed up a steep trail to the top of Sassafras Mountain. I reached the top of Sassafras first and waited for Freedom. After calling several times, I turned around and headed south to look for him. Freedom had developed physical problems and stopped about 90 percent of the way up the mountain. We talked for a while. He was convinced he couldn't hike very far today. We said our goodbyes, and he turned around to go find a ride to a hostel.

I hiked alone for the rest of the day and didn't meet any hikers. I passed a few who were inside their tents, sheltered from the rain. Today was hard. I climbed several steep mountains. It rained till 1:00 p.m., turning the Trail to mud. In some places, I felt like I was walking through a stream as rainwater flowed down the Trail. Not only was it wet and muddy, it was 40 degrees and cold. I hiked in thick clouds all day, and couldn't see much more than 50 yards most of the time. Besides the constant presence of rocks on the Trail, the ground was hard. Years of hiking had packed the ground into a dirt as hard as concrete.

I arrived at Woody Gap about 2:30 p.m. in a heavy fog and didn't see my wife right away. All the food was gone, so my pack was light today. There at the roadside, I met my first group of trail angels, and spotted my wife giving them a helping hand. She was being a trail angel, too! There was plenty of trail magic: hot food, drinks, snacks, a warm fire, and camp chairs for weary hikers. It was a wonderful end to a cold, wet, hard day. After I found my wife and enjoyed the hospitality for a while, we drove to the hostel at Suches, Georgia, to look for Freedom. He was staying at the Wolf Pen Gap Country Store and Hostel. We talked for a while. He said he was hurting and planned to stay another day. While we were talking, I noticed Joe Cool, the young girl from the Dahlonega festival. She was staying there to wait out the weather. Freedom and I said goodbye one more time, and I left. My wife and I checked into a deluxe mountain cabin she had booked near Dahlonega. A long, hot shower felt luxurious. Later that night, we dined at a restaurant in town. So far the Trail was much better than I had imagined.

DAY 3 MARCH 20: WOODY GAP TO NEEL GAP.
TODAY'S MILES: 10.7
TRIP MILES: 31.7

The trail plan called for me to hike to Neel Gap today. I woke up sore and tired. It would be a day of many firsts. The sun shone brightly all day, and the views were spectacular. The weather was warm, the Trail dry, and I was able to slackpack. Slackpacking means not carrying a full pack, just a small amount of emergency gear and lunch. It was also the first time I became aware of how deeply the Trail is eroded by hikers. In places the ground is eroded by as much as 12 to 18 inches, and feels like walking in a narrow ditch. The ditches quickly fill up with water, because the ground is rock hard from the pounding of hiker feet over the years. The Trail looks like a creek in places.

The Trail took me up and over Blood Mountain today. At 4,461 feet, it is the highest mountain I have climbed so far. It was a difficult climb, and the hike down was exceptionally steep and boulder-strewn. For the first time in my life, my knees hurt. I can't imagine how much my knees would be hurting if I had carried a full pack. When I got to the top of Blood Mountain, trail magic was waiting in the shelter—lots of cold bottled water. Perfect! I was out of water and had mistakenly assumed there was a well at the top, because I hadn't read the Guide properly. If I had read the Guide more closely, I would have noticed it clearly indicates there was no water. From now on, I need to read the

Guide more carefully. Without the trail magic, I would have been in a world of hurt. Trail magic—twice in my first three days!

Blood Mountain is the second most popular mountain on the A.T., and there were lots of day hikers on the trail. Blood Mountain got its name from a very bloody battle between the Creek and Cherokee Indians. Given that this mountain ends so many thru-hiker dreams today, it is still aptly named.

I met an older hiker named Bags and his little dog, Yeager, who seemed to be dragging his owner. Yesterday I met Rose, who is a member of the Wounded Warrior support team. She told me she completed a thru-hike in 2013. Rose is young and a bit plump. She gave me another great piece of advice: When it gets hard, only think about completing the next 10 feet. Then repeat. Don't look too far ahead, ever. It was surprising to hear that she had successfully thru-hiked. I assumed it was something only skinny people could handle. This assumption would be proved wrong repeatedly as I met more people attempting to thru-hike.

While at Neel Gap, I met trail legend Baltimore Jack. He has thru-hiked the Trail many times and was graciously giving assistance to new hikers and checking the contents of their packs. Frequently, he advised hikers: You don't need that much stuff. A nice guy, but looking at him, I found the legend hard to believe. Jack was hugely overweight. He said, repeatedly, that the Trail is more about mental endurance and putting up with the daily grind than physical strength. He thinks anyone can hike the A.T.—maybe not in one try, but anyone can do it.

I got my third Appalachian Trail passport stamp at Mountain Crossing Outfitters. A.T. passports are mostly designed for amusement and to advertise the various trail services along the way. It is fun getting your passport stamped, and I hope to collect as many stamps as possible. The first two stamps in my passport came from Amicalola Falls Lodge, and a hostel in Dahlonega.

My wife and I think Neel Gap is marvelous. Mountain Crossing Outfitters is located here inside an historic stone building. In front of the building, next to the parking lot, looms a huge tree festooned with hundreds of hiking boots tossed over the limbs by hikers who were either giving up the hike, or who had just bought a new pair inside the outfitter store. My wife spent time here waiting to pick me up after a day of slackpacking, and witnessed a lot of tired and sore hikers calling it quits. Some were crying and shouting into their cell phones, desperately trying to get help and arrange transportation to get them off the Trail. Neel Gap is the only place where the Appalachian Trail actually goes through a building. Hikers must walk through a wide, covered archway cut right into the stone building.

Just as we were heading back to our rented mountain cabin for the night, Bags and his dog, Yeager, hiked into Neel Gap. He asked if we could give him a lift to a motel in Blairsville. It gave us a chance to provide trail magic. When we finally arrived back at the cabin, I enjoyed another long, hot shower. Afterwards, we drove back to town for one more luxurious restaurant meal. I stocked up on four days' worth of food at Walmart, enough to see me to Dick's Creek Gap. Again, I bought bagels, summer sausage, cheese, candy, and trail mix. This combination was working. I was fine without a stove.

Despite advanced preparation, the first few days brought about some necessary equipment changes. My fanny pack broke on the first day, and I decided not to replace it. A second Platypus water bag was needed for storing dirty water before filtering it into another clean water bag. My method was to hang the dirty water bag from a tree and attach the Sawyer Mini filter to a tube running into a clean water bottle, or water bag. It takes ten to fifteen minutes to filter three liters of water, and it can be left alone while I work on other camp chores.

I also purchased a small shoulder pack at the last minute to store my camera/phone, mini-tripod, antibacterial soap, water filter, and enough toilet paper for immediate use. I wanted a separate pack that would give me quick access to these items, especially my phone/camera. Hygiene, especially hand washing, is important for staying healthy on the Trail. Many hikers hang a bottle of antibacterial soap from a shoulder strap.

I uploaded a digital version of the Trail Guide on my cell phone to avoid weight. The PDF format is handy, and I can easily access the Guide for trail information.

DAY 4 MARCH 21: NEEL GAP TO MILE 46.0.
TODAY'S MILES: 14.3
TRIP MILES: 46.0

The trail plan calls for me to hike 11.5 miles to Low Gap Shelter. My wife dropped me off early next to the Trail. We said our final goodbyes, and I was on the trail by 7:30 a.m. Having her nearby these last few days to lend support was great, but it added unexpected costs to the hike.

Today was another day of more firsts. It's the first day of spring. I wore sunglasses for the first time, hiked in a tee shirt, and got a little sunburned. It was a great day for spectacular views! I saw Blood Mountain from a distance and marveled that I had just climbed over it. At lunchtime, I ran into a trail angel named Sherpa. He gave me lots of fresh fruit and water. Trail magic three times in four days!

In the afternoon I hiked with a guy from Pittsburgh, and met a young German couple, plus another couple from Canada. It was becoming clear that all the cold weather training miles, along with stair climbing, had greatly improved my endurance.

I got to the shelter about 2:30 p.m. Several Wounded Warriors were setting up camp, along with many other hikers. This was a nice shelter, but it was too early in the day for me to stop, so I hiked on. The trail became a gravel road, which made for easy walking. Water sources were scarce, so when I finally found water, I filled up with four liters.

A young couple had pitched a tent near the Trail, so I decided to stop and camp with them. They were from Switzerland, and their names were Katrina and Mike. They had quit their jobs and flew to the States in order to hike the Appalachian Trail. I pitched my tent, and we built a campfire. After eating a meal together, we hung our food bags from a tree to keep bears from getting into them.

Hanging food from a tree is tricky. First, you have to tie your rope line to a rock. It's not as easy as it sounds. You have to find a rock with a suitable shape and weight. Too round and the line slips off the rock; too heavy and you won't be able to throw it over a branch. A rock that's too light doesn't throw well. The weight of the line holds it back, and it's unable to overcome the friction caused by tree bark. A rope tied to a too-light rock tends to get stuck and dangle in the air over the branch.

Bear line tossing was a skill I forgot to practice during my pre-hike training. After twenty minutes of watching the rock fly through the air as it slipped off the line, or having the line drop short and bounce off limbs, I was finally able to swing the bear line over the branch and pull the food bag up, and then tie the loose end to a nearby tree.

Mike and Katrina were laughing the whole time. Mike secured his bear line on the first try. He said he learned how to do it in the Swiss military. Mike showed me what to look for in a rock, the best size and shape, and then how to tie a line around it. I slept well that night knowing I had completed the most miles of any day so far. I had gone 14.3 miles and was ahead of the trail plan.

DAY 5 MARCH 22: MILE 46.0 TO TRAY MOUNTAIN SHELTER.
TODAY'S MILES: 12.6
TRIP MILES: 58.6

My trail plan had me stopping at Unicoi Gap, mile 52.9 on the A.T., and hiking 9.7 miles. I awoke feeling strong and knew I could hike the day's trail plan, but hoped to do even more miles. The Trail was hard. I watched the sunrise for the first time, because I was up before daybreak and hiking by 7:00 a.m. Trail magic was abundant. At Unicoi Gap, Mary Popplns, another Wounded Warrior support team member, offered hot dogs, candy, water, and fruit. At Tray Gap, another trail angel handed out baked potatoes, soda pop, and candy. I ate well today and never touched my trail food. Trail magic appears every day now. As a result, I have a lot of food—too much.

A half mile later, I arrived at Tray Mountain Shelter. The shelter is built on the top of Tray Mountain at an elevation of 4,199 feet. This is the first time I will be camping next to a shelter. I had hoped to sleep inside the shelter—it sleeps seven— but the shelter was overcrowded by the time I got there. It's supposed to rain tonight. I found a nice, flat campsite on the edge of a cliff overlooking a beautiful valley. As it got dark that night, I met my first ridge runner, an older retired gentleman named Razor, who funds his hiking hobby by working for the

ATC. Ridge runners are employed by the Appalachian Trail Conservancy to patrol sections of the Appalachian Trail.

As I ate my supper, a young man carrying a gun instead of a backpack walked into camp with his girlfriend. As soon as they filled up with water, they left. It was the first time I saw anyone with a firearm, and I wondered what they were doing.

Everyone at the shelter was young, except Razor and me. In the early evening, we all gathered around a campfire that some of the younger hikers had built. Two hikers brought out a guitar and mandolin, and they played and sang. Most of the young hikers drank alcohol and smoked pot. I didn't participate, although there were many generous offers. I was tired and turned in around 7:30 p.m., but not before taking a couple of naproxen sodium tablets for the first time to ease the pain in my right knee.

Tonight, I didn't have to exercise my arm by throwing a bear line. This shelter had a bear line system made with a horizontal steel cable secured high in the air between two trees, and a set of pulleys and cables hooked by carabineers running to the ground. All I had to do was hook my food bag to a carabineer, lift it with a pulley, then tie the end of the line to another carabineer attached to a tree.

DAY 6 MARCH 23: TRAY MOUNTAIN TO DICKS CREEK GAP.
TODAY'S MILES: 11.0
TRIP MILES: 69.6

The trail plan had me stopping at Addis Gap, but because I am so far ahead of schedule, I decided to get up extra early and hike to Dicks Creek Gap. Last night, I had a clear view of the entire valley below me. The lights were awesome. Again I had slept warmly, and the morning's temperature was 50 degrees. The forest is quiet. At night I only hear owls, and in the daytime, woodpeckers. I saw a squirrel scurry by on the trail today for the first time, and heard a songbird. The forest is still, and there are no leaves on the trees. It feels empty. I packed my gear early and was on the Trail by 7:00 a.m. I wanted to head out before the rain started. It started around 9:00 a.m., and rained off and on until 11:30 a.m. I hiked in and out of the clouds all morning. When the rain started, the temperature dropped a lot. By this time I was sweating and became chilled whenever I stopped moving.

I made it to the Gap about 12:30 p.m., a distance of eleven miles in only five and a half hours. I'm getting stronger and, luckily, the Trail wasn't so tough this morning. I've already hiked more miles than planned, making me a full day ahead of the trail plan. Hiking this Trail is amazing! I feel completely alone, but whenever I stop for a minute, someone passes me by. The only time I pass others is when they are snacking or taking a break. The Trail is so narrow and curvy that you never see anyone until you are nearly on top of them. Sometimes, it's spooky.

I tried calling the Budget Inn in Hiawassee, Georgia, to book a shuttle, but couldn't get cell phone reception. The shuttle wouldn't arrive until 3:00 p.m. I wore my rain gear, but still got cold standing on the side of the road. I am apprehensive about hitchhiking, but decided it was better than waiting for hours in the cold. I tried hitchhiking for half an hour, but everyone just drove by. Some even waved at me. It's been decades since I tried to hitch a ride. Maybe thumbing is out of fashion these days. Is that why they waved? I saw a sign advertising a new hostel, called Top of Georgia, only 0.3 miles down the road. Just as I decided to hike to it, a car pulled up. They said they worked for this new hostel, and would take me there. Another lifetime first— I was staying in a hostel and didn't know what to expect.

Top of Georgia was a pleasant place, and my fears vanished immediately. The owner had hiked the Trail many times and decided to open a hostel. After checking in, I got my A.T. passport stamped, cleaned up, and took the shuttle into town. Since I didn't need to buy groceries, I went to Dairy Queen for ice cream. It was the only place open, except the grocery store, because it was Sunday. With all the trail magic and being a day ahead of schedule, I still had plenty of food in my pack. Plus, some other hikers had given me their food because they didn't want to carry the weight as they were getting off the trail. I paid for dinner and breakfast at the hostel. Tonight's dinner was great. We ate ham, mashed potatoes with all the sides, ice cream, and brownies. It was all you could eat, and I am stuffed.

Seated next to me at dinner was another guy from Germany who goes by the trail name Confused. His English was marginal. Confused hiked with a dog, a massive Irish Wolfhound. He had been warned that within the next twenty miles, the Trail is so steep that dogs can't make the climb, unless they can climb ladders. He has arranged for someone to take care of the dog while he hikes through the Smokies.

Later that day, the enthusiastic kid from Montana showed up, along with others from the night before at Tray Mountain Shelter. It was nice to see them again, and I realized for the first time that I would keep meeting many of these hikers over and over again. The next few days are predicted to be cold with snow. It's going to be a real test.

DAY 7 MARCH 24: DICKS CREEK GAP TO MUSKRAT CREEK SHELTER.
TODAY'S MILES: 11.8
TRIP MILES: 81.4

I planned to hike to Muskrat Creek Shelter today. Eleven or twelve miles now seems like a low-mileage hiking day, because I'm feeling well and strong. The shuttle driver had to scrape ice off his car windows before driving Egret and me to Dicks Creek Gap. We started hiking at 9:00 a.m. after a wonderful, hearty breakfast at the Top of Georgia Hostel. Egret was the only hiker to leave as early as me. All the other hikers decided to sleep in, or take a zero day, because of the weather forecast. I didn't see the point because the storm was predicted for tomorrow, not today.

Egret is a slim nineteen-year-old girl who couldn't be much more than a hundred pounds, dripping wet. She is hiking alone and is tough as nails. Egret started hiking with the Wounded Warriors, but found their pace too slow. She confided that she wanted to hike with me because she was tired of all the attention from the young guys at the hostel. I must be harmless or fatherly. I hope it's the latter, but probably the first. Egret considers herself as a thru-hiker, but must complete the hike before heading back to school in the early fall. Like so many other young hikers, she has to keep up a fast pace, or run out of time.

The weather was cool and sunny all day. The Trail had changed a little—there were less rocks and more soil underfoot, making the constant clacking sound of my trekking poles against the rocks less sharp. The trees appear to be getting taller. The mountains are changing, too. Still winter grey, but tiny patches of green are starting to appear on the mountain sides. Those tiny patches are actually groves of pine trees and rhododendrons.

We both hiked at our own pace, stretching apart and snapping back like a rubber band all morning. Egret would pull away on the downhills, and I closed the gap on the uphill climbs. As the morning progressed, two very bizarre guys passed us. One was Jamaica, and the other Moccasin. Moccasin hiked without shoes. These two guys had enough pot to reach Maine without ever resupplying. We all stopped to take a break, and Jamaica asked me what my trail name, RW, stood for. I said, "What do you think it means?" He responded with Rastafarian Weed. His answer was so surprising that it gave me the idea to start asking others to come up with new meanings for RW. It could become a game, a challenge, to see if I could be renamed every day.

A short while later, Egret and I passed Jamaica and Moccasin while they were taking another weed break. Soon, however, they caught up to us and raced ahead. It wasn't long, though, before we passed them again. You guessed it! Jamaica and Moccasin were taking another smoke break. Back in college, pot mellowed us out. Apparently, some strains of modern marijuana act as a painkiller and stimulant. I noticed so many hikers using pot on the trail that I started to wonder just how they got it. As for me, my drug of choice was naproxen sodium— one tablet in the morning, and another one at night.

At 1:15 p.m. today, I crossed into North Carolina. There were a dozen hikers at the North Carolina border, including Jamaica, smoking his weed. Egret stayed behind. It was the last time we hiked together. I hiked the rest of the day alone, but was frequently passed by the younger, faster hikers. Jamaica was one of them. The first few miles of North Carolina were tough, but then it flattened out as I hiked the ridgeline.

At 3:30 p.m. I stopped at Muskrat Creek Shelter, located at an elevation of 4,580 feet. The area was packed with tents; at least 30 people were here. I considered hiking on to the next shelter, but decided this night could be interesting. Egret and many of the hikers I met at the hostel arrived later and set up their tents. In the evening, I hiked to a cliff half a mile away and enjoyed a spectacular view of the mountains. I wished I knew which of those mountains I had hiked up and over, because they looked intimidating. I also walked around the remains of a plane wreck that had occurred many years ago.

As the night progressed, a yogi (trail bum, hobo, or homeless person) with his dog showed up dressed in camouflage clothing, and he proved to be entertaining. He is the first homeless person I have met on the trail. He seemed nice. No one asked his name and he didn't say, but he regaled everyone with his stories of life in the woods.

The shelter and privy were overrun by mice. While using the privy just before retiring, I realized mice were watching me and slapped at them with my gloves. They moved a few feet, but then stopped and stared at me, completely unafraid. This was my first encounter with such bold mice. The night turned cold fast and talk around the campfire was of snow. I decided if the weather was bad in the morning, I would hike past my intended destination and get to Franklin for the night. It would be a massive 25.7-mile day.

DAY 8 MARCH 25: MUSKRAT CREEK SHELTER TO LONG BRANCH SHELTER.
TODAY'S MILES: 21.1
TRIP MILES: 102.5

RW means Really Winter.

Last night before getting into my sleeping bag, I decided to change the trail plan if the weather turned worse. The original plan had me hiking 12.5 miles to Carter Gap Shelter, but I would try to hike beyond that in hopes of getting to Long Branch Shelter. I gave up on Franklin after studying the distance and terrain. It was out of reach. I wasn't even sure Long Branch Shelter was feasible.

When I woke up and opened the tent flap, snow fell into the tent. Overnight, an inch of snow had fallen. I ate hurriedly, packed up, and hit the Trail at 7:30 a.m. before anybody else was up in camp. It was still dark, but I didn't use my headlamp because the Trail was bright with snow. I was blazing the Trail. It was clear no one had left camp before me. Only rodent, rabbit, and bird tracks were visible. The Trail was very difficult and slippery for the first few miles. Progress was slow, but eventually I made it to Standing Indian Shelter, a distance of 4.9 miles.

Some hikers had already left that shelter, so I followed in their footprints for several hours.

Around 10:00 a.m., it started to sleet hard. The sleet beat against my raingear and sounded like snapping rubber bands. The Trail became icy. Tree limbs glistened. Rhododendrons sagged under the heavy weight of ice. The wind picked up and the temperature was falling fast. I stopped for lunch at Carter Gap Shelter and was amazed to see I had made such good time. The cold kept me moving nonstop. Three other hikers were huddled in the shelter. They said they were going to wait out the weather. I wasn't about to stay there—the shelter was frigid and the wind howled directly into it. It looked like a good place to freeze to death.

I hiked on as the temperature plunged and the wind rose to gale force. The trees creaked and moaned. More than once, I turned around to see who was yelling. It was the wind and trees. They were shrieking! Then, the snow really started to come down. I began to think Mother Nature had it in for me today. When I got under the trees, I rested and hid from the storm. There usually isn't water in a place like this, so I wasn't going to stay and camp here in the storm without water.

About 3:00 p.m. I got to Mount Albert after a terrible uphill rock climb. I tied my trekking poles to my pack and climbed using my bare hands. Frozen boots made it tough to keep my balance on the icy cold, slippery rocks. Mother Nature, or a higher force, took pity on me during this torturous climb, and the snow, sleet, and wind subsided for a moment. But just as I crested the top, the wind was waiting to ambush me. It hit me with gale force as I climbed over the last rock, as if to push me backward off the cliff face. I hurried on as the wind picked up and the snow began falling again. The temperature was getting colder and colder. I had no choice but to keep hiking. A brief rest stop made my sweat freeze and sent shivers through my body.

I finally made it to Long Branch Shelter by hiking more than twenty-one miles, the most distance covered in a day so far. It was 5:00 p.m., and already the sky was dark and menacing. The shelter slept sixteen on two levels, but only four people were there, bunked on the top level. They had built a fourth wall with ground sheets to try and stop the wind from blowing into the three-sided structure. Fortunately, the wind was blowing against another side of the shelter, not the opening. This offered some protection from the wind, but not the cold. I figured the others knew what they were doing, so I joined them on the top level.

This was the first time I was sleeping inside a shelter. The others were all in their sleeping bags trying to stay warm. I climbed into mine and shivered uncontrollably for half an hour. My clothes were wet with sweat and snow, so I moved down to the lower bunk, changed my clothes, and wedged into a corner away from the wind. The new spot on the lower level, with dry clothes, was a good choice. I was slowly starting to warm up in my bag.

Two other hikers joined us. Scott, the guy from Montana who carried the latest in cold weather equipment, and a nineteen-year-old named Ben from Florida. This was the third night in a row that the guy from Montana and I had camped or bunked at the same location: Tray Mountain, the Top of Georgia Hostel, and now, Long Branch Shelter. Later, I learned more about the four people huddled on the upper level. One was a twenty-something guy from Cornwall, England, called Cornwall. Another man, in his thirties, was from Heidelberg, Germany, and the third guy never got out of his sleeping bag. The fourth person was a girl who emerged from her bag only once to take a pee. The German was dressed in arctic clothes, but still did calisthenics to try and keep warm.

Cornwall and I ran up and down a hill. The hydration tube connected to my water bladder was frozen solid and the water filter didn't want to work. I took a chance and drank unfiltered water from the stream because I was so dehydrated. The German was the only one who ate. Everyone else huddled in their bags, fearing the cold and wind. After a vigorous run, I climbed into my bag without dinner.

It was only 6:30 p.m., and Scott from Montana was already sleeping hard. He never woke up all night. Ben and I talked for a short while, but the cold was too much. We just laid in silence listening to the wind howl and watching the snow pile up on our sleeping bags. The four hikers on the upper level didn't move or make a sound. No one had taken precautions against the bears and mice. We were too cold. We slept with food in our packs. The cold must have kept the wild animals in their burrows, too, because we didn't see one mouse tail all night.

At 6:30 p.m. my thermometer read 20 degrees. I was confident my 12-degree sleeping bag could keep me warm all night. I slept in socks and clothes, but no hat. My regular hiking hat is good for rain and walking, but difficult to wear while sleeping. I found my bandana and wrapped it around my head. This worked surprisingly well and kept my head warm. Necessity is the mother of invention!

DAY 9 MARCH 26: LONG BRANCH SHELTER TO ROCK GAP.
TODAY'S MILES: 3.6
TRIP MILES: 106.1

RW means Risky Walker, a new trail name given to me by Simon. He was the German on the upper level of the shelter last night.

I slept restlessly all night and woke at 5:00 a.m. to find I was shivering uncontrollably. My 12-degree cold weather sleeping bag failed. I quickly started exercising in my sleeping bag, and stopped shivering after a few minutes. The movement not only warmed me up, it shook the snow off me, too. I went through lots of contortions putting on my pants and socks. I couldn't resist the call of nature, so I slipped out of the bag wearing every piece of clothing I had.

My boots were frozen solid. I pounded them mercilessly like a mad man. I'm sure everyone in the shelter was awake by now. I continued to beat the leather until there was enough room to wedge my feet in. I couldn't tie them because the shoestrings were icicles, so I hobbled to the privy in size eleven ice blocks. Back in the shelter, I beat my boots again and was finally able to tie the laces. I decided to hit the trail without breakfast, since the food was frozen. I packed up and checked the time and temperature: 6:30 a.m. and ten degrees. It was colder than my sleeping bag is rated for. When I slung the pack on my back, it hit like a cold block of ice. Not the familiar soft, warm feeling I had grown used to. My water bladder was frozen solid. Instead of life-giving water, it had become a useless block of plastic-covered ice pressed against the small of my back.

I donned my headlamp and started hiking. Yesterday, in my haste to get to the shelter, I forgot to scout the upcoming trail ahead of me. It was a habit of mine to scout the next day's trail map because I heard about hikers going the wrong way out of shelters and campsites. I didn't want to make that mistake. But now, I was confused in the darkness and sloshing down a running stream. I thought this was the Trail. I didn't want to walk in water with frozen boots. My feet were painfully cold. I retraced my steps, and sure enough, the Trail was the stream.

I walked as fast as I could, following the narrow tunnel of light beaming from my headlamp. After 30 minutes, I'd warmed up enough to take off a layer of clothes and didn't need the headlamp anymore. Another 15 minutes and my boots finally thawed enough to stop hobbling. It was really cold. None of the creatures ventured out. No animal tracks. The snow on the Trail was unmarked by life, so unlike yesterday.

I gazed down at the lights of Franklin in the valley below. There was only the glow of street lights, no cars were moving on the roads yet. The town was still asleep. A dirty brown crescent moon still hung in the east, and Mars or Venus in the west. After a while, I sensed the sun was rising on the other side of the ridge. I hiked over and saw a great red sun shining through the trees, setting them ablaze. The whole forest was glowing red. I marveled at the sight and heard a Voice speak: "You have passed today's challenge; you may advance to the next test." My heart filled with emotion, and I was renewed.

I charged down the Trail to Rock Gap and found six other freezing hikers. A trail angel drove by and gave three of us a ride to town. I checked into a motel, got my A.T. passport stamped again, and took a long, hot shower. I purchased a sleeping bag liner and another insulated underwear shirt at the local outfitter, more unexpected expenses. I needed a stocking hat, and luckily, found one in the hiker box. A hiker box contains anything hikers no longer want to carry. Most hostels and hiker motels keep a hiker box in the lobby or kitchen area.

While blogging in the lobby, I saw most of the hikers from last night's shelter check into this motel. Everyone except Ben, who said he was through. He was going home. We all tried to talk him out of quitting. I offered him the spare bed in my room, but he rejected all attempts to change his mind. The last time I saw Ben, he was on a shuttle headed for a larger town to catch a bus home.

41

I turned on the television and watched the weather channel. According to the National Weather Service, a powerful spring snowstorm had encompassed the entire eastern seaboard last night, March 25th, creating blizzards in New England and unusually cold, bitter temperatures throughout the Appalachian mountain range and the state of Virginia. This freak snowstorm was fueled by "bombogenesis", an unusual weather phenomenon that occurs when a storm quickly intensifies, usually over the ocean, just off the East Coast. On Wednesday, this storm was said to be similar in strength to a Category Three hurricane. After hearing this, and realizing the peril I was placed in yesterday, I decided to never do that again.

Egret and the couple from Switzerland checked into the motel later in the day. Egret was taking a couple of zero days while she waited for cold weather equipment to arrive from home. The town was filling up with hikers fleeing the mountains to find shelter from the miserable weather. Tomorrow I hit the Trail after breakfast. The First Franklin Baptist Church is treating hikers to an all-you-can-eat breakfast.

DAY 10 MARCH 27: ROCK GAP TO WAYAH BALD SHELTER.
TODAY'S MILES: 14.7
TRIP MILES: 120.8

RW means Righteous Walker, a name given to me by the ladies at the First Franklin Baptist Church hiker breakfast.

Yesterday I stocked up with food for two and a half days of hiking. I didn't need to buy much—quite a bit remained in my pack due to the weather and unplanned stop in Franklin. My trail diet is still bagels, summer sausage, cheese, candy, and trail mix. These last cold days have forced me to rethink my decision to hike without hot food. I still want to keep my pack light, but the extra clothing items I just purchased have already added more weight. Another reason not to carry the cook set.

I woke up early, packed, and waited for the 7:00 a.m. shuttle to the First Franklin Baptist Church. The church fed about 30 of us with all-you-can-eat pancakes and side dishes. They offer this freewill hiker breakfast throughout the trail season. I don't usually care for pancakes, but ate six of them anyway. The four hikers who had slept on the upper level of the shelter during the storm showed up and shared a table with me.

I learned the German's name is Simon, and Cornwall's real name is William. Wesley is from Florida, and the girl, Bree, is from New Hampshire. The five of us ate together and recounted our storm adventure. Scott didn't make it. He got very drunk the night before and said he wasn't leaving town until he finished all the beer he bought. The church volunteers took our photographs and handed out postcards so we could write home. I wrote a postcard to my wife and the church mailed it for free, along with a photograph of the five of us smiling together at our breakfast table.

The motel shuttle dropped us off at the trailhead. The other four had hiked a little further, so they started 3.7 miles ahead of me that day. They are all very strong hikers, so I don't expect to catch up to them, or see them, again. I got dropped off at Rock Gap with a hiker called Blue. Blue is a 46-year old mountain of a man, a retired Marine with lots of battle experience. Blue said he started the Trail two weeks before me and has been in total combat the whole time. Three days into the hike, he was hit with a double ear infection and took ten days off. Just before Franklin, Blue fell and twisted an ankle. He told me to go on without him because his pace would be slow until his ankle healed. As I rounded the switchback and looked back, Blue was standing upright, marching behind me using his trekking poles as a cane.

The day was cool and sunny, and the melting snow made the Trail muddy. The mountains were all high now, consistently over 4,000-foot elevations. During the storm I climbed Standing Indian Mountain at 5,498 feet. All the mountains were higher in North Carolina than Georgia. The air was still and the trees seemed peaceful, raising their limbs up to the heavens, giving thanks for surviving the storm. During the storm, the trees creaked and moaned as their branches smashed against each other. Many times during the storm, I thought someone was calling me, only to realize it was the trees straining in the winds.

As lunch time approached, I came across a 71-year old man called Walking North. In 2013, Walking North hiked 2,035 miles of the Appalachian Trail. He skipped 150 miles because of bad weather and jumped ahead so he could make sure to climb Mt. Katahdin. Walking North had planned to go back immediately after summiting and hike the remaining 150 miles, but never did. He was practicing now, hoping to go back in June and complete the section he skipped last year. As we hiked together, he told me many stories about his trail experience last year. We climbed to the top of Wayah Mountain, a 5,342-foot elevation, and walked the short distance to Wayah Bald Shelter.

I'm still following my trail plan, except I'm staying one day ahead of schedule. While crossing the bald, I climbed a tower and read signs posted at the viewing deck describing the mountains around me. One sign said Clingmans Dome was the highest peak on the Trail and located in the middle of the Smokey Mountains, but the clouds were too thick to see it.

At Wayah Bald Shelter, the homeless trail yogi I met at Muskrat Creek Shelter was cooking dinner on a fire. I learned his name is Russ. As dusk fell, Just Paul and his daughter, Tortoise (later known as Torta-Lean-Y), and Guy-On-A-Buffalo and his mother, Mum, arrived. We enjoyed our evening meal together in the shelter.

The poor and homeless are one of the general types of people on the Trail, although their numbers are small. This small group seems to be either running away from civilization, or unable to follow a code of behavior that society considers "normal." Some thru-hikers, young and old, have become temporarily homeless. In order to hike the Trail, they have to give up housing and place their belongings in storage until the hike is finished. Their decision may be based on financial conditions, or the inability to maintain a home while hiking for six months.

I decided to stay in the shelter because tomorrow's forecast called for rain, and I didn't want to pack up a wet tent. Later that night, Russ talked to me for an hour or more. He told me his sad life story. At 53, he looks more like an 80-year-old man. He thinks he has lived in the woods for 20 years. A kind man, Russ tries to help hikers when he can, and in return asks only for some brief company, and no trouble. Just Paul and Walking North joined us for a few minutes, but quickly realized they didn't want anything to do with Russ.

DAY 11 MARCH 28: WAYAH BALD SHELTER TO WESSER BALD SHELTER.
TODAY'S MILES: 10.6
TRIP MILES: 131.4

RW means Red and Wet, so says Mum.

It was a dark and rainy day, and we all slept late. During the night I went to the privy and spotted a mouse staring at me again. I tried to shoo it away, but it just sat and looked at me. I flicked its nose with my finger. It moved a few inches, then stopped and resumed glaring at me.

Walking North and I packed up our gear and prepared to leave at 8:30 a.m. I was exhausted. When I lifted up my pack and got into it, water started pouring down my back. Walking North left me behind. They said they were going to stop at Nantahala River Crossing, located 16.5 miles ahead. I stayed and unpacked my equipment, only to discover the hydration bag was leaking and had lost about a liter of water. I think the freezing during the storm damaged it. Fortunately, my gear was inside a plastic bag and stayed dry. I repacked and left about 9:30 a.m. carrying a very wet pack. Everyone else had left already.

I caught up to Just Paul and Torta-Lean-Y, and hiked with them most of the day in the rain. Just Paul had thru-hiked the trail in 1985. His daughter, Torta-Lean-Y, said she was hiking because of post-traumatic stress, but avoided explaining the reasons as she told me her life story.

The true thru-hiker falls into two broad categories. Some hike as a pilgrimage, using extreme physical activity to divine inner peace and meaning in their life. They hike to find purpose, to cure ills such as addictions, divorce, death of a loved one, post-traumatic stress (like the Wounded Warriors), financial ruin, and other events that have left emotional scars or voids in their life. They may find answers quickly, or they may return to hike the Trail, year after year. For some, it's the Trail that gives meaning and purpose to their life.

The second group of thru-hikers is seeking fun and adventure. For them, the Trail is an intensely physical, social, and interactive experience. Young hikers often falls into this category, as well as retirees hoping to complete a bucket list item. These groups are my own device, and few hikers neatly fit into any one category. Most are a blend. I'm a mix between bucket list adventurer and retiree seeking a new beginning at the end of a long career.

I'm also walking off the stress of lingering job bitterness. I worked 38 years as a bank examiner, and rose to a middle management position in a federal agency that closed during President Obama's administration. A transfer to another position in a different agency wasn't a good fit. So, after struggling for nearly twenty months, I called it quits and retired. I wasn't ready to retire, but couldn't tolerate my new job and needed to escape from an increasingly bad situation. I felt I had so much more to accomplish in my career, but would never be given the opportunity. Retirement unceremoniously ended a successful career. I needed to reset my life, and the Appalachian Trail seemed like an answer. I hoped to test my physical and emotional strength, and discover new insights from the experiences along the way. The Appalachian Trail fit the bill, plus I really enjoy camping and backpacking.

Later we caught up to Guy-On-A-Buffalo and Mum, and all five of us gathered at Cold Spring Shelter to eat lunch at an elevation of 4,945 feet. A little old man in the shelter called Merlin said he was a thru-hiker. He carried the best equipment I've seen so far, but was the most miserable person I've met so far and every other word was profane. Merlin complained that people wouldn't let him into the shelters, and that equipment manufacturers needed to make better equipment. His plan was to sleep in shelters, so he only carried a bivy-sack instead of a tent. A bivy-sack is basically a plastic bag. Merlin's plan was not going well. The shelters were usually full when he arrived, forcing him to sleep outside.

Merlin must have passed us in the morning, because he spent the night at the tower on Wayah Bald during the rain. He said the tower flooded and his waterproof pack was floating like a small boat. Merlin luckily stayed dry in his bivy-sack. We all left him as quickly as possible, so he could be alone in his misery. On the trail, I secretly laughed about his flood story, but was very glad it wasn't me. I am sure that if it happened to me, I would be in a terrible mood, too.

I pulled ahead as the rain and clouds moved in. The trail was a rain forest now, thick with moss, lichen, and fungus. The fog and clouds obscured visibility to within a few yards. As I neared Wesser Bald Shelter at 4,280 feet, I caught up to Walking North. We made it to the shelter at 3:15 p.m. I was exhausted and staying here for the night. This was the scheduled stop in my original trail plan. Up till this point, I had been able to stay one day ahead of the plan. Walking North said he was fine and left, determined to reach Nantahala River Crossing. Another six miles was too much for me.

Guy-On-A-Buffalo, Mum, Just Paul, and Torta-Lean-Y arrived later. Guy-On-A-Buffalo and Mum were from Olympia, Washington. Guy-On-A-Buffalo was a vegan and only twenty years old, and had already hiked the 2,600-mile long Pacific Crest Trail. Mum was his incredibly brave mother. In January 2014, she had a bilateral mastectomy due to breast cancer. Less than three months later, on March 10th, she started hiking the A.T. with her son.

We were asleep by 8:00 p.m. It was my best sleep yet on the Trail. It rained all night. I woke around 2:00 a.m. to use the privy and was blinded by darkness as black as a cave. Fog had saturated my sleeping bag. The headlamp barely made a dent in the fog and inky darkness, just enough to reveal the glare of beady eyes in the shelter. I shooed them away.

DAY 12 MARCH 29: WESSER BALD SHELTER TO NANTAHALA OUTDOOR CENTER (NOC).
TODAY'S MILES: 5.9
TRIP MILES: 137.3

RW means Rooty-Woo-Hoo-ty! Guy-On-A-Buffalo says this expresses his feelings about the Trail.

The morning started slow and rainy. As we roused, Guy-On-A-Buffalo found plenty of evidence to suggest that the mice had quite a party in his backpack last night. He spent half an hour cleaning it out, and laughed and joked about it the whole time. What a guy!

I headed out late again at 8:45 a.m., but was still the first to leave camp. The Trail had turned into a spider web of roots instead of rocks. Roots are just as difficult as rocks. They grab your feet and trip your every step. A short, but hard hike to the NOC was the trail plan, and that is what I did. I descended from 4,280 to 1,749 feet, a drop of 2,531 feet in only 5.9 miles. My knees are killing me. I am not used to knee pain. Usually, it's the Achilles tendons that give me trouble, but they seem to be doing well. It rained as I walked in clouds most of the day. This cloud rainforest is thick with mosses. It gets greener, descending, but only because moss grows on everything. The trees still look gray and lifeless.

I arrived at the NOC at 11:30 a.m. and checked into the hostel. Ate lunch, wrote in my journal, cleaned up, and bought food. I will air out all my equipment tonight, and hopefully start tomorrow dry and warm. The convenience store didn't have much, so I bought the usual bagels and cheese, but added snack bars and lunch meat to the mix. I couldn't find summer sausage, and only purchased two days of food. I bought a little Pocket Profile trail map published by AntiGravityGear, LLC. On one side, important data is listed, such as mountains, water, tenting, excreta, mileage indicators, and a terrain profile map with elevations. The other side gives an aerial view of the Appalachian Trail indicating important points along the track of the Trail through the mountains.

I checked emails, caught up on my blog, and read Freedom, Chiggabite, My-Way, and Achin's trail blogs. They're all still on the Trail, but Freedom seemed to be having a lot of trouble. My-Way was way ahead of me, hiking as much as thirty-one miles on some days, but the rest of the guys were several days behind me.

I received requests via my TrailJournals blog asking me to discuss gear changes due to the cold weather. Even though I carry a 12-degree bag, I still get cold, sometimes due to dampness. The moisture penetrates the sleeping bag especially in shelters, a little less in the tent. I purchased a sleeping bag liner, which has made an improvement in my comfort. It provides warmth, but the bag liner's biggest benefit is in combating dampness. I sleep dryer now, which translates into warmer. Because I don't carry a coat, a one-shirt layer of long underwear wasn't enough to keep me warm at night after hiking all day, so I purchased a second long underwear shirt. Now I'm more comfortable in the evening after a day's hike. It is not that they provide warmth so much as they fight dampness. I still wouldn't bring a coat. Liner gloves are working well so far. My hands don't usually get cold anyway.

I will end this journal entry now and celebrate by purchasing a Great Smokey Mountain National Park permit for twenty dollars. How nice that feels! But the permit expires after thirty-eight days, and is only good for eight days in the park. This means no loitering while hiking the 71 miles through the Smokies.

DAY 13 MARCH 30: NANTAHALA OUTDOOR CENTER TO STECOAH GAP.
TODAY'S MILES: 13.4
TRIP MILES: 150.7

RW means Re-wind, a name given to me by the waiter at the NOC restaurant.

It stormed all night and I shared a cabin with Geo, a geologist from Louisiana. We talked for a long time and he showed me pictures of a garnet he found on the Trail. We ate breakfast and I hit the Trail at 8:40 a.m. The Trail climbs 3,313 feet in only 7.9 miles, up to the top of Cheoah Bald. While it rained at the hostel, it was snowing in the mountains. I used the Pocket Profile instead of the Guide on my cell phone. It worked great and is now my go-to resource, with the Guide as back up.

While hiking, I admired the snow-covered mountains of the Great Smoky Mountain National Park in the distance and wondered if they would still be covered in snow when I crossed over them. I ran into Black Horse, a 65-year-old man from Maine. He took his trail name from the military unit he once served in. We hiked together for an hour or more, and he talked about his family and his lifelong dream of hiking of Appalachian Trail.

Constantly ducking snow-covered branches provided me with another new meaning for RW: Rhododendron Weeping. The Rhododendrons are heavy with snow and their branches bend low on the Trail. As I push them aside, snow falls on me, and as the snow melts, their leaves drip water. They look like they're crying out for relief from the cold, heavy snow.

Near the top of Cheoah Bald summit, I met Opie, Small Spoon, Super Scout, and Murphy. They were slackpacking and I hiked with them for the rest of the day. My trail plan had me hiking 10.5 miles to Locus Cove Gap. I intended to hike to Brown Fork Gap Shelter, a distance of 15.8 miles, but ran out of steam at

Stecoah Gap, at 13.4 miles. At the urging of the slackpackers, I joined them and took a shuttle back to NOC to stay in a hostel. The shuttle cost ten dollars one way; that means another ten dollars tomorrow. Add to this one more night at NOC, and another day of slackpacking... more unexpected expenses.

It must be fate. I found Scott, Blue, and the homeless yogi at the hostel. I telephoned my wife and father. I try to call them when possible, especially my father. He was using an atlas to track my progress on the Appalachian Trail and wanted regular updates. He enjoyed letting me know what to expect ahead on the Trail. I talked to my wife regularly, but found texting more efficient. Frequently, it's easier to text than get a voice connection on the Trail because of weak cell signals.

DAY 14 MARCH 31: STECOAH GAP TO FONTANA DAM SHELTER.
TODAY'S MILES: 15.1
TRIP MILES: 165.8

RW means Really Winded, according to Murphy.

Sorry about not posting for so long. There is virtually no cell service in this area. This post was sent on April 3rd. Cell service is becoming a problem—at best, it is intermittent. Because I use my phone as a camera, I leave the phone on airplane mode all day. This way my battery lasts long enough to get to the next electrical outlet where I can recharge it. Making emergency calls is not possible most of the time, and there is nothing I can do if someone calls me from home with an emergency. I am too remote to provide help.

The decision yesterday to return to the NOC and slackpack today was one of my best to date. Again, the Trail is hard. I didn't realize the infamous climb, known as Jacob's Ladder, was just ahead at Stecoah Gap. Jacob's Ladder is a vertical, straight up and down perpendicular climb without switchbacks, 546 feet in only 0.8 miles. Exhausting and terrifying, especially for those afraid of falling.

The five amigos—Opie, Super Scout, Little Spoon, Murphy, and me—alternated carrying the day pack as we hiked together all day. The Trail between NOC and Fontana is the hardest yet, and very wet. We could see that some peaks in the Smokies were still covered with snow. The day was pleasant and sunny. By the end, we all had sore knees due to the steep up and downs. Near Fontana we started a five-mile downhill trek that hurt our knees even more. The first signs of spring were evident: snowdrops, windflowers, and trillium dotted the Trail.

We tried to call the Fontana shuttle at the parking lot designated as a calling point, but the phone was broken and none of our cell phones could get a signal. Fortunately we found a working phone at the marina office, and we were soon heading to the little village of Fontana. The others had mail drops to pick up, and I needed to buy more food to get me to Newfound Gap.

When we picked up our packs, I discovered the guy who provided the slackpack service had bought me three days of food, on the house. He did this because I told him I needed food in Fontana and he was concerned that I wouldn't make it into town before the store closed. Trail magic from a wonderful shuttle driver!

That night we opted to sleep in our tents near the lake, rather than in the shelter. The Fontana Shelter is nicknamed the Fontana Hilton because it is well-built and spacious. The view was beautiful from the tents overlooking the lake. My trail plan had me staying here the next day, one day ahead of the plan, and I started to congratulate myself on my planning ability.

I had expected the pain in my knees to go away over time, as my physical condition improved, but it didn't. I still wasn't anywhere in the same level of knee pain as Little Spoon and Opie. Opie, a retired Colonel from the 101st U.S. Army, was wearing knee braces. It turns out Opie knew my late uncle, who also spent forty years in the 101st. What a small world, meeting someone in the wilderness who knew a family member of mine! Super Scout is his son. Murphy is a grade school teacher in her early thirties, taking a sabbatical leave to hike the A.T. Students and colleagues track Murphy's progress by reading her online journal. Murphy chose her name and it stands for Murphy's Law: Anything that can go wrong, will go wrong.

MONTH TWO: APRIL
DAY 15 APRIL 01: FONTANA DAM SHELTER TO RUSSELL FIELD SHELTER.
TODAY'S MILES: 13.8
TRIP MILES: 179.6

RW means Retired Willingly, according to Opie.

It was a warm night with rain for about an hour. We woke early and fixed breakfast. Around the time we were ready to leave, Steve, our slackpack driver, pulled up with coffee, eggs, and biscuits for everyone. This guy's generosity never ends! Little Spoon decided to take a zero day because of sore knees. We're all hurting. The remaining four of us hiked over Fontana Dam and entered Tennessee and The Great Smoky Mountain National Park. We climbed Shuckstack Mountain, a tough 3.4-mile climb up 2,100 feet.

As we rested, the four super hikers arrived: Bree, Will, Simon, and Wesley. I never expected to see them again, but they took a zero day in Fontana, so I was temporarily ahead of them. The day was hot and the Trail dry. Unlike North Carolina, there isn't much water in the Smoky Mountains. We ran out of water and found only one source after a long, dry, thirsty hike. The forest seems vacant. Trees are spaced far apart without undergrowth.

My trail plan had me stopping at Mollie's Ridge Shelter, but the water is unreliable here, and it was early, so I hiked another 2.8 miles. This put me 13.8 miles ahead of plan. It was a hard day, mostly uphill on a ridgeline. We arrived at Russell Field's Shelter about 5:30 p.m.

This is my first time in the park, and already I have heard many stories about it. Hikers are required to sleep in shelters because of bears. However, if a day-hiker arrives with a permit, and the shelter is full, self-sufficient thru-hikers must vacate the shelter to provide the day hiker with a place to sleep. There were no day-hikers at this shelter today, so we all were able to stay inside.

Smoky Mountain shelters are bigger and better than any I've seen so far, but offer no better protection from bears. They are still only three-sided structures. There are also no privies, so the area around the shelters is a bit disgusting since everyone is forced to go wherever.

Many hikers hadn't buried their "used" food or TP, as required. Walking in the woods around the shelter was treacherous. The ground soil is shallow, with rocks lying just below the surface. Most of the time, digging a hole seems impossible. I gathered some loose dirt and leaves, and buried as best as I could. I carried a tent stake instead of a trowel for digging cat-holes, because of the reduced weight.

DAY 16 APRIL 02: RUSSELL FIELD SHELTER TO SILERS BALD SHELTER.
TODAY'S MILES: 14.7
TRIP MILES: 194.3

RW means Rocky Top Wind. I gave myself this name. It's windy on top of Rocky Top Mountain.

We got up early after a warm night. The shelter was crowded with fourteen people. The water source is a little stream about fifty yards downhill.

I had a hard time filling my water bladder because the stream is shallow. My water system is not working well. I rely on dipping my dirty water hydration bag into the water, and then filtering it. The Sawyer Mini water filter is slow, but effective. I need something faster that can be used in shallow water. I never had this problem before the Smokies.

Opie uses a water treatment called Sweetwater Purifier Solution®. With only a couple drops and a few minutes' wait, the water becomes drinkable. Unfortunately, it makes the water smell and taste like bleach.

The four of us hiked hard all day, and the Trail was difficult. Opie and his son, Super Scout, carried detailed topographical paper maps of the Trail. They provided good information, but I found them to be no better than what I was already carrying and they were a lot more trouble, in my opinion. I use the Guide loaded on my cell phone and a Pocket Profile map. They worked fine.

We have to climb four mountains today. Russell Bald Shelter is located up at 4,360 feet. The morning started with a short downhill, and then we began climbing the famous Rocky Top

Mountain, with a 5,440 feet elevation. The sky was clear and the day grew hot, even though patches of snow still existed in the shady places. Some insects were moving about the water source. They are the first insects I have seen on the Trail. After Rocky Top, we climbed Thunderhead Mountain at 5,527 feet and met a ridge runner named Fletcher. He said this portion of the Trail is the hardest in the Smokies.

At lunch time, we ran into three of the four super hikers at Derrick Knob Shelter. They said Bree went on without them because they were too slow for her. They were stopping for the day after only 9.4 miles. My original trail plan had me stopping here, but the day was young, so we moved on.

The forest is changing again. Instead of wide open views with large trees, the forest is cluttered with densely-packed smaller trees. After a grueling day, we arrived at Silers Bald Shelter, located at an elevation of 5,460 feet. We were totally wiped out and it was only 5:30 p.m. Surefoot, Buzz, Tandem (Buzz's daughter), Sensei from Alabama, and Inflammable were already there. Inflammable is a French Canadian hiking back to Canada.

I was now about 17.5 miles ahead of schedule. I finally got a cell connection and contacted my father to arrange for tomorrow's pick-up at Clingmans Dome. He wanted me to hike to Clingmans Dome tonight, but I was too exhausted. By 7:30 p.m., everyone in the shelter was asleep.

The Smoky shelters provide ropes hung from the ceiling and rafters so hikers can raise their backpacks off the ground. I always try to hang my pack from a rope. People have attached aluminum cans and plastic pop bottles halfway up the ropes to try and prevent mice from climbing into the packs. It doesn't really work. Mice can still get in your backpack.

To reduce mouse damage, I unzipped all the zippered pockets and loosened every opening, so the mice could easily crawl inside. Hopefully, when they realize there's nothing edible, they leave without chewing their way out.

DAY 17 APRIL 03: SILERS BALD SHELTER TO CLINGMANS DOME.
TODAY'S MILES: 4.6
TRIP MILES: 198.9

RW means Reindeer Watching. I saw my first large animal today, a deer.

We got up early after a warm night and were back on the trail by 7:30 a.m. The skies threatened to rain, so we all donned rain gear. Out west, lightning could be seen. Sensei and Surefoot joined the four of us.

The forest was changing again. Instead of small trees, the forest was made up of large fir and pine trees. Clouds moved in and the wind picked up. We could hardly see thirty or forty feet in front of us as we climbed Clingmans Dome. The wind gusted 25 to 30 miles an hour. We made it to the top of Clingmans Dome around 10:00 a.m. Clingmans Dome, at 6,643 feet, is the highest mountain on the Appalachian Trail.

My father was waiting for me in a nearby parking lot when we came down the mountain. He had driven over from Indiana to spend a few days zeroing with me in Gatlinburg. He was a trail angel today, too, because he gave Buzz, Tandem, and Sensei a lift into Gatlinburg.

DAY 18 APRIL 04: ZERO DAY.
TODAY'S MILES: 0.0
TRIP MILES 198.9

My first zero day and I enjoyed it with my father. It rained hard all day, making it a great day to be off the Trail. My father had hoped to take me to Dollywood, one of his favorite places. I was glad for the rain because I was tired and just wanted to rest. A zero day is fantastic. My knees, ankles, and stomach are so much happier. After eating all day, I am finally full. I had no idea I was so hungry. I was curious to find out how much weight I had lost, and how much my pack now weighed, but I couldn't find a scale.

I learned today that Mum stopped hiking at NOC while her son, Guy-On-A-Buffalo, continued hiking alone. He's very strong and I expect he will catch me within a week.

I have had a difficult time trying to filter water, so I added the Sweetwater Purifier Solution® drops to my water system. I wish I had started with it, and used the Sawyer Mini as a backup. I purchased more food than in the past because I've been so hungry lately. I stuck with the same diet, just added larger quantities. Now I had five days' worth of food, the most carried so far, and needed to buy a bigger food bag. I also bought gaiters because the Trail is so muddy. I want to keep my socks as dry as possible. Spring weather will keep the Trail muddy for a while. My pack keeps gaining weight. Extra gear and unexpected expenses keep mounting. The plan is to leave for the Trail early tomorrow.

DAY 19 APRIL 05: CLINGMANS DOME TO ICEWATER SPRINGS SHELTER.
TODAY'S MILES: 10.9
TRIP MILES: 209.8

RW means Rock Wrangler.

The view from Clingmans Dome today is spectacular. I am using the computer at the Hiker Mission in Hot Springs, NC, to post all the journal entries due to the lack of cell service. There is no cell service here in Hot Springs. Cell service is rare along the Trail, and computers even rarer.

My father drove Buzz, Tandem, and me back to the top of Clingmans Dome, the place where we left the Trail two days ago. During the drive back, Buzz, a computer wizard, taught me how to use a cell phone to write, cut, and paste text onto my online journal.

The day was clear, and all the clouds lay below us as Buzz, Tandem, and I slackpacked from Clingmans Dome to Newfound Gap, where my father was waiting for us with our gear. This is an enjoyable and beautiful section of the Trail. At the Gap, trail angels provided sandwiches, chips, pop, and candy. The entire day was warm and pleasant. Buzz and Tandem collected their gear and decided to head for Pecks Corner Shelter after a short rest. I continued on toward Icewater Springs Shelter.

I had thought about going to Pecks Corner Shelter, but the group of hikers staying there were partiers, much too wild for my liking. The partiers seemed to be turning the hike into a drug and alcohol binge, and using shelters as personal party houses. They slept through most mornings and hiked late into the evening. Their raucous noise woke everyone up when they finally entered the shelters. Hike-Your-Own-Hike, or HYOH, is a catchphrase on the Trail, but in this case I thought it was a very poor Trail edict. Their own selfish pleasure was ruining the experience for other hikers.

Icewater Springs Shelter was crammed because tent camping isn't permitted, unless the shelter is full. I liked this shelter, but the crowd was incredibly noisy. I camped outside and didn't worry about bears. All the Smoky shelters provide good bear lines for hanging food bags. My tent is now home. There were other thru-hikers here that I've seen before on the Trail, too many to list.

DAY 20 APRIL 06: ICEWATER SPRINGS SHELTER TO CROSBY KNOB SHELTER.
TODAY'S MILES: 20.3
TRIP MILES: 230.1

Got up early and watched a spectacular sunrise after a very cold night. It dropped down to about 28 degrees. I was back on the Trail by 7:30 a.m., hoping to put in a big mileage day and separate myself from this bubble of rowdy hikers. They're drunk, high, and obnoxious to everyone. I hoped to skip over them and get as far away as possible.

I learned that Guy-On-A-Buffalo has already passed me and is way ahead. He is a super strong hiker. I don't expect to see him again. For the first time, the Trail was somewhat level in many places. At one point the Trail turned into a narrow catwalk spanning rock walls, six or seven feet wide, with steep drop-offs on both sides. Beautiful and sunny, the views to the left and right were great, but I had to be careful not to step off the cliff while enjoying the views.

Vaquero and Stargazer passed me by, hiking hard to get ahead of the obnoxious partiers. Vaquero is a strong hiker in his twenties. I met him last night at the water spring where he and a few other hikers were holding a safety meeting. A "safety meeting" is Trail code for getting together to smoke weed. In the beginning, whenever I saw someone rolling joints, I thought they were filled with marijuana. Later I learned pot smokers preferred to use a pipe. Rolled joints were mostly handmade tobacco cigarettes. Making your own cigarettes is popular with the younger hikers. They say it is cost effective and a fun skill to learn.

Stargazer is a young, tall, beautiful woman from Germany who dressed mostly in black, like other Germans on the Trail. I met her before in the NOC when she was ill and taking a few zero days to recover.

I arrived at the shelter around 5:30 p.m. and it was crowded. Someone said a large number of hikers were close behind me. The park's ruling on shelter sleeping, compounded with the recent snow storms, was causing hikers to bunch up. I pushed into the shelter because I didn't want to be one of those self-sufficient thru-hikers forced to tent camp outside in the rain. After the evening meal, I noticed a hiker drinking his cooking fuel. I asked him what he was using for fuel. So far, everyone I'd met was using poisonous chemicals, like Heet or denatured alcohol.

He told me the dealer who sold him pot was also selling moonshine, so he bought some. Moonshine is a perfect multi-use backpacker fuel. It can be used for cooking, heating, as a nightcap and sleep aid, or as an antiseptic for first-aid emergencies. His only concern was scoring it, since many pot dealers didn't like to haul heavy containers of moonshine into the woods. It amazed me how quickly these hikers found drug dealers. He said it was easy, but I hadn't seen any, and I certainly had never been approached on the Trail. It must be an age thing. I am just too old to fit the dealers' demographics.

I met Fletcher, the ridge runner, again. He hikes the Trail five days a week, patrolling to keep the peace. I also met Wildlife, a young girl from Switzerland who was hiking the Trail because of Bill Bryson's book, "A Walk in the Woods." Most of the Germans said they became enthusiastic about hiking the Appalachian Trail after watching a film documentary and reading Bryson's book. As of today, I am 23.3 miles ahead of the trail plan.

DAY 21 APRIL 07: CROSBY KNOB SHELTER TO PAINT BRANCH CAMPSITE.
TODAY'S MILES: 12.8
TRIP MILES: 242.9

RW means Rock Welder.

It rained hard all night, turning the Trail into a mountain stream deep with running water. I was glad to be hiking in ankle-high waterproof boots. Most hikers wear trail runners, and their feet get wet all the time. Trail runners are much lighter than boots and rely on airflow to keep your feet dry, except in wet conditions. Then, your feet never dry.

Due to the rain, I left a little later than normal, about 8:45 a.m., but was still one of the first to leave the shelter. I dodged deep pools of water in the pouring rain. At about 10:30 a.m., Stargazer came from behind and passed me by. Later, when she stopped for a short break, I caught up and passed her. Minutes later, I heard her scream and turned around. Stargazer was lying in the flowing water on the Trail, clutching her leg in agony. She had fallen and cut her leg on a sharp rock. I helped her to stand and get out of the water. After a while, she felt better and refused my offer to carry some of her pack weight. I walked slowly ahead, keeping an eye on her as she limped behind me. Other hikers started to appear, so I picked up my pace, knowing that Stargazer wouldn't be left alone as she struggled on the Trail.

I left the Smokies about 12:00 p.m. and arrived at Standing Bear Hostel around 1:30 p.m. It was too early to stop hiking for the day, so I just bought some candy bars and trail mix and cooked a frozen pizza in their stove. After lunch, as I was leaving, Stargazer limped in. She said she was going to stay here tonight, and then go into town and find a doctor tomorrow.

I hiked another three miles, partly up the five-mile climb to the top of Snowbird Mountain, and stopped for the day at the Paint Branch Campsite at 3:30 p.m. The sun still set early this time of year and I hated to pitch camp in the dark. Besides, arriving late at campsites guarantees getting stuck with the spots nobody wants: wet, rocky slopes. By starting early and quitting early, I could claim better tent spots at shelters and campsites.

At an elevation of 4,263 feet, I would have to climb another 2,852 feet tomorrow to reach the summit of Snowbird Mountain.

Two 18- or 19-year-old boys named Prom Queen and Trail Wife were camped next to me. Prom Queen had made his own raingear and kilt out of plastic bags; it even had pockets. They were an interesting couple from Maine. Many other hikers were there, too many to list. As the evening progressed, the campsite got crowded. We built a nice campfire and everyone became excited about reaching Hot Springs, North Carolina, only two days away.

It felt great to be camping in my tent again in a good campsite with a reliable water source. The national park shelters in the Smokies were cold, damp, crowded, noisy, dirty, and mouse-infested. I started arriving late just so I could sleep outside in my tent, but other thru-hikers were more successful at using this strategy, and I ended up sleeping in a shelter almost every night in the Smoky Mountains.

This campsite has decent water, but I regret not putting in a few more miles. Tomorrow will be hard. I searched for a rock and a suitable tree branch to hang my food bag. It took a little while, but eventually I found a workable rock in the stream and a tree fifty feet away, with a limb about fifteen feet above the ground. Many of us used the same tree limb. By the time I crawled into my tent, ten food bags were hanging from it, all tangled by now.

DAY 22 APRIL 08: PAINTER BRANCH CAMPSITE TO MILE 261.6.
TODAY'S MILES: 18.7
TRIP MILES: 201.0

RW means Ridge Walker.

I knew it would be a long day, so I was the first one up and out of camp. It took about ten minutes to untangle my food bag from everyone else's. This required untying many of the other bags. I left the food bags on the ground, knowing the rest of the hikers would be getting up soon and figuring a bear wouldn't pass by in the next few minutes. I started up the mountain at 7:30 a.m. The Trail was dry, not too cold, maybe forty degrees, but damp and windy. Clouds enveloped me until 10:30 a.m. I wore several layers of clothes to fight off the cold wind and dampness. The Trail was an uphill hike until 12:30 p.m.

After summiting Snowbird Mountain, the Trail became a steep descent that abruptly turned back into a sharp ascent to the top of Max Patch Bald. Atop Max Patch Bald, I could see for miles. The land below had once been cleared for farming and there were no trees to block the views. I didn't linger to enjoy the view; cold winds were blowing all around me.

I hiked alone all day. A woman who called herself "I Believe" passed me, headed south. She was slackpacking today, and we talked for a few minutes. I Believe's husband was driving her from point to point for the next few days so she could slackpack and rest a bit. Yesterday, she had hiked twenty miles carrying a full pack. I Believe started out from Amicalola Falls on March 10th, eight days before me.

Just before Walnut Ridge Shelter, I ran into Opie, Super Scout, and Murphy, who were all slackpacking southbound. It was good to see them again. When we separated after Clingmans Dome, I wasn't sure if we would ever meet up again. They invited me to share a ride to Hot Springs and slackpack with them tomorrow, but I declined. The Trail would be mostly downhill from now on, and my pack was light since most of the food was gone.

Vaquero and I reached Walnut Ridge Shelter on top of Walnut Mountain at about the same time, 4:30 p.m. He decided to keep hiking for another ten miles to get to the next shelter, just shy of Hot Springs. This would be a 28-mile day for him. I wasn't up to that kind of mileage. I didn't like the looks of Walnut Ridge Shelter. It was cold, broken down, drafty, and mouse infested. So, I filled up with four liters of water and headed down the Trail.

Ever since my father's visit, I had rarely been treating my water, and was drinking it straight out of streams and springs. A risky move, but I was beginning to trust my ability to know the difference between good water and bad. Bad water was a stream running on flat ground from an unknown source. Good water was a spring or stream running down a steep hill with no obvious signs of human activity around the stream. Besides, I was in a hurry. Filtering takes at least thirty minutes, and I didn't like the taste and smell of bleach from the water purifying drops.

As I hiked, I thought about Russ, the old homeless yogi, and realized my life was starting to resemble his in some ways. I appeared homeless; each day brought me to another temporary and unfamiliar location. And although I was getting acquainted with many of the other thru-hikers, our short-lived encounters felt transitory and illusive as we continually passed each other on the Trail. They were simply people I kept running into. Daily hiking was the only permanent thing in my life now. The Trail is all about movement. Not moving means not advancing toward the goal—Mt. Katahdin. I treat every day like a work day. I get up, break camp, hike, set up camp, and sleep. Repeat the next day. Towns are a treat.

One more mile brought me to a stand of pine trees in Kale Gap. It was a beautiful site, so I decided to camp here on my own. Up till now, I had always tented in groups or near shelters. I breathed in the heavy scent of fir trees and scooped up pine needles to form a soft mattress underneath my tent. Dry wood was plentiful, and the trees offered protection from the weather. In the process of building a campfire, a piece of wood that I was splitting hit me on the nose. Blood gushed, and I tried to stave off the bleeding by using most of my precious toilet paper. Toilet paper is the most valuable item in anybody's backpack. Woe to those who run out! Hikers who think a leaf is a good alternative to toilet paper should try it once before yogiing for TP.

I turned on my cell phone and reversed the camera view to look at my face. Not too badly injured, I thought. After wiping the blood off and treating my nose, I went back to building a fire and used the bloody TP and hand sanitizer, which is mostly alcohol, as kindling to start the fire. It was amazing how easily antibacterial soap ignites and burns. It is now my favorite fire starter. Soon I had a warm fire that took the chill off, and I began drying my socks and shoes.

One thing about hiking in these mountains is that they are always wet and damp. The forest floor and wood are always wet, and the air damp and cold. Even 45 degrees feels cold because of the constant dampness. After a meal, I found a tree to hang my food bag, and made the toss over a limb on the first try. Another first!

For the past few days, campfire talk has centered on getting to Hot Springs—taking a zero day, buying supplies, making phone calls, and soaking in the hot mineral springs. Hot Springs is now nirvana in most hikers' minds, and we can't wait to get there. I didn't know what Hot Springs looks like, but I imagined it as a scenic tourist getaway with large pools of mineral spring water filled with people luxuriating in the healing waters, surrounded by rustic cabins in a heavily forested mountain setting.

I crawled into my sleeping bag about 9:00 p.m. and discovered my headlamp was dead. Even though my cell phone was down to a 20 percent charge, I was forced to use it as a light. The night was quiet and very dark as I fell asleep dreaming of Hot Springs and the mineral pools. At 4:00 a.m. I woke to answer Nature's call and had to check to see if my view was blocked by the sleeping bag, and then double-check to see if my eyes were actually open. It was so black that I couldn't tell if my eyes were open or closed.

DAY 23 APRIL 09: MILE 261.6 TO HOT SPRINGS.
TODAY'S MILES: 12.3
TRIP MILES: 273.9

RW means Really Wanting to be in Hot Springs, North Carolina.

It started raining early around 5:00 a.m., so I waited until 7:30 a.m. before breaking camp. With a partially dead headlamp, I finally started hiking around 8:30 a.m. and reached Hot Springs at 12:30 p.m. When I finally walked out of the woods, I found myself on a road in a subdivision without any sign of a white blaze. What happened to the Trail? I searched and searched for a blaze. After five minutes, I finally spotted an Appalachian Trail symbol embedded in the sidewalk cement. I followed the sidewalk, and it led me into the center of town. More firsts! The Trail was marked differently, and ran directly through a town.

Hiking into town, I passed the Alpine Court Inn motel and checked in for two nights. It's cash-only, and cost more than what was left from the fifty dollars I started out with from Springer Mountain. I had to find an ATM to get cash and replenish my fifty dollars of traveling money. Up to now, credit cards were sufficient.

Hot Springs is accommodating and hiker-friendly, but nothing at all like I imagined. It wasn't touristy. It has a paved main street lined with commercial buildings, restaurants, and bars. The hot springs were located inside a small building at the edge of town. And from what I gathered, the mineral waters were simply piped into bath tubs. Sorely disappointed, I soaked my frustration in the motel room tub.

I'm spending most of my time at the Hiker Ridge Ministry Center, a volunteer center for thru-hikers. It provides Internet and other social services. While there, I checked up on Chiggabite, My-Way, Freedom, Achin' and Murphy. They were all still on the Trail. Murphy was just ahead and My-Way was 150 miles ahead of me, but the rest were behind. Freedom was the farthest back, over one hundred miles behind, still struggling to get to Fontana. We had spread out so much, in such a short time! I uploaded several YouTube videos to my online trail journal, including a video of the flooded trail in the Smokies and a how-to video on filtering water.

During the day I ran into hikers who I had met on the Trail. They were all taking zero days to rest. The three super hikers showed up at the same restaurant where I was already seated and joined me. Our dinner conversation was enlightening. Wesley has adopted the trail name Cowboy. Simon, now called Gargamel, and Cornwall talked about the complicated process of obtaining a six-month visa for travel in the United States.

I had no idea it was so difficult. A visa application requires proof of financial means while staying in the country, proof of employment, plus many other documents. They both fibbed about having jobs waiting for them back home, because they both had to quit their jobs in order to hike for six months. We also talked at length about our shared trial by snowstorm. Everyone agreed it was the most intense experience so far on the Trail.

DAY 24 APRIL 10: ZERO DAY IN HOT SPRINGS.
TODAY'S MILES: 0.0
TRIP MILES: 273.9

RW means Roaming Wilderness.

My cell phone charger died today and the Hikers Ridge Ministry Center gave me a replacement. Trail magic! I haven't been able to get cell phone service in this town, and haven't had any real service since Franklin. Former thru-hikers told me to expect poor cell reception for the first weeks on the Trail, but I could usually pick up a signal on mountain tops. Now the phone never worked, not even on top of mountains. AT&T is my service provider. Verizon customers seem to have better service more often.

I hung out all day in Hot Springs. Thought I might head out today if I felt okay, but realized I needed a day off when I woke up this morning. I weighed myself at the outfitter store. With all my clothes on, I was three pounds lighter than when I last weighed myself at home without clothes. So far, I have probably lost eight pounds.

A hiker told me that only 12 percent of A.T. thru-hikers actually completed the Trail in 2013, and that 50 percent or more had dropped out before Hot Springs. While at the Hiker Mission, I looked up the completion rates on the ATC website. Her facts were inaccurate, which is not uncommon on the Trail. In 2013, nearly 50 percent of north bounders, or NOBOs, made it to Harpers Ferry, and 26 percent made it to Mt. Katahdin.

I ran into Katrina and Mike, the young couple from Switzerland, while doing laundry. I met them a long time ago in Georgia, and again in Franklin, after the big snowstorm. They told me they had skipped the Smoky Mountains and jumped to Hot Springs because of Katrina's serious knee problems. No longer attempting a thru-hike, they have decided to enjoy as much of the Trail and the United States as much as possible before their six-month visas expired. They have trail names now. She is Swiss Miss, and he is called Matterhorn.

Tonight the town provided trail magic in the form of free dinners for all the thru-hikers. There must have been about forty of us, including Swiss Miss, Matterhorn, Buzz, Tandem, and the three super hikers. Trail angels served pizzas, hot dogs, salads, desserts, and beverages.

During the dinner, we learned about a large Trail festival starting tomorrow. I wasn't interested in spending more time in town. If I had known in advance about all of the Trail festivals that take place along the route, I might have altered my trail plan to enjoy some of them.

Tomorrow I start a long 70-mile section to Erwin, Tennessee, with no resupply points along the way. I will have to carry four days of food. I purchased food at the Dollar General and a few other convenience stores. Summer sausage wasn't available, so I replaced it with lunch meat, individually packaged Spam slices, and single servings of tuna fish for protein. They were out of bagels, too, so I bought soft-shelled tacos, peanut butter, and more protein bars. Food is expensive in this little town, especially at the convenience stores, but they are the easiest places for hikers to shop.

DAY 25 APRIL 11: HOT SPRINGS TO CAMP CREEK BALD.
TODAY'S MILES: 20.9
TRIP MILES: 294.8

RW means Right Whales, according Caveman One.

I headed over to the restaurant at 6:00 a.m. and ate a wonderful breakfast. After buying a take-out sandwich for my lunch, I hiked out of Hot Springs at 7:00 a.m.

I climbed several mountains today. This required a lot of energy. Every thousand feet of climbing requires the same expenditure of energy that it takes to hike two miles on level ground. Hot Springs is situated at a 1,326-foot elevation, and I am currently standing at 4,750 feet. Earlier, I came across a group of workers conducting a controlled burn of the forest. They were all wearing forest-fire gear. Afterwards, the acrid smell of burning smoke followed me for hours.

There weren't many hikers on the Trail. Almost everyone stayed in Hot Springs to enjoy the hiker festival starting today and lasting all weekend. I did meet Caveman One and his partner, Uncle Fool. They had left from Springer Mountain on March 8th.

This is Caveman One's second thru-hike attempt. Last year, he fell and sustained a concussion near Erwin, Tennessee. Both of them have already been off the trail ten days this year due to sickness and injuries, and were now sick again. I hurried along, not wanting to catch whatever they had, and washed my hands with antibacterial soap as I hiked away.

Later on, I came across a hiker called Caveman Two. He was 22 years old, and had been doing 20-miler days early in his hike. By the time he reached NOC, however, his calf muscle was pulled. Now his tent poles were broken, and he was hurrying to pick up a mail drop with replacement parts waiting for him at the next hostel.

The forest here is mostly hemlock. A posted sign said the Boy Scouts of America were maintaining the hemlock trees near Hot Springs in an effort to save them from destruction by Chinese beetles. No other trees have even started to bud. The mountains are a stark contrast to the lush vegetation growing in Hot Springs. There, the townspeople were already mowing grass, and garden flowers were in full bloom. Up here, only a few wildflowers are beginning to peek out, and most of the trees are bare and leafless.

Hiker logbooks can be found at most shelters. I usually sign them so people know whether I passed through or stayed there for the night. I consider signing logbooks to be a safety measure. If something happened to me, and I needed to be found, rescue parties would have a rough idea of when and where I was last hiking on the Trail. Some hikers refuse to sign the logbooks because they want to remain anonymous. Some are trying to avoid a particular hiker for whatever reason, and don't want to reveal any clues as to their whereabouts. Other hikers just consider shelter logbooks to be stupid.

I signed the logbook at Spring Mountain Shelter when I stopped for lunch. As I ate the take-out sandwich from the Hot Springs restaurant, I skimmed through the logbook pages and recognized the signatures of a lot of hikers who are just a little bit ahead of me. I decided to push harder tomorrow and try to catch them, even though I seem to be developing a blister on my heel. My first blister!

I arrived at Camp Creek Bald at 6:30 p.m., where communication towers and a lookout tower had been built on the summit. After exploring the mountain top, I sat and watched the sunset. I had the whole mountain to myself and was enjoying it.

After eating dinner, I hung my food bag from a tree and began writing in my journal. Writing about the events of the day had become a nightly ritual for me. I had never written in a diary or journal before, and found this new experience to be very satisfying.

DAY 26 APRIL 12: CAMP CREEK BALD TO HOGBACK RIDGE SHELTER.
TODAY'S MILES: 20.2
TRIP MILES: 315.0

RW means Randall White, a name given to me by a day-hiker.

I started the day early at 7:00 a.m. thinking the Trail would be easy, but it wasn't. After the first hour, I encountered a blue blaze sign indicating an alternate bad weather trail route. Blue blazes were usually considered to be the route chosen by those looking for a short cut, or an easier way. That wasn't my way. I considered myself a dedicated white blaze hiker. For the first several hours on the white blaze trail, I walked over boulders and broken rocks overlooking a sheer ledge. I enjoyed the view, but progress was very, very slow. Any misstep could cause a real injury.

I was grateful for the good weather. Suddenly, I realized just how dangerous this route would be in bad weather. I carefully made a mental note that I needed to consider following the blue blazes in bad weather, especially on the more hazardous sections of the Trail.

The temperature heated up as the day progressed. The forest floor in the lower mountains was now covered with green plants. I walked by graves of Union soldiers killed during the Civil War. This wasn't the last time I saw grave markers on the Trail. Grave sites are more common than you would think. So far, I've seen grave markers for Union soldiers, forest rangers, forest firefighters, notable A.T. hikers, and Trail maintainers.

At lunch time, I finally met two other thru-hikers named Listener and Tank. They were moving slow, and I ended up passing them. The terrain is difficult. The mountains are high, and unlike the Smokies, each mountain is separated by a steep gap. I'm climbing up or down rugged slopes all day long.

By the end of the day I was extremely tired. If someone had asked me to stop hiking at this point, I might have said yes. For the first time, I really felt like quitting.

When I finally reached the Hogback Ridge Shelter, I knew a lot of the thru-hikers: Surefoot, Merlin, Time-to-Eat, Rob, and Nick. They each greeted me by name, and I felt so much better.

It was a great end to a very hard day. I hung my food bag and noticed several lines hanging from the tree limb. Other hikers had tangled their bear lines and couldn't get them back down, so they left them hanging like vines on the tree.

DAY 27 APRIL 13: HOGBACK RIDGE SHELTER TO SPIVEY GAP.
TODAY'S MILES: 15.8
TRIP MILES: 330.8

RW means Roy Wilson, renamed by a trail angel who said I looked like his friend named Roy Wilson.

We all packed up early and headed for Sam's Gap because of the promise of fantastic trail magic. When we arrived, Paul was serving scrambled eggs, hash browns, and all kinds of sides. What a wonderful Palm Sunday breakfast!

Except for the free dinner in Hot Springs, this was the first trail magic since Newfound Gap, nearly 111 miles ago. Merlin hadn't read the sign carefully and missed the small detour needed to get to the trail magic. When he realized that he'd ended up walking past it, Merlin had a lot of four-letter words to say about his mistake!

The day warmed up and there were no noticeable changes in the wildlife, except for the growing presence of insects and songbirds. Rob, Surefoot, and I hiked together most of the day. Merlin and Time-to-Eat walked together. Time passed quickly with pleasant company, but the hiking proved to be hard again because of the many steep elevation changes. We ended the day early at 4:30 p.m. Merlin and Time-to-Eat arrived about 6:00 p.m. By the end of the day, I had left North Carolina behind me. Two states down!

The water source was good here and the five of us settled in for the night. After about six tries, I finally got my food bag hung. Rob and Surefoot tied their food bags to my line as well. The wind picked up and the trees rustled loudly most of the night. We were camped near a road and noticed the sound of traffic, off and on.

During my limited hiking so far, I had been warned against camping near roads. Roads are risky places to camp, because human predators consider lone campers easy prey. I wasn't worried about it tonight because there were five of us, but I was determined never to camp near a road alone.

DAY 28 APRIL 14: SPIVEY GAP TO ERWIN.
TODAY'S MILES: 10.7
TRIP MILES: 341.5

Rob says RW means Ridge Wizard.

Last night was warm and we camped in a grove of large hemlock trees next to a stream. A few day hikers had warned us earlier about predicted rainstorms, so we got up early and left by 7:30 a.m., hoping to reach Erwin, Tennessee, before the rain. As usual, Surefoot, Rob and I hiked together, with Merlin and Time-to-Eat hiking behind us.

The Trail was easy and we made Erwin just after twelve noon. We planned to stay at Uncle Johnny's Nolichucky Hostel and Camp Store, but there were only two beds left. I was looking forward to buying new socks at the camp store, but they didn't have much of a selection. Rob and I decided to check into the Mountain Inn and share a room. The Mountain Inn is wonderful: fantastic service, clean rooms, easy walking distance to supplies, and the nicest people you will ever want to meet. Tank, Listener, and Time-to-Eat checked in later.

A brief description of the people I have been hiking with: Merlin is super skinny and stands about five feet three inches tall. He appears to be in his sixties, and is very intelligent and interesting. Now that he is retired, Merlin lives and travels all over the world. He chooses adventure over possessions, such as a car or house. Merlin worked his entire life in sewage treatment and never filters his drinking water, believing he is immune to all waterborne diseases. Merlin claims he never gets sick on his world travels and ignores all precautions about drinking the local water. This is his third attempt to hike the Appalachian Trail. The first two attempts, combined, lasted about 100 miles, and he started in Maine. He will likely make it all the way this time.

Surefoot had been a nurse, but decided to make a new start after dealing with the stress of career burnout. I think she'll complete the trail. Rob is a retired corrections officer who developed and administered training for inmates. He was looking for adventure and a way to put the years of working for a prison system behind him. I think he is dedicated to thru-hiking the Trail, and will make it. Time-to-Eat is a section hiker. He's in the United States Army and enjoying his time on the Trail.

Once again, I didn't eat all of the food I carried because of trail magic and making faster time than projected, as much as a day. We went to an all-you-can-eat pizza place, and then walked back to the motel where we did laundry and chores. Around dinner time, we learned about a trail angel named Miss Janet. Miss Janet shuttles hikers around and has the biggest, most decorated van you'll ever see. It is totally rigged for hikers. She drove Rob, me, and a few others to town for groceries and a cooked meal. I bought two and a half days' worth of food to get me to the next resupply point, including a large Subway sandwich for lunch tomorrow. I also did laundry, caught up on my online journal, and called my wife. Freeze warnings are predicted for tonight with snow in the mountains. I will wait and see about hiking tomorrow.

Here's an odd, horrifying fact about Erwin, Tennessee. In 1916, a five-ton elephant known as "Murderous Mary" from the Sparks Brothers Circus killed a man. The local people demanded justice. In front of a crowd of 2,500 people, a crane was used to hang the elephant to death.

DAY 29 APRIL 15: ERWIN TO BEAUTY SPOT GAP.
TODAY'S MILES: 12.2
TRIP MILES: 353

RW stands for Royal Whiskers, a name given to me by Listener.

Weather occupied all our discussions this morning at the Mountain Inn during breakfast. Rob decided to hike out and joined up with Surefoot, Merlin, and Nick, who had stayed at Uncle Johnny's hostel. Due to the poor weather, Listener decided to slackpack, so he called a shuttle driver, and I joined him. It was a good decision. My heels were hurting from blisters and I was tired. I think I have a cold coming on.

While talking to the shuttle driver, I mentioned that two days ago while crossing Big Bald Mountain, a man who treated my feet with blister patches thought the blisters were caused from socks folding up in the back of my boots. She quickly pulled out a pair of smaller socks and gave them to me. Trail magic! This brightened my mood and attitude about hiking in such foul weather. I hiked all day with the donated socks, and am now ninety-nine per cent sure that I need new socks. I will purchase smaller socks the first chance I get.

The shuttle took us to Beauty Spot Gap, and for the first time, I hiked southbound on the Trail. The weather was awful, cold and wet all day long. The wind was blowing and gusting, and the driving rain came at us horizontally. As we hiked down the Trail, the weather turned even worse, with sleet, hail, and falling snow.

We met a guy known as Father John. He had coffee and warm brownies, just the type of trail magic needed on such a miserable day. As I hiked out of the mountains, I passed Prom Queen, Trail Wife, and the three super hikers, Cornwall, Cowboy, and Gargamel. They were all heading into the mountains. I also saw Rob, Surefoot, Nick, and Merlin at Curly Maple Gap Shelter. A sturdy shelter, but it will be a very cold night. I am glad to be sleeping at the motel tonight, and not in the mountains.

Listener is hard to keep up with because he's such a strong walker. We discussed many interesting topics during our hike. Including the definition of hiker. We decided a backpacker was a subcategory of hiker. So slackpacking is hiking, but backpacking only includes carrying a backpack.

Even though I wore rain gear, my clothes were damp by the time I got back. Snow is predicted in the mountains tonight. I will stay in the motel and eat in town. That night, I wrote in my online journal: "I want everyone who is reading my journal to know that I am having the time of my life. There are hardships on the Trail, but that does not diminish the enjoyment. I continue to meet the best and most interesting people. The mountains are very beautiful, and my days fly by very fast."

After I updated my online journal, I checked up on the original hikers I had met at Amicalola Falls. Chiggabite and Achin' were still on the Trail, behind me. On April 13, Freedom left the Trail at Fontana due to severe hip pain. My Way was at least 230 miles ahead of me, but hadn't posted any new entries during the last few days. His last post mentioned ankle problems. I was 46 miles ahead of my original trail plan.

For the last two days, a shuttle driver named Miss Janet has driven me to a restaurant for dinner. Her huge van is plastered with various A.T. and hiker support stickers. She is a true A.T. legend. Miss Janet is a very capable and knowledgeable shuttle driver who lives in her van during the hiking season and follows thru-hikers all the way to Maine. She supports herself by providing shuttle service on a donation basis, and she knows everything there is to know about the Appalachian Trail. Miss Janet is frequently the savior of injured, stranded, lonely, weather-beaten, and depressed thru-hikers. Miss Janet is one of the must-meet people on the Trail!

DAY 30 APRIL 16: BEAUTY SPOT GAP TO CLYDE SMITH SHELTER.
TODAY'S MILES: 14.40
TRIP MILES: 368.1

RW means Renegade Wanderer. The shuttle driver came up with this name.

He drove me back to Beauty Spot Gap for a charge of $35. An unplanned expense added to an unplanned motel bill, and the cost of meals in town.

At 9:00 a.m. I left Beauty Spot Gap clearing and arrived by 5:30 p.m. at Clyde Smith Shelter. Overnight, it had snowed hard. Beauty Spot Gap was beautiful, and so were the snow-covered mountains. I hiked in the cool morning sunlight surrounded by stunning views. With snow and ice crunching under my feet, I hiked up the mountain, but hardly noticed the steep climb because of the breathtaking scenery. As I climbed, the snow deepened into drifts, making the trail difficult to follow. On one occasion I lost the Trail and had to backtrack to find my way.

The day went by fast and I passed very few people. At the end of the day, I finally made it to Clyde Smith Shelter. There were some people I knew at the shelter, and some I didn't. Cowboy, Gargamel, and Cornwall were already there. They said yesterday was the worst day yet on the Trail, even worse than the March 25th storm.

I met Frankie the Sleeper for the first time. Frankie the Sleeper is an anesthetist who quit his job to hike the Trail. In 2010, he made a thru-hike attempt and completed 463 miles before calling it quits due to injuries. Two young girls arrived in the evening. Their trail names were Alaska, from Alaska, and Happy, who was perpetually happy. These two girls had hiked at least 25 miles today, and planned to hike many more 25-mile days. They didn't even seem tired. The rest of us were amazed. They were both Harvard University students and members of the rowing team. They planned to hike 100 miles in three days in order to be in Damascus for Easter.

We had a hard time finding low-hanging branches to secure our food bags. This shelter didn't have a cable system, so Frankie the Sleeper solved the problem by throwing one end of a rope over a tree and attaching a carabineer to the rope, and then throwing the other end of the rope over another nearby tree. We attached our food bags to the carabineer and tightened both rope ends to raise the food at least ten feet about the ground. With no privy, and the thin soil a mere few inches deep, we had to maneuver our way through landmines of partially-covered human piles when walking in the woods.

DAY 31 APRIL 17: CLYDE SMITH SHELTER TO OVERMOUNTAIN SHELTER.
TODAY'S MILES: 15.0
TRIP MILES: 383.1

RW means Roan Wireless.

Very cold this morning, my thermometer read 28 degrees. There was a crust of ice in my water bottle. Today was a big day with a major milestone. I climbed the dreaded Roan Mountain. The mountain reaches 6,212 feet, the second highest on the Appalachian Trail. The climb was hard, and because of the weather, was the most treacherous yet. Overnight, the Trail flooded and transformed into a trail of ice. Every step was slippery and threatened to put me on the ground. As a result, it took a long time to climb the mountain. I am not sure which is worse—a trail turned into a running stream, or a steep, frozen river of ice. The day started cold and warmed up a little in the afternoon, but not enough to melt the ice on the Trail, or the snow on the mountains.

Overmountain Shelter, at an elevation of 4,654 feet, is a big, rickety barn that was once used as a film set in the movie "The Following." As I surveyed the inside of the shelter, I could see the wind whistling through the spaces between the boards. I decided not to sleep in the barn; it was too cold and drafty. Most of the crowd from last night was going to sleep in the barn, anyway. My tent is warmer.

Everyone from last night is here, except Happy and Alaska, who planned to hike a marathon day. Rob arrived soon after me, exhausted. He had hiked tremendous miles to make up for the seven-mile lead I had on him two days ago.

There is no sign of spring in these mountains, except for small patches of green grass. The trees aren't even close to budding and there are no visible flowers. Spring will not show up for a long time.

I am almost completely out of food, something that hasn't happened to me before. I thought I had purchased extra, but I was so hungry that I ate more than expected. While Rob made a reservation at the next hostel, I asked him to include me, too, so I could buy food. I had to walk nearly a hundred yards from camp before I found a tree with a suitable limb to hang my food bag. The line got tangled on the first cast, and I eventually had to cut the rope because it wouldn't break free. I decided to sleep with my food bag. Everyone else was doing the same thing that night. I'm writing this journal entry inside my sleeping bag because it is so cold and windy. It is only 6:30 p.m. Everyone else is inside their sleeping bag, too, because of the cold weather.

DAY 32 APRIL 18: OVERMOUNTAIN SHELTER TO US HIGHWAY 19E.
TODAY'S MILES: 8.7
TRIP MILES: 391.8

RW means Roan Whistler, after the windy day in the Roan Highlands.

I climbed the Balds today. Theories abound as to how these famous mountain tops became bald. Some believe fires, caused by lightning, are the reason. Others say overgrazing, and some blame logging. Nobody really knows for sure. Was it nature or man?

We crossed a log bridge over a small stream at the 400-mile mark today. Someone had made a sign out of sticks to mark the 400-mile location. I thought this was a fun idea and decided to make a sign every hundred miles.

A short day, I stopped at Mountain Harbor Hostel. This was the second hostel I have ever stayed in. Rob and I shared a clean, private room while the other hikers were packed into the bunk house. After cleaning up, the owners shuttled us all to town for a hot meal and shopping. I bought five days' worth of food at the local grocery. It should be enough to get me to Damascus.

I've been startled lately by thru-hikers pretending to be action heroes or historical figures. A trio of thru-hikers dressed in kilts, with blue face paint, like Mel Gibson's Braveheart, charged by brandishing handmade machetes. Yesterday, "Rambo" popped up from nowhere, and earlier, a masked Bat Girl caught me by surprise. It's popular for hikers to choose a superhero as their trail name, but some of these people were taking it to the next level by assuming the persona of their favorite character. The scariest people on the Trail so far!

DAY 33 APRIL 19: US HIGHWAY 19E TO MOORELAND GAP SHELTER.
TODAY'S MILES: 18.9
TRIP MILES: 410.7

RW means Reckless Whirlwind, because I broke a picture at the hostel where I stayed with Rob and many of the thru-hikers I met in the past few days.

Caveman Two tented outside. In the morning, we were provided with a fabulous breakfast. I ate so much I was almost too full to hike. During the meal, I heard about a 71-year-old lady named Vagabond who hiked the A.T. last year in less than six months. She plans to hike it again and set the record as the oldest woman to thru-hike.

Merlin walked into the hostel and upset the staff with his rudeness. He didn't stay, just purchased a few food items and left. I figure it's his diet that makes him so angry. As a rule, he adds water to dehydrated potatoes at night, and then eats them cold in the morning. Lately the potatoes have been half frozen in the morning, and he swears at them. It is just one of many food choices that can make a difficult hike miserable. I am amazed he is still hiking. He just gets more miserable every time I see him. I bet he finishes the Trail, though.

I weighed myself today. I gained back some of the weight I had lost. Seems improbable, but the scales at the hostel say it's true. Today Rob and I hiked together all day. We left the hostel at 9:30 a.m. and by 5:30 p.m. had hiked 18.9 miles. The day was cool and drizzly. We hiked along the Upper Laurel Fork River for several hours. Hiking was easy, and we did more miles than expected. After dinner there was lots of campfire talk about politics and Damascus. Just before bed I saw the strangest rainbow. It went straight up out of the top of Roan Mountain. Unfortunately, there were too many trees to get a good picture.

Rob and I hung our food bags together, and then learned a new trick from one of the other thru-hikers. She put the rock into a little nylon sack, synched the sack tight, and then threw it over the branch. We liked the idea—no more trying to tie a line to a rock. Why didn't we think of this earlier?

DAY 34 APRIL 20: MOORELAND GAP SHELTER TO WATAUGA LAKE SHELTER.
TODAY'S MILES: 16.6
TRIP MILES: 427.3

RW means Really Wise, according to Sprout, a hiker I met a few days ago.

It's Easter Sunday and Rob and I hiked together all day. Spring weather is taking hold in the lower elevations. Columbines were in bloom today. While hiking over a series of picture postcard wooden bridges, we passed the spectacular Laurel Falls. The trail to the falls was steep, rocky, and difficult, but Laurel Falls is beautiful. We hiked along the stream for hours. In July 2012, a father and son went swimming near the falls, in hot weather, after a hard day of hiking. Nobody knows what happened next, but their drowned bodies were found along the edge of the stream bank.

We were a little disappointed that there wasn't any trail magic today, since it is Easter. The only exception was at breakfast when a thru-hiker gave everyone a piece of chocolate. Gargamel, Cowboy, and Cornwall passed us going into town for supplies. Gargamel seems sick. I will know more at Damascus. We are making great time to Damascus and hope to be there by Wednesday. We met a young couple from London, England, who were quite overweight, but still hiking high mileage day after day. I am amazed by the number of people who appear seriously out of shape, but hike great distances carrying a full backpack. Maybe being fat and fit is possible for some people.

After Laurel Falls, the trail followed a small path between a cliff and the river, and then cut steeply up toward the ridgeline and over a mountain called Pond Flats. What a misleading name for this steep climb. I found a blue blaze above the river trail. The sign said it was the high water trail. Since the water was low, we chose to hike the white blaze trail along the river. The day was perfect.

Near the end of the day, we arrived at Lake Watauga, located at a lower elevation of 2,084 feet. Lake Watauga is a man-made lake, actually a large reservoir. Its dam is over three hundred feet tall and was built in the late 1940s. When we reached the lake, we had to hike around it. Many people were picnicking at the beach, and several fishermen tapped the shoreline with fishing lures while casting from their boats. I was envious of them and dearly wished I could stop to fish.

Tonight, Rob, Red Dog, Caveman Two, and I will stay in a shelter near the lake, but not close enough to see or enjoy it. This is a popular recreational area and many local campers and weekend hikers stay here. If it wasn't Easter Sunday, this shelter would be packed. We all slept inside the shelter instead of tenting because of the threat of rain for the morning. Cell phone reception has improved. I was able to make calls for the last two days.

DAY 35 APRIL 21: WATAUGA LAKE SHELTER TO DOUBLE SPRINGS GAP CAMPSITE.
TODAY'S MILES: 27.0
TRIP MILES: 454.3

RW means Romantic Whippoorwill. Just after dawn, a singing whippoorwill flew close to our shelter. Red Dog sat up and shouted, "Romantic Whippoorwill, that's what RW means!" Then he went back to sleep.

Red Dog is a retired high school shop teacher who needed some time away from the classroom. I left camp at 7:30 a.m. intent on catching up to Rob, who had left fifteen minutes before me. I hiked hard all day, but never caught up to him.

I didn't study my Guide closely enough before leaving the shelter and hadn't noticed how scarce water would be on the

Trail today. After crossing the Watauga Dam, the Trail began a long steady climb up to Vanderventer Shelter. I was supposed to pass a spring along the way, but I didn't see the spring and ran out of water. Caveman Two caught up to me and kindly gave me some sips of water, even though he had little to spare. I didn't want him to suffer because of my mistake. A few more miles and I would be at the Shelter. When I got to it, I couldn't find water. Now what? I was out of water and, according to the Guide, the next water source was nearly four miles away. No problem, I thought, I had done this before.

Unfortunately, the weather had been hot today. So far I had only gone without water on cold days. My mouth was dry. I walked for two more hours, nearly seven miles, before finding a stream. A female backpacker was sunbathing next to the stream, but I was so thirsty that I rushed past her and plunged my face in the water, frantically drinking my fill of unfiltered water. It was only afterwards that I realized she was in her underwear, staring at me like I was crazy. I had never been so thirsty before! I said, "Hello!" and she introduced herself as Phase 2. After a brief conversation, I filled up my water bottle and scurried away.

At 3:00 p.m. I discovered a large box of soda pop and snacks sitting next to the Trail. A sign said the box was kept supplied by a local church group. This trail magic appeared at an opportune moment, because I was once again almost out of water. I was drinking more water than usual because of the warm weather. Water sources are spaced surprisingly far apart and are meager on this section of the Trail. Water had been abundant until yesterday.

I got to Double Springs Shelter at 5:00 p.m. and was feeling good, but still hadn't caught sight of Rob. He had talked earlier about doing a 28-miler today, but I thought he had changed his mind. Rob hadn't signed any shelter logbooks, so I was stumped about his whereabouts. I didn't like the look of this shelter. It was small, dirty, and overrun with mice. The tent sites were poor, too. I studied the Guide and found a campsite at Double Springs Gap. I decided to go for it and arrived at 6:30 p.m.

My first marathon day! I hiked 27 miles. The miles were moderate-to-easy all day. Caveman Two was at the campsite, building a fire. We were the only people there. As night fell, sitting around the campfire, we spotted the beam of someone's headlamp approaching us on the trail. As the person got closer, he appeared naked, and was moving incredibly fast. When we finally got a good look at him, the only thing the hiker was wearing was a pair of shoes and an extremely brief bikini swimsuit.

He was Indiana, a young, very tall man from Hawaii who wouldn't explain why he chose Indiana as his trail name. He said he was doing a 40-miler today and wasn't stopping until he made it to Damascus. If it takes between 4.6 million and 5.7 million steps to hike the entire A.T., then Indiana, with his super long legs, might finish in only four million steps. No wonder he hiked so many miles in a day!

DAY 36 APRIL 22: DOUBLE SPRINGS GAP CAMPSITE TO DAMASCUS.
TODAY'S MILES: 13.3
TRIP MILES: 467.3

RW means Reading and Writing, a name given to me today by Blue Jay.

Caveman Two and I stayed at a nice campsite last night and left early by 6:45 a.m., headed for Damascus, Virginia. The Trail was mostly downhill and smooth. On the way into town, I crossed the Virginia state line. Three states down so far! I ran into Murphy, who I hadn't seen since Gatlinburg, Tennessee; and Surefoot and Merlin, who I hadn't seen for the past four days. Surefoot had a whole new hiker look. Hikers rarely change their appearance. I can recognize hikers a hundred yards away just by their clothes. Everybody wears the same clothes every day. Now, Surefoot was sporting bright pink knee socks. She said they were compression socks and they helped ease the swelling in her legs. No one had seen Rob.

I made great time and arrived in Damascus at 11:30 a.m., and had lunch with Caveman Two, Merlin, and Blue Jay. Merlin couldn't have been happier; he was downright pleasant! It turns out he hates cold weather, and as the weather warmed up, so did his mood.

Damascus is a small town, and like all towns on the Trail, I couldn't get a cell signal. Maybe Wi-Fi if I am lucky. I posted this entry from the public library. The Appalachian Trail runs through the center of Damascus. As a result, the town's economy has developed around catering to backpackers. There are several outfitters and a lot of hostels and bed and breakfast inns. Rob is not in town. I must be ahead of him, but how and when did this happen?

I saw Phase 2 as soon as I got into Damascus. She was squeaky clean and carrying a large sack of groceries. I asked her how she beat me into town. There was no way she out-hiked me during these past two days. After pressing her, she confessed that she got tired and hitched a ride about fifteen miles before Damascus. She said it was fine with her, because she was still making an honest effort to thru-hike. What was the harm in skipping a few miles?

Tomorrow will be a zero day. My ankles are hurting. I am tired and hungry. I plan to check out the three outfitters in town and buy new socks, a water bag, and possibly new hiking boots. My boots feel fine but are falling apart after hiking 467 miles of hard mountain trails, not to mention all the breaking in and training miles in Illinois. I bought a portable backup charger for my cell phone to compensate for the long periods of time between electrical power outlets on the Trail. All these items were adding more weight and unexpected costs to the hike.

DAY 37 APRIL 23: ZERO-DAY IN DAMASCUS.
TODAY'S MILES: 0.0
TRIP MILES: 467.6

RW means Rainbow Walker, as a reminder of the rainbow jutting out of Roan Mountain a few days ago.

Last night was not good. I had checked into Dave's Hostel and my room flooded because of bathroom plumbing problems. On top of this, some guy was sick all night and kept everybody awake with his noisy and disgusting stomach ailments. I stayed up most of the night. First thing in the morning, I complained to the manager and demanded a refund. He said I must have slept some of the time, so he only gave me half my money back.

I walked down the street and checked into the Hikers Inn Hostel, the best in town. Now I have a very clean, private room. Another reason I left Dave's Hostel is because I don't want to get sick. Rumors of contagious hikers were circulating around town and became the topic of conversation in every café. Some say

Norovirus is spreading throughout the hiker community. I hope not. I'm taking extra precautions with cleanliness and limiting physical contact with other people now. "Noro" is a nasty virus. Talk has been going around for weeks about last year's devastating viral infection that had been picked up in the Damascus area.

I finally saw Rob again in the morning. We had separated two days ago when he had left the Watauga Lake Shelter fifteen minutes before me. Rob said he became disoriented and confused right after leaving the Watauga Lake shelter. Usually, shelters are situated uphill, and the Trail continues to rise when exiting them. This isn't always true, but it sure feels that way. On our arrival the night before, Rob and I hadn't noticed that the Watauga Lake shelter violated the norm. The next morning, Rob followed his regular routine and started hiking uphill. Uphill, in this case, was the wrong way! He headed south for over a mile before realizing his mistake. Rob was behind me from the start! He had hiked 21 miles that day trying to catch up to me.

Today is beautiful and a zero day. I stayed in town and noticed the arrival of many more hikers. I saw Buzz and Tandem, and recognized others, but not by trail name. No matter how many miles I hike, there are always hikers right behind me, hiking just as hard. Many are taking a zero day in Damascus.

After breakfast, I went to Sun Dog Outfitter and purchased new socks, called Fits, and a pair of hiking shoes, Salomon XA Pro Low trail hikers. This will be my first time hiking in low profile trail shoes without waterproofing. I hope they work, or I will be in a world of hurt when I start hiking again. I'm wearing the new shoes in town today, hoping to break them in a little before hitting the Trail. I mailed my old boots, old socks, and compass back home for only $9.99 postage. I sent the compass home because I never used it. The Trail is so well-marked, I just don't need it. So far, the compass, pocketknife, and braided survival wrist rope were the most useless items carried. The braided wrist band got ditched in a hiker box. I only use the knife to open food packages, so I am glad it's miniature in size. I purchased some Epson Salts and plan to soak my feet and rest tomorrow. Feet, knees, and ankles are sore.

Merlin and Murphy left town today. Merlin is carrying eight days of food and is now moving fast. It's most likely I won't see him for a long time, if ever. I probably won't see Murphy again either. She is a strong, fast hiker.

I am scheduled to meet my son on May 5th in Bland, Virginia, 120 miles to the north. Right now, I need to decide on how many days' worth of food to buy, and when and where to make food stops before reaching Bland.

DAY 38 APRIL 24: ZERO-DAY IN DAMASCUS.
TODAY'S MILES: 0.0
TRIP MILES: 467.6

RW means Really Wrecked due to my poor physical condition. My left Achilles tendon is very sore. Walking is difficult.

I am still in Damascus and plan to stay another day. Once I get back on the Trail, I plan to hike slowly for several days. I ran into Tandem this morning at breakfast. She said her father, Buzz, was at the clinic. He had open sores on his feet that weren't healing.

I saw more hikers that I know. I ran into Cornwall, Gargamel, Cowboy, and Stargazer at the library. Gargamel and Cowboy were sick for three days with Norovirus, and never stopped hiking. They pushed 16 to 27 miles every day, vomiting the whole time. Trail lingo for this is "brown blazing", which means leaving a streak of human waste along the Trail because of illness.

These guys are invincible and unstoppable. Cornwall has escaped the virus, so far. Stargazer, the young woman who fell on the trail two weeks ago, said she went to the hospital after her accident and spent three days in a hostel recovering. Since then, she hasn't stopped hiking, afraid that her six-month visa will expire before she is able to complete the Trail. They all plan to leave Damascus tomorrow.

Last night I saw Razor, the A.T.C. ridge runner. I first met him at Tray Mountain Shelter on my fifth day of hiking. He's driving north in order to hike south and gather information about sick hikers. He said it seems like Norovirus is spreading on the Trail. I really need to heal and get out of town as soon as possible. The Center for Disease Control has signs posted everywhere with instructions for Norovirus prevention. I noticed antibacterial soaps in shelters. I've purchased bleach cleansing wipes for hand washing, and supplemented my antibacterial soap with regular soap. Cleanliness, no food sharing, and minimal human contact are recommended prevention measures.

Spring has arrived in Damascus and the surrounding mountains in a big way. Dingy mountain brown is sprouting vibrant colors of green. Dogwoods are dressed up in pink and white, and the other tree blossoms are ready to pop. Tulips, dandelions, and spring flowers brighten up town flower beds, and the residents are happily mowing grass and planting vegetable gardens.

What a great day to take it easy and heal! I soaked my feet yesterday and plan to soak them again as I sit outside in warm sunshine, gazing up at the deep blue, cloudless sky. This reminds me, I need to buy sunblock. I hope soaking my feet completely distracts me from my fear of Norovirus.

Just before my arrival in town, I ran into a swarm of mosquitoes. I also need to get bug repellent for the trail, while I'm still in town. I tried to purchase a pair of short pants today and went to all three outfitters, but nothing fit. My waist size is down three or four sizes. I weighed myself on the scale at the hostel. I dropped ten pounds.

Damascus is gearing up for Trail Days, which will be held this year on the weekend of May 14-16. During that week, the town's population of nine hundred explodes with an estimated twenty thousand festival goers. With its economy hinged on the Appalachian Trail, many local businesses depend on the success of the annual Trail Days festival.

I highly recommend the Hiker Inn Hostel. It's clean and well run by hospitable owners. It is now my favorite hostel. The Top of Georgia hostel in Hiawassee would be my second choice. Hiker Inn Hostel has comfortable mattresses on the bunk beds. Up till now, the best hostels provided hard vinyl cushions for sleeping pads.

The worst sleeping accommodations were two-by-four wooden bunks with plywood bases. Hikers have to use their own sleeping pad and sleeping bag as a mattress. Must go and buy food now. If you don't hear from me for several days, it means I left town for the Trail.

DAY 39 APRIL 25: ZERO-DAY IN DAMASCUS.
TODAY'S MILES: 0.0
TRIP MILES: 467.6

RW means Recovering Wounded. I went to the clinic yesterday and received bad news. My Achilles tendon is inflamed and needs to rest a few days so that it can heal. I can barely walk now. They gave me a cortisone shot and some medication to help with the pain and swelling.

Monday, I hope to start the Trail again by slackpacking for one day. If all goes well I will begin hiking again at a very slow pace for about a week. I am still fifteen miles ahead of my original trail plan. This injury is the result of my inability to distinguish between temporary pain and pain caused by serious damage. I thought it was just normal trail pain that would eventually go away. Instead, it got significantly worse.

Right now, I am sitting in the hostel resting my ankle. Most hostels have a policy of limiting the time a hiker can stay, generally no more than two days. But because of my injury, the owner agreed to let me stay until I recovered. No further news on the Norovirus, and no other illnesses noted in town today. This makes me feel better, since I can't leave.

The fact that I am not hiking today doesn't upset me. It has rained hard, all day long. Rainwater pours down the main street of Damascus. I can't imagine how badly the Trail is flooded today. It seems a higher force is looking out for me. Whenever I am not hiking, the weather seems to take a turn for the worse. Rob left for the Trail today in this rain. I hope he stays dry.

Now, many of the people that I have been hiking with for the last several weeks will be significantly ahead of me. I will be meeting a whole new group of hikers when I get back on the Trail. There is still time for me to make Mt. Katahdin.

Last night I went to dinner at Joe's Taco. Two thru-hikers who carry a banjo and violin played for tips. During the evening I met Grandma Jo, a 52-year-old woman from Germany. She has been in town for almost two weeks with the worst case of blistered feet I've ever seen. Her feet are just raw. Another one of the walking wounded in town.

DAY 40 APRIL 26: ZERO-DAY IN DAMASCUS.
TODAY'S MILES: 0.0
TRIP MILES: 467.6

RW means Rusty Wheel.

This is a very special entry and day. On March 30th, I hiked with a 65-year-old man named Black Horse while climbing Cheoah Bald. This kind and gentle man shared with me his hopes and dreams for hiking the Trail, and we both talked at length about our family and friends.

Black Horse is from the state of Maine. He was excited about hiking home to his family and friends. Every step on the Trail brought him closer to that dream. That morning, we climbed a mountain in the snow and were rewarded with beautiful mountain scenes.

Yesterday, I emailed his wife a photo of Black Horse taken on that day. She emailed me back to inform me that he had suffered a tragic accident on April 12th. Shortly after he left the Smoky Mountains, Black Horse fell off a cliff in Pigeon Forge and was seriously hurt.

It was a miracle that people were whitewater rafting directly below him at the precise moment he fell. They saw him fall from the cliff and came to his aid. Black Horse is now in the hospital with multiple broken bones and internal injuries. He is preparing for his fourth surgery.

The Trail can take anyone, at any time, any way it chooses. I wish him the best and want to let him know that for those few hours, he touched my life. I'm still recovering from an Achilles tendon injury, but knowing what happened to Black Horse gives me a new perspective on my own setback.

DAY 41 APRIL 27: ZERO-DAY IN DAMASCUS.
TODAY'S MILES: 0.0
TRIP MILES: 467.6

RW means Reborn and Wondering if I can walk. I went to a worship service at the local Presbyterian Church. The inspirational sermon was about Timothy.

Damascus is quiet today. Other hikers are reporting Norovirus and sickness on the Trail. I hiked for about two hours on the Trail today without a pack. Minor aches, but no pain, so I plan to hit the Trail on Tuesday, moving slowly for a few days.

Yesterday, a Baptist Church group brought food for all the thru-hikers at the Methodist Church Hostel, also known as The Place. I appreciated the good food. Today, a trail angel found out it was a German thru-hiker's birthday, so she brought cake and ice cream for everybody staying at the hostel.

I received another email from Black Horse's wife. She said that Black Horse is looking forward to providing trail magic for me in Maine when he is stronger. I look forward to seeing him again as a trail angel.

While wandering around town, I found a manhole cover next to a gas station on a hill where I was able to use my AT&T phone. I talk to my wife now every day at that spot. This manhole cover is the only place where I have been able to get cell service. If I move a few feet away, I lose service. It is so frustrating.

My wife is a miracle of encouragement during this hard time being injured and off the Trail. She wants me to stay put until I can get back on the Trail strong and healthy. She is my greatest supporter.

DAY 42 APRIL 28: ZERO-DAY IN DAMASCUS.
TODAY'S MILES: 0.0
TRIP MILES: 467.6

RW means Random Wobbler. I'm still here in Damascus and walking around town fairly well now. My Achilles tendon is getting better.

Tomorrow I hope to slackpack about seven miles as a test, but with a forecast of severe thunderstorms, I may skip hiking if the weather is bad.

The three injured Germans—Grandma Jo, German One, and Little German—all shared a shuttle ride this morning headed for a larger town. Because of their injuries, they may take a bus and travel several hundred miles north in order to hike an easier section of the Trail.

I purchased a monthly Verizon phone plan and cell phone. Another unexpected expense, but I hope it solves some of my communication problems. Staying in town for so long is really adding to the expenses. I am now way over my planned budget, more than $1,000. Today, I gave up budgeting and decided it will cost what it costs. I just need to deal with it.

I leave tomorrow to get back on the Trail. I am behind my trail plan for the first time, by sixteen miles. Am I returning too soon? Do I really have what it takes to hike the A.T.?

I went to church again this past Sunday and prayed for strength to hike the entire A.T., a rather self-serving prayer. I don't want to give up and fear what failure could do to me emotionally at this point. I'm not ready to quit hiking, just as I wasn't ready to quit working when I retired.

While preparing to leave Damascus, the biblical story of the exodus came to mind. I made it to Damascus in 36 days. The Hebrews, travelling about the same distance, walked in the desert for 44 days before reaching Mount Sinai. The Appalachian Trail may be harder miles, but at least I didn't have to cross the Red Sea.

DAY 43 APRIL 29: DAMASCUS TO SAUNDERS SHELTER.
TODAY'S MILES: 9.2
TRIP MILES: 476.8

RW means Right or Wrong.

Yesterday I purchased a paperback version of the A.T. Guidebook, ripped out the pages pertaining to the sections I had already hiked, and mailed them home. I will carry the rest of the guidebook with me because the PDF version on my cell phone is too hard to use. I tore out the page detailing today's hike, put it inside a plastic sandwich bag, and slipped it in my pocket for quick access. The rest of the guidebook is stowed in my pack.

After the thunderstorms passed, I ate breakfast at my favorite coffee house, bought two large Subway sandwiches, and hit the Trail. I skipped slackpacking because I needed to test myself with a full pack. If it didn't work out, there were plenty of opportunities in the next fifteen miles to catch a shuttle back to town. I took three naproxen sodium tablets and began to walk slowly. The new trail shoes and socks worked well, but six days off the Trail had affected my physical fitness level. My legs were tired and the injuries sore.

I hiked along the Laurel River for several miles. The morning storms had swelled its banks and the river roared. The gully I was walking in thundered with the sound of rushing water. This section of the Trail closely parallels, and even merges for a short distance with, a bicycle path called the Creeper Trail. The Creeper Trail could serve as an emergency route, if I found I couldn't walk today. I hiked up and down Iron Mountain, the most useless and pointless PUD on the Trail so far. The Trail climbed straight up to Iron Mountain from the Creeper Trail, and then right back down to the Creeper Trail. No point at all, no view, and nothing to see from that mountain top.

The forest has livened up since I left the Trail six days ago. Many of the trees were pushing out leaves, giving the forest a subtle green hue. The forest floor is green with new growth. Trees are starting to blossom. Insects are emerging, too.

The Trail is surprisingly dry, even with the recent rain, and the temperature is comfortable. The humidity is sweltering, however, and I am soaked with sweat. Rumblings in the distance give warning of yet another approaching storm.

I am staying in a shelter because of the predicted rain. Trail angels had left a spray can of Lysol, and we spray everything to try and kill Norovirus. I hung my food from a sapling using a new bear line, a five millimeter, water-resistant smooth poly-rope. The weak sapling bent under the weight, causing the food bag to sag only seven feet off the ground. I let it go and hoped a bear wouldn't come by. I took three more naproxen sodium tablets before sleeping.

DAY 44 APRIL 30: SAUNDERS SHELTER TO THOMAS KNOB SHELTER.
TODAY'S MILES: 18.6
TRIP MILES: 495.4

RW means Roaring Wind.

No bears last night. The wind must have been 35 miles per hour all day, with the Trail offering next to no protection. I climbed White Top Mountain, the second highest mountain in Virginia at 5,235 feet. Standing was difficult. The wind caught my pack like a sail and forced me to stumble and lean to one side for hours. I entered a large area of Balds where the scant trees were leafless due to the high elevation. I was back in a winter environment. Spring was still weeks away from here.

The map indicated an ideal campsite that was located farther away than I wanted to hike, but I hiked on anyway. Sixteen miles to find protection from the wind! When I got there, a sign said the campground was closed in order for the meadow to recover from overuse. I hiked two more miles to the next shelter and ended up hiking far more miles than intended with my sore Achilles tendon. I took three more naproxen sodium tablets and tried using both phones, but neither could get cell service. Maybe purchasing another cell phone plan wasn't such a great idea.

The shelter was crowded with eighteen young people. I am the ancient old man here. We all just huddled, thankful to be staying inside such a well-built shelter instead of a tent. The shelter was located just below the top of Mt Rogers. At 5,490 feet, this is the highest mountain in Virginia. I saw a wild horse just before reaching the shelter. This is wild horse country and everybody in the shelter talked about the horses, hoping to see more tomorrow. The night was cold and rainy, and by 6:00 p.m., everyone could see their breath. The wind picked up and howled and buffeted the shelter all night long.

I ate my cold food ration and was still hungry, but forced myself to stop eating anyway. Afterwards, I hunched down by the shelter entrance and watched some latecomers prepare their dinner. It was terrible. One guy cooked the most tantalizing meal I'd ever seen. It smelled delicious. I stared at his food while he ate it, desperately wanting to snatch it away and eat it myself. After an agonizing several minutes, I became aware of how conspicuous I was and crawled inside my sleeping bag, dreaming of food—pizza, burgers, ribs, hot bread, on and on and on, until I finally fell asleep.

MONTH THREE: MAY
DAY 45 MAY 01: THOMAS KNOB SHELTER TO FOX CREEK. TOTAL MILES: 12.7
TRIP MILES: 508.1

RW means Received Wave.

I woke up with a sore Achilles tendon and took three more naproxen sodium tablets. I used naproxen sodium instead of ibuprofen because I just wanted the swelling to go down, and didn't want the painkiller associated with ibuprofen.

It's cold and windy, and heavy clouds and mist surround the shelter. I started hiking with anticipation as I entered Grayson Highlands State Park. Wild horses live in these mountains, and after the brief encounter with one horse yesterday, I hoped to see more. The terrain is mostly treeless grassland, ideal for horses. The Trail, though, is hard on the feet and ankles because of broken rocks and deeply eroded soil. I hiked with my head down in an effort to avoid tripping. Keeping your head down makes it hard to enjoy the awe-inspiring scenery.

After a while I noticed four horse legs on the Trail and looked up. Just a few feet ahead of me was a small herd of wild ponies! I had walked right into a herd before I ever saw them. Many beautiful horses and colts stood all around me, calm and tame. I petted a horse standing next to the Trail. Throughout the day I came across four herds, 30 or 40 horses all together.

The cool air and heavily overcast sky threatened to rain all morning. A hiker I had never met before named Forester Gump caught up to me. We started walking together and ended up talking for a long time. Just before noon, Forester Gump and I crossed the 500-mile mark. I made a milestone marker next to a stream using rocks. Forester Gump's trail name reflects his life story. He is a forester from Michigan and walks with a limp after being struck by an uninsured drunk driver. The doctors told him he would never be able to walk again. For the past twenty years, he has undergone many operations in an attempt to repair the damage to his legs.

The sun finally came out after lunch, and I took a terrible fall. I had been limping and favoring my right leg all day due to the sore Achilles tendon. The tumble strained my right thigh. The last 20 to 25 miles of trail had been mostly broken rock, and the rough terrain overtaxed my ankle. I lay on the ground trying to decide what to do and checked the guidebook for an emergency exit.

Eventually, I hobbled to the nearest road at Fox Creek and tried hitchhiking into Troutdale, Virginia. This second attempt at hitchhiking on the Trail was even more unsuccessful than the first try. Today's meaning for RW stands for the people who waved at me while I tried to hitchhike. What is with the waving?

At one point I stood in the middle of the road, frantically trying to hail down a car. The driver almost ran me over. He didn't even slow down. There were no shoulders on the road, and several cars purposely rode the white line, forcing me to jump into the ditch. I limped and prayed for a ride the entire three and a half miles into town. No ride. It was the worst experience that ever happened to me on the entire Trail.

I walked to the small hostel run by a Baptist Church. No one was there, so I just entered and staked out a bed. A sign pointed to the water and shower locations. This hostel is nice and clean, but Troutdale is a dead town. No gas station, food, restaurant, stores, or anything else. Not even cell service. Fortunately, I was able to walk to a tiny bank branch while it was still open, and the employee kindly let me use their phone to call a shuttle. I tried to be nice, but I wasn't. The hitchhiking experience and the pain in my leg had taken a toll on me. I called Miss Janet first, but she didn't pick up. I called Gypsy Dave, the shuttle driver who had offered to help me slackpack back in Damascus. He charged $45 to pick me up in Troutdale the next day and drive me back to Damascus.

As the night wore on, back at the Baptist Church hostel, five other hikers showed up, including Forester Gump and a homeless couple who camped outside with a vicious dog. All the thru-hikers described similar experiences while trying to hitchhike into Troutdale. Oddly, the homeless couple with their half-wild dog got picked up on that terrible road. By lights out, no one from the church had stopped in to check on us.

DAY 46 MAY 02: ZERO DAY.
TODAY'S MILES: 0.0
TRIP MILES: 508.1

RW means Riding not Walking. As expected, I am too injured to hike today, and besides, there is no place to resupply in Troutdale. This new injury has me walking so slowly that my food supply would run out well before reaching the next resupply point.

This Baptist Church hostel is a strange, but very clean hostel. It is co-ed, like all the hostels I've stayed at so far. Men and women share the same bunkroom. Ironically, many of the hikers that I met would prefer separate sleeping areas, because it would make dressing and changing clothes so much easier.

Every hostel so far, however, had an absolute rule against bed-sharing, even for married couples. I left the hostel today without seeing a caretaker or anyone from the church. I put some money in the donation box and wrote a thank-you note in their logbook. Except for the bank teller who let me use the phone, I didn't meet anyone else in Troutdale.

While waiting for Gypsy Dave to pick me up, I studied the mountains. The lower elevations were green with freshly-minted tree leaves. As the elevation rose, the mountain colors faded from green into a brownish gray at the top. The days are getting warm, but nights in the mountains still fall to near-freezing temperatures. Winter gear will be needed for several more weeks.

I provided a little trail magic for the other thru-hikers at the hostel. I paid for their trip to the Trailhead. Just like me, they dreaded the thought of walking back on that merciless road. The homeless couple remained at the hostel hoping to find work.

My wife is driving into Damascus today, or tomorrow, depending on how many miles she covers before stopping for the night. I will spend my time recovering while waiting for her. We are scheduled to pick up our son at the airport in Johnson City. My son and I will start hiking together and continue as long as we can before he has to fly back to California in a week. I am so looking forward to hiking part of the Appalachian Trail with him.

I've decided to start using my camp stove. Eating dry food all the time feels like deprivation. I want hot meals at night. I am sick of bagels with peanut butter, and the other dry food. Some of it I will still carry, but a stove will expand my food options. It might keep me from dreading meal times, in spite of the constant hunger pangs that never end once I'm back on the Trail. Food is the only thing I think about at night. I just don't seem to be able to carry enough food anymore. I carry more food than ever now, but it still runs out. I am forced to limit myself to one meal ration at night, and then go to sleep hungry. This same meal, forty days ago, would have been too much food for me.

Back in Damascus, I checked into The Place, a hostel run by the local Methodist Church. It costs only six dollars a night, which is a deal. I couldn't get into the Hiker Inn, the place where I stayed earlier. The Hiker Inn is more expensive at 25 dollars per night, but is clean and run by friendly people. It also has a modern bathroom, comfortable beds, and heat. The Place is a rundown old house set up with wooden sleeping racks in a crowded unisex bunkhouse environment. It isn't heated, and everyone shares one small bathroom. A warning sign is posted that states the building does not meet current building code standards for electricity and plumbing.

The weather in Damascus is so much warmer than in the mountains. I went from a long-sleeved shirt and jacket to shorts. I keep running into hikers I haven't seen since the beginning of the Trail. I saw Geo and Scott. I was surprised to find Scott still on the Trail. He's drinking beer in town and getting his fill before hitting the Trail again. The German girl, Stargazer, the one who fell in the Smoky Mountains, is still in town. She intended to leave days ago, but her knee is sore. Everybody is catching up to me, both the injured hikers and the healthy people who started a week or two after me.

When I begin hiking with my son on May 6th, I will be eighty miles behind my original trail plan, roughly six days behind schedule. I wrote about this delay in my online trail journal to alert Steve and Denise that I might not be able to reach Shenandoah National Park in time to hike with them as planned. I dearly wanted to be able to hike with them in that park.

DAY 47 MAY 03: ZERO DAY.
TODAY'S MILES: 0.0
TRIP MILES: 508.1

RW means Relaxing Well. Today, I just sat and rested my Achilles tendon and sore leg.

My Verizon phone has cell service so I kept up with my wife's driving progress from Chicago. She plans to pick me up tonight and drive me to a motel in Atkins, Virginia. I called Steve to tell him about my slow progress, and we agreed to hike together from the point where I was located when they arrived from Indiana.

I also checked the thru-hike status of Freedom, Achin', My-Way, and Chiggabite. Freedom was definitely done. Achin' quit the Trail on April 28th, and Chiggabite got off on April 18th. My-Way hadn't updated his journal since April 12th, which made me suspect he was off the Trail. I was the only one left from the Amicalola group, but I was struggling with injuries.

I was impatient to leave Damascus and knew my wife would have a hard time finding me. I sat on the street curb at the town's entrance and leaned against the stop sign. I studied every pickup truck that drove by, hoping it was her. Two hours later, long after dark, my wife arrived, and we drove to Atkins, Virginia for the night.

DAY 48 MAY 04: ZERO-DAY.
TODAY'S MILES: 0.0
TRIP MILES: 508.1

RW means Reconnecting with the Wife!

This is Cathy, RW's wife, filling in as Pat's journal writer. Here we are in Atkins, VA. Yesterday, I drove in from Chicago and picked him up in Damascus, where he had to spend another day recuperating from his second leg injury. He seems to be on the mend and his energy is good.

We drove around the area today and saw Owl Bear at the Grayson Highlands Visitor Center. RW met him in Damascus during his first injury. We gave Owl Bear a lift to a hotel where he planned to stay for the night. The rest of the day was spent shopping for food and gearing up for the next seven-day hike. Our son, Mark, flies in from California tomorrow. He'll hike for a week with his dad. Once we pick him up at the Johnson City airport tomorrow, father and son plan to head out on the Trail that evening.

DAY 49 MAY 05: FOX CREEK TO HURRICANE MOUNTAIN SHELTER.
TODAY'S MILES: 3.3
TRIP MILES: 511.4

RW means Rustling Woods.

For the first time since starting the Trail on March 18th, I went to a barber shop in Marion, Virginia. I got a haircut and beard trim, and I feel like a new person! One thing about hiking the A.T.: men rarely shave and beards get long. Many of the women don't shave either, so there are a lot of hairy hikers on the Trail. All this hair soon becomes a disguise. I have re-met many men I couldn't recognize because of their big beards and long hair.

Today was a very special Cinco de Mayo. My son, Mark, flew into the Tri-City Airport, where Cathy and I picked him up in the afternoon. I rested during the day while waiting for Mark to arrive. His flight connection in Phoenix was delayed so he didn't arrive until 4:40 p.m. The weather is beautiful right now and the Trail is decked out with spring flowers and tree blossoms.

By early evening, Mark and I were geared up and ready to head out on the Trail near Troutdale. We fine-tuned our packs and posed for a few parting photographs, and said our goodbyes to my wife, who had dropped us off at the trailhead parking lot. During this time, we met two other hikers: Union Jack from England, and a veteran section hiker from Pennsylvania who recently had both knees replaced.

By starting today, instead of tomorrow, it places me roughly sixty-one miles behind the original trail plan, not eighty miles as I had earlier mentioned. Maybe with some good days, I can get close enough to Shenandoah in time to hike there with Steve and Denise. We finally hit the Trail at 7:00 p.m. I felt better than I had in weeks. We got to our campsite just after 8:00 p.m. and set up in the dark. We camped below the shelter next to a stream and ate Subway sandwiches. We ate and talked for a long time, and then went to bed. Mark had tied his hammock between two dead trees. During the night, the wind picked up and bent the trees, causing the hammock to stretch and twist all night long.

DAY 50 MAY 06: HURRICANE MOUNTAIN SHELTER TO STREAM AT MILE 524.3.
TODAY'S MILES: 12.9
TRIP MILES: 524.3

RW means Raccoon Wilderness. It's the name of the forest we hiked in today.

Mark and I slept late, and then prepared a hot breakfast of oatmeal and coffee. This was my first hot breakfast on the Trail since I started two months ago. After packing up, we were back on the Trail by 8:45 a.m. A cool day, a smooth trail, and lots of water! We walked by a roaring waterfall where we intended to fill up with water, but a warning sign said it was unsafe. We still had enough water to make it to the next water source without worries. I showed Mark my system for filtering and purifying water. Gatorade bottles have replaced the smaller plastic water bottles. The wide mouth of a Gatorade bottle is perfect for scooping up water from streams. The bottle fills easily and is lightweight, cheap, and sold everywhere. Many hikers use Gatorade bottles instead of the expensive store-bought water bottles. Mark used a Lifestraw to filter his water. A Lifestraw is just that—a filter designed like a straw. Lifestraw works, but Mark discovered it was slow and cumbersome when filtering several liters of water for later use. Many hikers tried Steripen, which uses light to kill germs, but few hikers carried it for long. A Steripen can't filter sediment and breaks easily.

Mark joined me at a remarkably good time. Flowers were blooming along the trail and trees provided just the right amount of shade. We hiked through pastures several times. I couldn't ask for a better hiking day. We talked like we never talked before.

We met two people from Germany, another from England, plus many more interesting hikers. Stopping early at 4:30 p.m., we set up camp in a scenic spot next to the Trail. To our good fortune, the ground was level with plenty of clean water and firewood close at hand. We relaxed and leisurely watched the cows grazing in a nearby pasture. Soon, Tex joined us. She was a young girl from Texas who had never backpacked before. This was her first day on the Trail. We helped her pitch a tent and prepare for the night. In the evening we cooked our meal over a fire and ate well. The night air remained warm, and we both slept without using rain flies. Every time I woke up, I looked up at the stars.

DAY 51 MAY 07: STREAM AT MILE 524.3 TO CHATFIELD SHELTER.
TODAY'S MILES: 13.9
TRIP MILES: 538.2

RW means Remembering Wishes.

We woke early and enjoyed another hot breakfast of coffee and oatmeal, then packed up and hit the Trail. Mark got his first taste of mountain fog, which didn't burn off until 9:30 a.m. We enjoyed the feeling of hiking in the cool fog. Once the sun came out, the day really started to heat up. May-apples were flowering alongside our route. I had never seen May-apple flowers before. The Trail was fairly smooth all morning. By 10:45 a.m., we had reached the Mt. Rogers Visitor Center.

I called Pizza Hut to order a pizza. I had heard it's one the few places where you can get a pizza delivered to the Trail. To my great disappointment, they told me they didn't deliver before 4:00 p.m. While there, I introduced my son to the Kallin family. They had camped the night before at the nearby shelter. The Kallin family is a husband-and-wife team hiking with their two children and dog. The son, Robin Hood, is nine years old, and their daughter, Cartwheel, is six. The Kallin family started hiking the Trail two weeks after me and passed us yesterday. The children are being home-schooled by their parents while they hike the Trail. If the Kallin family succeeds in their attempt, Cartwheel may become the youngest female thru-hiker, and the second youngest 2000 Miler on record.

For a fifty cent fare, we boarded the 11:00 a.m. bus with fifteen other hikers and rode into Marion. About half the people on the bus showed up at the same pizza place as us. Wrecking Ball joined our table. There were many other hikers at the pizza parlor, too, that I hadn't met before.

We took the bus back to the Trail, and were hiking again by 3:00 p.m. The weather was hot, 89 degrees at one point. According to the guidebook, potable water sources would be scarce for the next seven miles. We passed the homeless woman I had met a few days earlier at the Troutdale Baptist Church Hostel. She was waiting for her husband, who went searching for water. We offered some of our water, but she declined. We left hoping that her husband would return soon with water.

Later, we noticed a child-sized walking stick lying beside a water spring. It looked like Robin Hood's walking stick. We discussed bringing it to the next shelter, only a mile ahead. That was where we planned to stop for the night. If it was Robin Hood's stick, the family was probably miles ahead of us. We wouldn't see them today, and maybe never. Those kids hike eighteen to twenty miles a day and still have energy left to play.

Further down the Trail, we saw Mrs. Kallin hiking towards us. She was trying to find her son's lost walking stick and had already backtracked a mile. The family was waiting for her at the shelter. We told her where it was located and apologized for not bringing it with us. We'd just figured we couldn't catch up to them.

We reached the shelter at 6:45 p.m. The first thing I did was tell the rest of the Kallin family that the walking stick had been located, and their mother should be back in about half an hour. When Mrs. Kallin did return, the family continued hiking, intent on covering several more miles before calling it a day.

The shelter was crowded and few tent spots were left. A party atmosphere had taken hold. Many hikers brought in beer and liquor from town and were getting very drunk. Others smoked pot. One girl was so drunk that she shuffled to a corner of the shelter, dropped her pants, and peed in front of everybody. She was too drunk to make it to the privy only twenty feet up the hill. We were all wide-eyed and disgusted, especially the hikers lying on the floor next to the encroaching urine flow. The girl lost her balance and landed in her own puddle. Afterwards, she proceeded to put the make on several guys. They immediately ducked inside their tents. It was surprising to see a bunch of drunken guys running away from a horny, drunken girl.

Scott from Montana was there. His trail name is now Jalapeno, because he puts hot sauce on everything. Dependable Pete and Dirt were there. I met Dependable Pete and Dirt, both in their late 40s or early 50s, in Damascus. Like Mark and I, they went to sleep early, doing their best to avoid the drunken party animals.

I dug on the ground for half an hour trying to level out a spot for my tent. Afterwards, we cooked powdered eggs for dinner. Tasty, but it made a mess of our pots. I wouldn't do it again.

DAY 52 MAY 08: CHATFIELD SHELTER TO STREAM AT MILE 549.9.
TODAY'S MILES: 11.7
TRIP MILES: 549.9

RW means Refreshing Waters.

We were back on the Trail by 7:00 a.m. I met Monique and Optimist, a young couple who were college students from Florida. Very few of the partiers in the shelter were up yet when we left. They were still sleeping off their hangovers. The Trail headed downhill, and after two miles, we came to an interesting historic park called the Settlers Museum. The park site included two old farm houses and a visitor's center, besides the historic schoolhouse.

Inside the old schoolhouse, situated next to the Trail, we found a big box of free goodies for thru-hikers. We didn't take advantage of the trail magic because we were heading to The Barn, a restaurant in Atkins where my wife was waiting for us. As we neared the restaurant, a homeless man asked us if the Trail was a shortcut to Marion. We said there wasn't much water along that stretch and thought the road would be shorter. The man was wearing a heavy coat and didn't appear to be carrying a water bottle. He ended up hitchhiking to Marion.

A southbound, or SOBO, section hiker named Tiptoe joined us for breakfast. She is 78 years old and a great source of information about the Trail ahead. Breakfast at The Barn was good and plentiful, but the service was very slow. While we waited, I picked up a mailed box of food that I had shipped to the Barn from Damascus. It took us two and a half hours to get back on the Trail.

While there, I introduced my wife to the Kallin family, who showed up soon after we arrived. Robin Hood excitedly talked about the nice trout he caught in a stream yesterday with a stick, some line, and a hook. His family ate it, and he was so proud! It made me realize that I was missing the annual spring fishing trip with the guys. Hopefully, if all goes well, I can still make our fall fishing trip, but it will be close.

Mark and I stopped about 4:30 p.m. and camped next to a pleasant stream. The Trail had been easy and we hiked through several pretty meadows. My wife had purchased some trail food for us, too, so we were really well-supplied. Now we had various flavors of ramen noodles, summer sausage, oatmeal, coffee, candy, trail mix, flatbread, peanut butter, and fruit. As a result, we struggled under the weight of four days' worth of food. Mark is carrying most of the food weight, and all the bulky fresh produce.

We looked forward to a quiet and pleasant evening away from the crowds, so we set up camp in a grove of rhododendrons situated next to a stream. It is just the two of us in this location. Sitting here, we can watch the hikers walk by. We must be close to the interstate, because I had cell phone service most of the day. I hope this is a trend from now on. We didn't hike many miles today—partly because it was hot, partly because of our pack weight, and partly because we were in no hurry. We bathed in the stream and rinsed out our clothes, as well.

DAY 53 MAY 09: STREAM AT MILE 549.9 TO POND AT MILE 563.9.
TODAY'S MILES: 14.0
TRIP MILES: 563.9

RW means Rebalanced Wants.

The forecasted rain and thunderstorms never materialized as we walked through miles of grassy fields. In the morning, we met Lumberman, a past thru-hiker now in his late 70s. He was offering peanut butter and jelly sandwiches and soda pop to hikers on the Trail. Lumberman said he gave out over one thousand sandwiches last year. Great trail magic! Wrecking Ball was there, eating a peanut butter and jelly sandwich and enjoying a cold drink.

The temperature was hot, again. Mark and I were always refilling our water. We stopped next to a cow for a snack break. It must be very used to hikers; we were completely ignored.

We walked by the night hikers who were now sleeping during the day. Late last night, this group jolted us out of our sleep as they loudly hiked past our tents. They were very noisy and quite a sight, with their beaming headlamps and glow sticks eerily dangling off their clothes and packs.

I soaked my feet several times today in cold streams. Little fish nibbled at them. Soaking my feet in the middle of the day, and at night, minimized much of the Achilles tendon pain and was actually more effective than naproxen sodium tablets. Still, I take two tablets in the morning and two before bed.

It looked like rain as evening approached, so we stopped for the night in a small wooded area next to an old farm pond. It was an ideal spot. Trees blocked the wind from three directions, and a little dam on one side of the pond blocked the remaining side. The wind picked up to at least 30 miles per hour during the night, but didn't bother us in our protected location. We sat next to our campfire, listening to the wind howl through the trees. In the background, frogs croaked and owls hooted.

We reminisced about other backpacking trips together. When I was a Boy Scout leader and Mark was a Scout, we hiked together at the Philmont Scout Ranch in New Mexico. We talked about our three-generation trip hiking down to the bottom of the Grand Canyon when he was a teenager. Mark, his grandfather and I had backpacked for three days in the Grand Canyon as a Father's Day present to ourselves. Wonderful memories!

DAY 54 MAY 10: POND AT MILE 563.9 TO LAUREL CREEK CAMPSITE.
TODAY'S MILES: 16.6
TRIP MILES: 580.5

RW means Rough Weather.

It took a long time to break camp this morning. We were both slow, but at least it didn't rain. We quickly made it to the top of the mountain where Chestnut Knob Shelter is located. Many other hikers had already squeezed into it, trying to get out of the storm. They said storms were intense on the mountain top. A nice shelter, but the stench of so many unbathed hikers was overwhelming when we opened the door.

I recognized many hikers. There was Uphill and Roots. We had met while signing the hiking register on March 17th in Amicalola Falls. Their parents had emailed get-well wishes to me while I was recovering in Damascus.

Mark and I continued on our way and after a few miles came to the best trail magic yet. The Keen family had a 20-foot table set up heaped with food: fresh fruit, vegetables, desserts, and drinks. Every year, the Keens provide this trail magic on the day before Mother's Day. They handed out scenic postcards of nearby Burke's Garden, an oval bowl-shaped valley, four miles wide and eight miles long. It looks like a volcanic caldera, but was actually formed by the collapse of a huge underground cavern system. Supposedly, Burke's Garden has the richest farm land in Virginia. We ended up hiking half way around Burke's Garden in the afternoon.

It rained most of the day. A thunderstorm crashed above us as we hiked along a rocky ridge overlooking the valley. Despite all the rain, finding drinkable water wasn't easy. If it hadn't been a cool and rainy day, we would have suffered from thirst. We spotted an interesting salamander called a red eft. It was actually an immature red-spotted newt. Ever since the Smoky Mountains, these newts have been showing up, especially after a hard rain.

As we neared Laurel Creek, Mark and I called Fort Bastion, thinking to stay there for the night. We changed our minds, though, when we reached Laurel Creek, and decided to camp there instead. It's a spacious and pleasant campsite. And because of the rain, we had the place to ourselves.

A friendly British man who runs a private campground just up the road drove by and offered to take us there, but we preferred our own company. My-Way posted his final trail journal entry from this location. He was here over a month ago, on April 5th. I wonder what happened to him.

DAY 55 MAY 11: LAUREL CREEK CAMPSITE TO ROAD 611.
TODAY'S MILES: 15.9
TRIP MILES: 596.4

RW means Roman Warrior.

Happy Mother's Day! This is Mark's last day with me. He is a great hiking companion. I will miss him when I continue to hike the Trail alone. We started the day at 7:30 a.m. and made fantastic time. My tent and his hammock were still wet from yesterday's rain storms. We'll try to dry them out later today.

Last night, an almost full moon shone brightly through the trees. I woke up about midnight thinking someone was in our camp with a flashlight, but it was just the moon lighting up the place. There are plenty of camp sites here, and we had the whole place to ourselves. The rain must have sent everybody into the shelters and town.

We planned to meet my wife at noon, but this trail section is so well maintained that we had already covered the eight miles by eleven o'clock. Here in Virginia, the Trail is more like a park trail, with few roots and rocks and lots of switchbacks. Cathy picked us up in the trailhead parking area and then drove to the motel, where we cleaned up and washed clothes. We celebrated Mother's Day afterwards with a nice dinner at a nearby restaurant. On the way back, I bought some trail food and prepared for tomorrow's hike. My pack will be heavy in the beginning, because I plan to hike a lot of days without stopping to buy food.

Mark and I decided to end our time together with a night hike that evening. We hit the Trail at 6:45 p.m. and hiked along a high, dry ridgeline. We brought headlamps, but never used them. Tonight's eight-mile hike checks off another bucket list item: night-hiking under a full moon.

By 8:15 p.m., the sun set and the forest grew darker and darker. We slowed our pace and crept quietly along the Trail. Once or twice, we heard what sounded like large animals rustling nearby in the darkness, but we never saw them.

A surprising number of thru-hikers had pitched their tents practically on top of the Trail. Most of them were already asleep and didn't hear us, except for one when we nearly tripped over her tent. We tried to reassure her that it wasn't a bear, just night hikers passing through.

While hiking with my son in this part of Virginia, I observed rapid undergrowth changes along the Trail. Frequently, one side of the mountain is covered with large trees and sparse undergrowth. The leafy trees act as a shade canopy. It is also more humid and less airy. When you cross over a ridgeline, the trees become smaller with denser undergrowth. In many places the spreading ground plants reach out and cover the Trail. I used my trekking poles to push small branches out of the way. Grasses, flowers, and other plants are abundant. The ridgelines are barren, dry, and hot, a stark contrast to the dense undergrowth in lower elevations. Fewer animals are seen on the ridgelines because of the lack of water. I carry more drinking water now, due to the long distances between water sources located only in the lower elevation gaps between mountains. Locating water will surely become an even bigger problem during the upcoming summer months.

DAY 56 MAY 12: ROAD 611 TO DISMAL CREEK CAMPSITE.
TODAY'S MILES: 15.4
TRIP MILES: 611.8

RW means Recalling Walk.

Mark and I slept in late after our night hike. We were tired and didn't get to bed until midnight. I packed after a good breakfast, said my goodbyes, and was back on the Trail by noon. The beginning of the trail section was difficult and rocky for the first eight miles with very little water. After this hard stretch, the Trail became easier and water was plentiful. Fortunately, the weather wasn't too hot.

I hiked along Dismal Creek for almost seven miles on a relatively flat surface. The Trail tunneled through arching rhododendrons and the soft ground was covered with leaves and pine needles. While making great time, I reflected on the past week as best as I could, and relished the memories of hiking with my son. This easy Trail allowed me to get lost in my thoughts. Time passed and before I knew it, I had hiked farther than planned. Today was another milestone. I crossed the 600-mile mark! I made a sign out of rocks on the Trail and took a picture.

I stopped at 6:15 p.m. next to a beautiful stream called Dismal Creek. Doesn't sound nice, but it is. The campsite is in a forest of huge old-growth pine trees. Even though I covered a long distance today, I saw very few people, only five all day. Two of them were camped with me tonight. They are from Quebec, and call themselves Kit and Kat. I talked to Kit, the guy. He is a retired Canadian Army officer. Kat might not know English, because I only heard her speaking in French.

This is the end of eight weeks, or 56 days, or two months of hiking and living in the woods. I am averaging only 10.9 miles a day, and 63 miles behind schedule.

DAY 57 MAY 13: DISMAL CREEK CAMPSITE AND FOOTBRIDGE TO PEARISBURG.
TODAY'S MILES: 19.5
TRIP MILES: 631.3

RW means Real World.

Today started out easy enough but soon became difficult. The Trail was flat with readily available water sources. As the day progressed, I climbed up a ridge, and boulders and rocks took over the Trail. At Docs Knob Shelter, I thought about stopping for the night but decided to camp on the ridge near a water source.

I left the shelter with only a half-liter of water, expecting to find two water sources within the next few miles. Unfortunately, the recent dry spell had caused both locations to dry up. This left me in a predicament. I didn't have enough water to camp here for the night, and it was eight miles to the next water source. Wearily, I decided to keep hiking to Pearisburg, Virginia.

On my way, I ran into Blue Jay. I met her in Damascus a few weeks ago. Blue Jay is in her early sixties and loves hiking. She decided to hike the entire A.T. just for the fun of it and is actually more than 125 miles further up the Trail, but skipped this ten-mile section so she could hike with her son.

What a break for me! She couldn't give me water, but we shared a big bowl of juicy strawberries and tomatoes. There was enough water in this fresh produce to get me through the rest of the six miles into town.

Today, the Trail was dry and hot, and the ridge rocky. The trees hadn't completely leafed out yet, so the sun beat down on me all afternoon. I have been noticing a fungus growing on the forest floor that looks like a corn cob. I looked it up on the Internet and discovered it is called Bear Corn. It isn't a fungus, it's a parasite, and edible if roasted or boiled after several soakings in water.

When I got to Pearisburg, I recognized a great number of hikers. They were all in town to resupply. I checked into the Holiday Lodge Inn/Hostel.

DAY 58 MAY 14: ZERO DAY.
TODAY'S MILES: 0.0
TRIP MILES: 631.3

KW means Relaxing, Wednesday.

I woke up this morning and found my left little toe swollen to the point where my foot wouldn't fit inside my shoe. I will take a zero day and rest my feet. My last zero day was May 5th, nine days ago, 123 miles back. The unexpected extra miles yesterday, lack of water, heavy pack, hot weather (91 degrees), and inability to soak my feet during the day, are all partly to blame for my current foot injuries. Shoe inserts may also be crowding my swelling feet during the day in this hot weather. I will remove one of the insoles tomorrow to see if it makes a difference.

The weather forecast indicates a 100 percent chance of rain and storms tomorrow, with cooler weather and rain for the next few days. Cooler weather should help my feet, but it may get cold during the night. Nighttime temperatures are expected to drop down to 41 degrees. Drinking water will be a concern for the next 70 miles featuring many long, dry ridgelines. I hope the springs and streams fill up with rain water. Yesterday's difficulties were caused by the fact that several important water sources had dried up.

I switched to summer gear a few days ago. My summer bag is rated for 45 degrees. Mark gave me his Reflectex insulation to add to my sleeping system. I used it for the first time two nights ago. It seems to have solved some overheating problems on warm nights. We'll see how well it works in colder weather this week.

While shopping around for food menu ideas, I noticed another hiker smashing bags of potato chips into small bits, and then storing the crushed chips in sandwich bags as trail food. An eight-ounce bag of potato chips contains between 1,200 and 1,400 calories, depending on the brand. It is amazing how many bags of potato chips can fit inside a sandwich bag once they're smashed. One thing I have learned on this hike is the value of calories. I now shop for calories—the more, the better. If the package says light, low calorie, low fat, or nonfat, it's not suitable food. Some bagels, which many people might think are healthier than regular bread, contain more than twice the calories of a slice of bread. Muffins contain higher calories than donuts. I bought a tiny package of muffins that listed its contents as two servings totaling six hundred calories. I ate both servings in three bites.

This morning I ate breakfast with several older thru-hikers like myself. We are all taking a zero day. One of them, a man named Mark, told us that when he was young, he completed his thru-hike in a remarkable one hundred days, and was one of the first to finish the Appalachian Trail that year. Today Mark seemed down, and he talked about how hard the Trail is, and how far behind schedule he was. It sounded as if this second attempt to thru-hike was not going well, and I wondered if he would be ending it soon.

Everybody except Mark planned to hike far more miles in the next four days than me. Even though I enjoyed their company, I planned to say my goodbyes tomorrow. Mark said he wasn't up to hiking in the rain tomorrow and was taking another zero day.

I'm recognizing other hikers, especially the group my son and I had met at the shelter. They checked into the motel today. I read the online journals of other hikers, but still no word from My-Way. Achin' left the Trail on April 28th and returned on May 5th. He seems to be back in the groove.

Achin' wrote in his trail journal that getting off the Trail was the second biggest brain-fart of his life. My second biggest was getting my wife a water softener for her 24th birthday at our first house. The biggest brainfart was buying that house in the first place. If this was his second worst, Achin' was doing well with brain farts. Chiggabite got off the Trail on April 13th, and then resumed his hike on May 8th.

I had lunch with Owl Bear today.

DAY 59 MAY 15: PEARISBURG TO PINE SWAMP BRANCH SHELTER.
TODAY'S MILES: 19.3
TRIP MILES: 650.6

Dark, gloomy, and raining hard this morning when I walked to the Dairy Queen at 6:00 a.m. for breakfast. I met Isn't Black and Curious George. Curious George is an ex-fighter pilot and retired American Airlines pilot. He likes the storybook character Curious George, and carries a little stuffed Curious George monkey strapped to his pack.

Isn't Black is a 52-year-old man from Germany who stands taller than all of us, well over six feet tall. His trail name sprang from the fact that he wears black clothing all the time. His black rain suit wasn't keeping him dry, so he decided to buy a new one. He told the story in this way: "On an unbelievably FUCKING rainy day, I walked into the outfitter at Neel Gap to buy a replacement rain suit, and all they had was a FUCKING green poncho, and I kept telling the guy, it isn't black, it's FUCKING green!"

I learned later that Bear Bag had taught Isn't Black how to swear in American English. As a result, every time Isn't Black retold the story of how he got his trail name, he took the opportunity to pepper it with this new vocabulary.

We started the Trail together in heavy rain this morning. As soon as we left town, we had to climb one thousand feet to reach the ridgeline. It rained hard until 2:00 p.m., and then let up for a few hours. We were soaked and our shoes squished. I wanted to stop for the day and camp on the ridge, but the rain was too much, and except for rain puddles, I couldn't find any drinking water. We made it to Pine Swamp Shelter at 4:30 p.m. after a thousand-foot downhill climb. After finding a few pieces of dry wood, we made a small fire in the shelter, but it didn't last or dry anything out.

Bear Bag got his trail name in 2009 during his first A.T. thru-hike attempt. He sleeps in a hammock, and after other hikers began to comment that he looked like a bear bag hanging from the trees, the name stuck. Bear Bag is Jewish, around five feet seven inches tall, talkative, and blessed with a great sense of humor.

A young man and his mother entered the shelter. He said his mother had taken a bad fall and was injured. The young man went ahead to find a road crossing, and came back an hour later with help. The rescuers assisted the mother to her feet, and they all left together in the rain at nightfall.

Afterwards, the young couple, Optimist and Monique, walked in and slept on the floor. I met them once before when my son was hiking with me. They huddled together in a light blanket because they had already gotten rid of their winter gear. They were soaking wet and deeply in love. Optimist went out in the rain, even though he was obviously cold, to search for dry wood. Hardly any dry wood was available, but he built a small fire that went out quickly. The two clung to each other, shivering on the floor.

DAY 60 MAY 16: PINE SWAMP BRANCH SHELTER TO LAUREL CREEK SHELTER.
TODAY'S MILES: 18.5
TRIP MILES: 669.1

I regret shipping my winter gear sleeping bag back home. I shivered half the night and heard Monique crying because she was so bitterly cold. Curious George said he froze during the night because his sleeping bag was rated for only 50 degrees. We all woke up early and put on our wet clothes. After breakfast we hit the Trail. The loving couple stayed behind. As I left, Optimist was searching the forest for dry wood in hopes of building a fire.

My back was badly chafed from yesterday's wet hike. The pack had dug into my skin all day long.

We hadn't gotten very far when we discovered the Trail was submerged under a stream that had turned into a small river. We quickly found several large logs and built a bridge. Curious George was the real hero. He waded across the violent stream and single-handedly managed the building of our little bridge on the other side of the torrent. No longer was I suffering from a lack of water, like in the last few days! The day was cool and the Trail very wet. At least, it wasn't raining. Then, we hiked up another thousand feet to another ridgeline.

During the day we walked through several gaps in the forest, located underneath high tension power towers. It felt good to be able to look up and see the sky. I spotted some unripe wild strawberries and pointed them out to the group. Isn't Black had never seen wild strawberries before and was amazed at how tiny they were, compared to store-bought strawberries. I hope we find another strawberry patch in about a week, when they are ripe.

We had walked over eighteen miles by the time we stopped at a shelter. The shelter was very small, so I am tenting tonight. We were able to get a fire going and I used it to cook my dinner tonight. Other hikers are staying here tonight, beside our group of four, aka G4.

DAY 61 MAY 17: LAUREL CREEK SHELTER TO PICKLE BRANCH SHELTER.
TODAY'S MILES: 22.5
TRIP MILES: 691.6

RW means Really Weary.

The night was frigid again and I struggled to stay warm. I cooked breakfast and was the last of the G4 to break camp. This morning was miserably cold. I caught up with Bear Bag and we talked for a while. He started thru-hiking this year on March 28th, ten days after me.

I learned that the three of them—Bear Bag, Isn't Black, and Curious George—had met early on in Georgia and have continued to hike together whenever possible. Staying together all the time is just not practical. Everyone needs to hike at their own pace. Groups regularly split apart, and then meet up again somewhere down the Trail.

Bear Bag's pack, with all his gear, weighs less than ten pounds, rarely more than fifteen pounds with food and water. He owns his own gear company, called Bearbaggear.com, and makes super-lightweight gear. We walked through farm fields and passed the largest oak tree growing on the southern half of the Trail. Bear Bag told me about his campaign work for President Obama.

The Trail took us along a knife-edge ridge with spectacular views of the mountains. The ridge was demanding and we moved slowly. It would be a very long day. We passed the grave of Audie Murphy, the most decorated American soldier of World War II. He starred in a few Hollywood movies and died in a plane crash near this location.

In the late afternoon we came upon a young couple from South Korea standing at a gravel road intersection. They both wore matching knee braces. I had seen them regularly for the past week. She had fallen and was hurt. They had been standing by this gravel road for about half an hour, hoping to get a ride to town for medical treatment. Just then a pickup truck approached. I jumped into the road and stopped the truck. The driver agreed to give them a ride to a hostel.

We finally arrived at the shelter about 7:30 p.m. and set up our tents. Tenting was the better option, because of the cold weather and the fact that the shelter was in poor condition. Water was located far from the shelter, forcing me to carry four liters up a steep hill for a mile, a grueling climb. Water is just so heavy. Water had been a concern all day. There were many times when it was scarce, but thankfully, it never ran out.

It was already cold as I set up my tent and tried to steel myself for a third nearly-sleepless night of shivering. My feet and Achilles tendon were really sore today. We were all exhausted. Tomorrow promised to be another hard day, but one rewarded with spectacular views.

Bear Bag and Isn't Black plan to get up before sunrise and hike several miles to watch the sunrise from the top of the Dragon's Tooth, a famous rock spire just ahead.

DAY 62 MAY 18: PICKLE BRANCH SHELTER TO VA ROAD 311, CATAWBA, VA.
TODAY'S MILES: 12.6
TRIP MILES: 704.2

RW means Rhododendron Wonderland.

A milestone day! First, it was the start of my third month of hiking. Secondly, I crossed the 700-mile mark at 11:15 a.m. I tried to make a mileage sign, but the 700-mile mark was in a large, grassy field, without a stick or rock to be found.

This morning, the G4 split up into separate groups. Isn't Black and Bear Bag left camp at 4:45 a.m. to catch the sunrise on Dragon's Tooth. I left camp at 6:00 a.m., and Curious George left at 7:00 a.m. The hike to the Dragon's Tooth was brutal and my thighs were aching by the time I finished the four-mile climb. The Dragon's Tooth is a large rock spire overlooking a cliff. Many hikers have their picture taken standing on the top of the tooth. I partly climbed it, but didn't go to the top, since I was alone. If I had fallen, no one was there to help me. It wasn't worth the risk.

The next mile was the most difficult yet. I climbed down a near-vertical cliff. Several times, I dropped my trekking poles and backpack down to the next level as I climbed down the cliff. At one point, steel handholds drilled into the rock face had to be grabbed in order to continue down the cliff face. It was very dangerous. I slipped once and rolled onto my trekking poles, bending the left pole. Fortunately I was able to straighten it out nearly back to its original position. Much later in the day, I learned Curious George had fallen on this descent and severely damaged his right heel.

Hiking on, I finally saw rhododendrons in bloom and walked through a tunnel of blooming rhododendrons for a quarter mile. Awesome! Isn't Black had hiked off-trail to get to a small convenience store. He bought beer and lunch for everybody, and then carried the groceries back to a rock overlooking the valley, where he waited for us to catch up to him. When we finally arrived, we all enjoyed the view and his delicious trail magic. The day proved to be hard hiking, but by 2:00 p.m. we were already at Road 311 in Catawba, Virginia.

We tried unsuccessfully to hitchhike to the Homeplace Restaurant this Sunday, but none of us got a ride. Expecting someone to stop and pick up four hikers seemed improbable from the start, but it was worth a try. So far, all my hitchhiking attempts have failed. Curious George even held up a sign that read, "AT Hikers Ride into Town." On the other side it read, "AT Hikers Ride to Trail." It didn't work.

We hiked the one and a half miles to the Homeplace, an AYCE, or all-you-can-eat restaurant, famous on the Trail. The food was fantastic and we ate till we burst. We had planned to keep hiking, but we were so full that we called a shuttle and stayed the night at Four Pines Hostel.

It was a three-car garage converted into a hostel. Not bad, but far from the best. At least we were warm and dry. The beds were full, so we all slept on couches and the floor. Monique and Optimist arrived and had to sleep in a barn with llamas.

Phase 2, the girl I met sunbathing just before Damascus, was also staying here, along with many other hikers. Phase 2 had skipped ahead about twenty miles to get to the Homeplace Restaurant, because it was only open on weekends.

I learned that the Korean couple had stayed here the previous night and left for New York today to meet up with other Koreans.

DAY 63 MAY 19: VA ROAD 311, CATAWBA TO DALEVILLE.
TODAY'S MILES: 19.8
TRIP MILES: 724.0

RW means Road Work.

The day started out great. We stopped at a small convenience store for coffee and sweet rolls, and then hit the Trail by 7:00 a.m. We climbed to the top of McAfee Knob, the spot where the most pictures are said to be taken of hikers standing on a rock outcropping. Later on we hiked over Tinker Cliffs. All the views were stunning and I took lots of photographs. As the day progressed, my left toe and Achilles tendon started hurting a lot. It was a good thing we planned to zero tomorrow. By the end of the day we were all tired, so we checked into the Howard Johnson in Daleville, Virginia, located only a tenth of a mile off the Trail. We had trail magic twice today: pop and candy.

Curious George is really hurt. He called his doctor, who said he needed to take seven to ten days off the Trail due to yesterday's injury. He is a very tough man. He's walked at least 25 miles on his badly injured heel.

DAY 64 MAY 20: ZERO DAY.
TODAY'S MILES: 0.0
TRIP MILES: 724.0

RW means Reclining and Wondering about the next eighty miles.

Just resting and eating. I am 57 miles behind my trail plan and have lost about fourteen pounds, so far. I went to the outfitter to buy a new pair of boots, but couldn't find a pair to fit properly. I ended up purchasing another pair of socks. I carry different brands and consider myself to be quite an expert now on hiking socks.

In the evening we ate a wonderful meal at a local barbeque place. Because we were thru-hikers, we received a free ice cream dessert. This wasn't the first time I got a free dessert. We often heard about places that gave enticing freebies to thru-hikers by way of comments in shelter logbooks and conversation on the Trail. Conversation on the Trail always revolves around food.

To do list: wash clothes, buy food, plan tomorrow's hike, and eat. It looks like it could be 80 miles before the next resupply point, so I will purchase at least five days of food. I don't plan to try crushed potato chips, but I will add dehydrated packages of potatoes, and other pre-cooked noodle dishes.

I am already tired of ramen noodles. Instead of summer sausage, I am buying packaged thigh slices of spam and salmon. I still enjoy bagels, and I'm making coffee most mornings now I should arrive at the Blue Ridge Mountains tomorrow and will start hiking along the Parkway.

DAY 65 MAY 21: DALEVILLE TO BOBBLETS GAP SHELTER.
TODAY'S MILES: 18.5
TRIP MILES: 742.5

RW means Rapturously Warm.

It was a day to remember, full of many remarkable things. Last night, Bear Bag's girlfriend drove down to see him from New

Hampshire. We all met for breakfast at 6:30 a.m. Isn't Black and I said our goodbyes to Curious George, who is taking several days off to recover from his heel injury. He hopes to catch up to us, or meet us, somewhere ahead. We said goodbye to Bear Bag, who is taking another zero day to be with his girlfriend. By 7:20 a.m., we were back on the Trail.

Another beautiful day for hiking, the Trail was gentle, and thick layers of leaf litter cushioned our footsteps. Hiking was easy despite our heavy packs loaded with food. Water was available most of the day and the temperature mild. I didn't carry a lot of water in an effort to reduce the pack weight. The new socks helped my toes, and the chafing on my back finally healed after four days of misery. Wearing a pack all day with a chafed back was really painful. Overall, my trail pains were light and ordinary—the Achilles tendon, ankles, knees, feet, and toes had a normal soreness level today. Yesterday's rest did me a lot of good. We are hiking so many miles now that I am starting to catch up to other hikers.

We spent much of our time hiking in heavy undergrowth. The Trail became a narrow corridor crammed between four-foot walls of trees and bushes. Mountain laurel and other bushes were very thick; a bear could have been standing a few feet away and I wouldn't have see it. By now I was hoping to see a bear. Other hikers had seen bears, but not me.

The dense tree canopy provided shade most of the day. I walked through tunnels of huge lavender-colored rhododendron blooms and tiny cup-shaped pink and white mountain laurel flowers dotted with delicate red spots. Mountain laurels bloom in massive groupings of thirty to fifty flowers clustered on the tip of each branch. I wish I could put them in my garden. Time flew by because of the distracting flowers.

We started hiking close to the Blue Ridge Parkway around noon. The trail was located only fifty feet away from the parkway. At three o'clock, we discovered great trail magic. A trail angel and his three assistants were offering fresh strawberries, cake, and Cokes to thru-hikers at a scenic parkway overlook. He provides trail magic every year on the anniversary day of his thru-hike completion in 2009. It took him ten months to hike the A.T that year.

We crossed the parkway several times and enjoyed the views. A posted sign said the Appalachian Trail was the longest and oldest continuously marked trail in the world. We got to the shelter about 4:30 p.m. It was already full of thru-hikers I hadn't met before. We didn't want to sleep in the shelter anyway. Not much space here for tents, and the guidebook described it as a non-tenting shelter. I cursed the rocks and slopes as I pitched my tent on a rocky slope.

Shortly after setting up the tent, Bear Bag and his girlfriend showed up. They had parked near the trail on the parkway. Bear Bag and his girlfriend drove us into town and treated us all with Sonic hamburgers for dinner. Trail magic again! Then we discovered that Bear Bag had lost four hundred dollars, his driver's license, and credit cards at a scenic turnout on the parkway earlier in the day. We decided to drive back to the scenic overlook and search for his wallet, even if there wasn't much hope of finding it.

Incredibly, sitting in the middle of the scenic view parking lot lay his belongings, in plain sight of every car and hiker. Four hundred-dollar bills were clearly visible. We decided the reason the money was still there was because no one had gotten out of their car when stopping to look at the view. If they had, they would have seen Bear Bag's valuables sitting right at their feet. Invisible trail angels were protecting Bear Bag today!

Too often, people miss out on opportunities because they would rather stand back and watch. Scenic views aren't just to be looked at from a distance, they should be experienced. The reward is not found sitting inside a car.

It was supposed to start raining at four o'clock today, but the sky is still clear at nine o'clock. It is expected to be warm tonight, with a low of 61 degrees. Finally, NOT COLD!

DAY 66 MAY 22: BOBBLETS GAP SHELTER TO CORNELIUS CREEK SHELTER.
TODAY'S MILES: 18.4
TRIP MILES: 760.9

RW means Roanoke Waving because I left the Roanoke area today.

Last night was warm and I used my sleeping bag as a blanket most of the night. It did rain for about one hour, which woke me up and gave me a chance to climb out of the corner of the tent that I had slid into during the night. I stayed dry, but Isn't Black's sleeping bag got wet.

We left at separate times in the morning—Isn't Black at 6:00 a.m., and me at 7:00 a.m. We hiked separately for a good part of the morning and carried plenty of water, because the next water source was eight miles away.

Shortly after leaving camp, I almost stepped on a big black snake. I didn't get a picture because my cell phone wasn't turned on yet. The snake dashed into the bushes before I could take a picture. It was a Black Racer, and moved incredibly fast. I couldn't have moved out of its way fast enough if it had wanted to bite me. It was the first of two Black Racers that I would see today. Both were about four feet long, but they moved so fast it was difficult to tell how long they really were. They were big.

The Trail paralleled and crossed the Blue Ridge Parkway several times before turning into the mountains. After that, I didn't hear or see the Parkway again. The temperature was about 80 degrees all day. The forest floor was covered with lily of the valley, poison ivy, sassafras, and small trees. In some places, the Trail was hemmed in, confining our view strictly to the path. It all depends on which of the various micro-climates you are hiking through at different elevations. Only a few flowers today, and no rhododendron. We mostly saw large oak and maple trees.

We introduced Isn't Black to sassafras tea by making it from the roots of the sassafras plant. He liked it and started carrying roots with him for tea in the evening. Several days ago, we met a thru-hiker who had hiked the A.T. five times and knew a lot about edible plants. He pointed out several of the plants to us. As a rule, we ate very few wild plants, but observed people eating ramps and fiddleheads. We were told to expect to see patches of wild onions, blackberries, blueberries, and raspberries, as well as a great variety of other edible plants, if we knew where to look.

None of us were very knowledgeable about wild plants and didn't plan on eating them unless we were absolutely sure they were edible. There aren't enough edible plants near the Trail to sustain a community of hikers. Anyone seriously planning to feed themselves with wild plants on the trail is likely to go hungry.

We had trail magic today! Around lunchtime, we met a couple parked by the road next to a stream and swimming hole. They gave us soda pop and beer. As we sat next to the stream, enjoying our drinks, a kaleidoscope of butterflies appeared. Up till now, butterflies had been black with brilliant indigo wingtips. Today we saw hundreds of yellow and black butterflies fluttering in a giant swarm ball. After this memorable break, we climbed Floyd Mountain, a 2,349-foot climb. It was the longest climb on the Trail in the last 150 miles.

Even though I was the last one to break camp in the morning, I was the first one to reach camp in the evening. The others had stopped during the day to take a long nap. This gave me plenty of time to pitch my tent and set up camp. By 8:00 p.m. I was asleep in my tent.

DAY 67 MAY 23: CORNELIUS CREEK SHELTER TO MATTS CREEK SHELTER.
TODAY'S MILES: 17.7
TRIP MILES: 778.6

RW means River Water, in honor of the good water at this location.

Last night, the shelter next to our tent area was nearly vacant. Moe, an older man from Wisconsin, was the only one who stayed inside the shelter. He is section hiking half the Trail this year, and plans to hike the second half next year. Nobody wants to stay in the shelters in nice weather—or bad weather, for that matter. Now that the insects have emerged and are active, mosquitoes and mice both take turns harassing hikers inside the shelters.

We all left early and by 10:00 a.m. had covered seven miles. I took over for Bear Bag this morning and began explaining to Isn't Black the nuances of American-style speech and the multi-layers of meaning one word can have. Bear Bag sometimes added Hebrew and Yiddish words to the conversation. Since Bear Bag is a good teacher, language lessons could go on for hours. Isn't Black is a wonderful student and eager to improve his American English. He was already familiar with some Yiddish words. For his part, Isn't Black often taught us German words. This was our form of entertainment on many days, discussing all three languages. Isn't Black would constantly repeat a new pet phrase, but not always appropriately, such as, "That's what she said!"

Later on, we spent a lot of time high up on the mountain ridgelines, at nearly 4,000 feet, enjoying the sunlight and gentle breeze. It is still spring up here. Flowers are in bloom and leaves are still opening. The lower elevations have already flowered and are now just green foliage.

We saw Kit and Kat, the Canadian couple, several times today. They didn't carry backpacks and had come up with an interesting system for traveling along the Trail. Together, they would drive in the morning to a designated trail section and park their car. Kat would hike down the trail, and Kit would bicycle along a road for ten or twenty miles, stow his bike at an A.T. road crossing, and then start hiking toward her. They would meet in the middle, eat lunch, and then continue in opposite directions. Kit would hike to the car, drive to where he had left his bike, and pick up Kat. Kit was trying to simultaneously hike the white blazes, plus cycle on the yellow blazes, for the entire length of the A.T. We had seen them doing this routine for several days in a row.

We arrived at Matts Creek Shelter about 5:00 p.m. and camped along a stream in a valley near the James River. We'll cross this river tomorrow. The only other thru-hikers here are a few Wounded Warriors who I mentioned at the beginning of my hike. Not too many of them are still hiking. I remembered most of the Wounded Warriors, and they recognized me. We talked for a long time and I enjoyed their company. Only Major Tom, a young guy from Maryland, and his dog, Lucky, slept in the shelter. Everybody else slept in their tents. Major Tom wasn't a pot smoker. Pot smokers are getting rare, as are the younger hikers. I'm running into older hikers like myself now, either retired or near retirement. In general, the number of hikers on the Trail is noticeably lower.

Now that the weather is nice, shelter areas and trails are filling up with local hikers and weekend campers. It's Friday, and a family is here at Matts Creek Shelter on a weekend camping trip. They ask questions about our thru-hike experiences, and we enjoy telling our stories. Each of us told them how we got our trail names. Isn't Black "unpeppered" his story for the benefit of the children.

DAY 68 MAY 24: MATTS CREEK SHELTER TO CAMPSITE MILE 798.0.
TODAY'S MILES: 19.4
TRIP MILES: 798.0

RW means Rescued Willingly because the Boy Scouts came to our rescue.

Today was the most amazing day with incredible trail magic. Last night I slept very well and felt rested this morning. I am still taking at least two tablets of naproxen sodium three times a day to combat the swelling in my Achilles tendon. My daily drug use is increasing.

We all got up early and left camp by 6:30 a.m. At the James River, we crossed over on the A. T.'s longest foot bridge. The whole morning was spent climbing 2,000 feet to the top of Bluff Mountain. At the top of Bluff Mountain, I called the Blue Dog Art Cafe and Hostel in Buena Vista to confirm our reservations for tomorrow. The person running the place told me the restaurant was closed for the Memorial Day weekend, and the shuttle wouldn't pick us up because she was going to church this Sunday. She was the shuttle driver.

I didn't even realize it was Sunday, or that tomorrow was Memorial Day. I kept track of the date, but no longer paid attention to the day of the week. I told her we would enjoy going to church with her, but she declined. She said she might pick us up after church, maybe, around 1:00 p.m. This left us in a bad spot because our food was nearly gone. I tried calling other shuttle drivers but couldn't get either phone to work.

Luckily, the Boy Scout Troop 911 from Virginia was camped right next to us. I asked John, one of the scout leaders, if he would drive us into town to buy food and bring us back. He agreed and within two hours, we had resupplied and were back on the Trail. We bought extra food for Bear Bag so he wouldn't have to stop. We sent him a text message saying we had bought him food. He was doing high-mileage days in an effort to catch up to us.

We hiked another seven miles and thought we had found the lakeside camping area listed in the Guide. After we climbed down the steep hill to the shore of the lake, a sign said, "No Camping— Restoration Area." We climbed back out and began to worry about nightfall. It was already dark. We kept hiking and found a level campsite next to a good stream. While surveying the site, we spotted another tent a little ways off into the woods, and decided to stealth camp. Stealth camping means camping in a non-designated camping location, usually just off the Trail. Isn't Black and I bathed in the stream. Afterwards, I soaked my feet for half an hour and my Achilles tendon really appreciated it.

All day long I texted Bear Bag to give him our situation and location. Phone reception was remarkably good. After setting up camp, Bear Bag texted and said he was going to Buena Vista for the night because he needed a zero day. So we had extra food. We should reach Waynesboro, Virginia, in three days. Steve and Denise will meet me there on Wednesday. I am still 69 miles behind my trail plan.

DAY 69 MAY 25: CAMPSITE AT MILE 798.0 TO SEELEY-WOODWORTH SHELTER.
TODAY'S MILES: 18.6
TRIP MILES: 816.6

RW means Regina Watching.

Last night was so damp that, by morning, my sleeping bag was damp and cold and my clothes were still wet with yesterday's sweat.

Every hundred miles, I make a sign on the trail using rocks or sticks to commemorate the milestone. This time I used sticks and placed them on a bench near the Trail. Other hikers passing me said they wondered who'd made those mileage signs and told me they enjoyed seeing them. It felt good to know others found my little amusement helpful and fun.

After half an hour of hiking, just after passing the 800-mile mark, we met Regina, a ridge runner. She is the first ridge runner I've seen since Damascus. Regina told us trekking poles are a major source of trail erosion. Poles cause the Trail to widen at an alarming rate. I hadn't thought about the damaging effect of trekking poles until she brought it to my attention. Paradoxically, trekking poles are a lifesaver, and I can't imagine giving them up. It was a conflict—wanting to be a conservationist, yet relying on trekking poles in order to keep on hiking.

Today was a brutal day. All morning, we climbed a steep mountain called Bald Knob, a 2,963-foot climb. I thought

Virginia was going to be easy; it is not. I also thought climbing mountains would get easier after hiking 800 miles, but it is still hard. I am going to bed early. I'm tired, my feet hurt, and I have blisters. There are about fifteen hiker tents set up around the shelter. Nobody is sleeping in the shelter because of bugs. Wrecking Ball and other thru-hikers are here. Everybody is tired and asleep by 8:30 p.m.

DAY 70 MAY 26: SEELEY-WOODWORTH SHELTER TO HARPERS CREEK SHELTER.
TODAY'S MILES: 14.2
TRIP MILES 830.8

RW means Regenerative Waters.

It's Memorial Day and I only hiked 14.2 miles today because my feet and Achilles tendons are hurting. Yesterday, I skipped my zero day and hiked, so I thought I would take it easy today. I've already finished a tough climb up Priest Mountain today, but another long, tough climb is directly ahead of me. I will tackle it first thing in the morning. Earlier, while hiking, I said my customary hellos to Kit and Kat as they each passed me from opposite directions. They were now fixtures on the Trail. My shoes, Salomon Trail Runners purchased in Damascus, continue to hurt my feet more and more. I am getting blisters on my heels. I must stop and treat them before they get worse.

We passed Priest Shelter, home to the most interesting hiker logbook I have seen so far. The Priest Shelter is located on Priest Mountain. According to hiker tradition, hikers must confess their Trail sins in the Priest Shelter logbook. Many hikers confess personal transgressions in the Priest's logbook, which everybody ends up reading. Last night I played a game of chess with a young boy named Packrat, and told him I wasn't very good. That isn't totally true. I am better than average and quickly became the winner. I confessed in the Priest logbook that I'd misled him about my skill level. In my defense, bluffing your opponent is part of the game of chess. I am sure Packrat read my confession, because he was only a few miles behind me.

Later, I took a long break on Spy Rock with Isn't Black, and told him I was making a short day of it. He decided to keep hiking alone. And so, our group of four is now completely broken up. I hope to catch up to him tomorrow when I am feeling better.

We agreed to meet at the Paul C. Wolfe Shelter tomorrow, 22 miles away.

About eight miles before camp, I came to a wide and deep stream. Many other thru-hikers joined me, all just as hot and sweaty as me. We jumped into the stream with our clothes on to cool off and swim. Wrecking Ball was there, soaking and relaxing. The stream was very refreshing and I got to rinse my clothes for the first time in days. The cool water energized me for the thousand-foot climb up to the shelter. The revitalizing effect of the water didn't wear off until I had almost reached the shelter. I was napping in my tent by 3:30 p.m. on this very warm Memorial Day.

Several section hikers arrived who have all hiked the A.T. before. We have been close together on the Trail for the past several days. Wrecking Ball and Hey Everybody eventually showed up at the shelter. The section hikers slept in the shelter and the thru-hikers tented. I pitched my tent on a modest slope with soft ground, built a warm fire, cooked dinner, and was asleep early, completely exhausted.

DAY 71 MAY 27: HARPERS CREEK SHELTER TO PAUL C. WOLFE SHELTER.
TODAY'S MILES: 22.0
TRIP MILES 852.8

RW means Rattlesnake Winding.

I got up early, refreshed from a good and long night's sleep, and started hiking at 6:00 a.m. while the morning was still cool. I had to climb two thousand feet up to the top of Three Ridges Mountain. Since I was the first one out of camp, I was the first to clear the spider webs off the Trail. Wrecking Ball was stirring in her tent as I was leaving. Sunrise was breaking, so I had just enough light to see the Trail without using my headlamp. In the valley below, no lights appeared from the houses or cars yet, and the woods were still dark.

I hadn't gone more than a hundred yards when I almost stepped on a snake. I don't know what kind of snake it was. I was too startled to get a good look. After that, I studied every root and stick before stepping on it, just to make sure it wasn't a snake.

My plan yesterday to rest my feet and save my energy for this climb was a wise decision. I felt good. The climb didn't take a lot out of me, even though it was steep and very rocky. I thought I was moving fast, but Wrecking Ball caught up and passed me at the top of the mountain. She is such a strong hiker. I ended up chasing her for the rest of the day.

Just before reaching Maupin Field Shelter, I nearly stepped on a big black RATTLESNAKE! My right foot was inches from its nose. When I saw how close my foot was to its head, I jumped four feet in the air. It was still early morning, so I hoped the snake was more interested in warming itself than in striking at me. The snake eyed me intently, but never threatened. I took my trekking pole and straightened out its tail to prove that it really was a RATTLESNAKE! It let me push it around and never rattled. Then I curled it back into a ball and hiked away. I wanted to leave a note warning the next hikers to watch out for the snake, but didn't have any paper. Later, I spoke to the hikers who were behind me, and none of them had seen the snake. I was relieved it had crawled away without attacking anyone.

I ran across Major Tom trying to leave camp. He was having a hard time with his dog, Lucky, who didn't want to hike. The dog kept lying down, not moving, as soon as Major Tom tried to hike out. Major Tom was yelling at Lucky, who stubbornly refused to move. Dogs are tough, but not as strong as humans. I am sure this dog had given his all. He needed a break and was doing his best to tell his owner, "Let's take the day off!" I hoped his owner got the message.

At lunch time I cooked some food on top of Cedar Cliffs. I usually don't cook lunch, but had lots of extra ramen noodles, and the view was stunning. Wrecking Ball came by and we hiked together. She intended to stop for the day on Humpback Mountain, but the weather looked threatening, so she hiked with me to the next shelter. She didn't want to camp in bad weather on an open cliff ridge. Good decision. I considered camping near a spring after eighteen miles instead of meeting up with Isn't Black. I was getting tired, but thunder and lightning changed my mind.

Wrecking Ball and I hiked as fast as possible to get to the next shelter before the rain started. We needed to get off this cliff ridge and down to lower ground. We didn't make it. The heavens opened up with a tremendous thunderstorm. I counted the lightning to see how close it was. "One thous—crack!" Less than 0.2 miles away, we must get off the top of this mountain! Again, "One thousand one, one th—crack!" We were nearly inside the thunderstorm. The wind howled and rain poured down in buckets. The Trail was all mud and the creeks overflowed their banks. We were soaked, despite wearing all our rain gear.

We had managed to get off the top of the ridge line without being hit by lightning, but were drowning in the rain. It lasted an hour and stopped just as we reached the shelter. How considerate! The little stream in front of the shelter was now a dangerous flash flood river. We couldn't just wade through it to get to the shelter because of the raging water. We ended up hiking several hundred yards upstream to where a fallen tree was lying over the stream, and inched our way across the roaring water.

Isn't Black was there, smiling. He was dry and enjoying the storm. He had decided not to wait for me and was just about to walk into town when the storm hit. He was glad he hadn't left for town, and I was happy he waited. We changed clothes and cooked a hot meal. Soon other hikers, including Hey Everybody, arrived and the shelter filled up, forcing late arrivals to sleep in their tents. We were all wet, but thankfully, the temperature wasn't too cold. After changing into dry clothes, we spent a comfortable night in the shelter.

I had treated my backpack and rain cover with water-sealer before leaving Daleville a few days earlier. I had also lined the inside of the pack with a heavy duty trash bag, and stored my clothes and sleeping bag inside a plastic bag. Multiple layers of water protection worked. Everything stayed dry, except me.

DAY 72 MAY 28: PAUL C. WOLFE SHELTER TO ROCKFISH GAP.
TODAY'S MILES: 5.0
TRIP MILES: 857.8

RW means Riding to Waynesboro.

Late last night after the storm, a young man and woman stopped by the shelter looking for a certain backpacker. None of us knew the person. They were carrying a mandolin this hiker had accidently left behind in a shuttle van 35 miles back. The couple had hiked 35 miles trying to catch up to this person! When they realized he wasn't at our shelter, they continued on, intent on hiking all the way to Waynesboro before stopping. A whopping 40-mile day to return a mandolin to someone they didn't even know. Now that's trail magic!

I was awakened by the sound of the shelter alarm clock, the whistle of air rapidly escaping from someone's sleeping pad. Time to get up and go! Morning shelter edict calls for silence. Some hikers sleep late and some rise early. Only the sounds of cooking stoves, deflating air mattresses, and packing are permitted. By now I was expert at recognizing different types of stoves by their sound. An alcohol stove is silent. The king of all stove noise is JetBoil. It boils water incredibly fast and sounds like a jet taking off.

Isn't Black, Wrecking Ball, and I left camp early, headed for the town of Waynesboro, Virginia. When we got to the US 250 road and trail intersection, a woman pulled up in a van with a section hiker. He got out, and we got in. By 8:30 a.m. we were in Waynesboro eating breakfast. Afterwards, we went to the YMCA, showered, and then headed out to the laundromat and library to update our journals.

While reading other hiker journals, I noticed Chiggabite got off the Trail on May 21st because of a bad knee, and Achin' got off May 25th. I didn't know about My-Way. It felt like I was the only one of the original Amicalola five still on the Trail. I called my aunt to ask about my cousin, who planned to join me for a few days' hike. My aunt told me my cousin had to cancel the trip.

I expected my friends, Steve and Denise, to arrive late that night, but they called at 3:00 p.m. and said they were already in town. They picked me up, along with Isn't Black, and drove us to the local outfitter. I purchased my third pair of new hiking boots. Steve and Denise dropped Isn't Black off at the Lutheran Church Hostel, and we checked into the Best Western Motel. They treated me to a great meal that evening.

Afterwards we mapped out the next four days of slackpacking in Shenandoah National Park. Amazingly, I am only eight miles behind my trail plan! By hiking more miles and skipping planned zero days, I made up enough miles to hike the Shenandoah National Park with Steve and Denise.

DAY 73 MAY 29: ROCKFISH GAP TO TURK GAP.
TODAY'S MILES: 12.1
TRIP MILES 869.9

RW means Raining in Waynesboro.

I met Steve and Denise at 6:30 a.m. this morning for breakfast. By 7:30 a.m., Steve and I started slackpacking on the Trail in Shenandoah National Park. The weather was cool in the mid-sixties, and drizzling. Fog and dense forests limited our views most of the day. The Appalachian Trail in the park is similar to the Trail elsewhere, but extremely well blazed, and the mountain climbs are shorter and more gradual. Maybe this is the start of the Trail section that finally starts to flatten. Rain made the Trail wet and slippery at times, but not muddy. My new hiking boots performed well.

I introduced Steve to Kit and Kat as they passed us on the trail, coming from opposite directions. We met one section hiker, a man in his mid-sixties, who was hiking about two hundred miles and hoped to complete his third hike of the entire A.T. soon. Another veteran hiker told us she planned to complete her second thru-hike this year. She said she once owned a gear company, but got tired of big commercial manufacturers stealing her gear ideas.

Steve and I hiked the Trail at a comfortable pace, about two miles per hour, and spent our time catching up on events. The last time we backpacked together was over thirty years ago. We compared our past hikes in Glacier and Banff to the Appalachian Trail. We hadn't seen any bears yet, which was disappointing since everybody told me bear sightings were common in this park. Maybe tomorrow.

We completed the day's hike around 2:00 p.m. Denise picked us up at an intersection. At five o'clock, we went to the All-You-Can-Eat (AYCE) Chinese restaurant in town. The New Ming Garden Buffet and Grill is widely regarded by hikers as having the best Chinese food on the entire Appalachian Trail.

Tonight I will get a good night's sleep at the motel. Tomorrow, Denise and I hike together, and then I plan to stay in a park campground that evening.

At 6:30 p.m., I spoke with Isn't Black at the Lutheran Church Hostel. He is joining Bear Bag and will hike the same mileage in three days that I plan to complete in four. It is a good thing I have a twelve-mile start on them. Curious George is back on the Trail but several days behind us, and doing well.

DAY 74 MAY 30: TURK GAP TO LOFT MOUNTAIN STORE.
TODAY'S MILES: 16.0
TRIP MILES 885.90

RW means Running Wild Beast.

After breakfast, Denise and I started slackpacking at approximately 7:30 a.m. Once again, the day was cool and very foggy. The dripping trees and wet grass soaked our feet and clothes. We did not spot any wildlife, but we did see more flowers today than Steve and I had yesterday. I was able to show Denise the beautiful mountain laurel, rhododendrons, and honeysuckle in bloom.

Denise and I talked about many things and got to know each other. Our pleasant conversations made the day pass quickly. I introduced her to other thru-hikers on the Trail: Kit and Kat, the Canadians, Blue Jay, and the Kallin family. I have discussed them before. Everybody was exceptionally friendly. Before we knew it, we arrived at Loft Mountain Store and saw Steve, who was waiting to pick us up.

We hiked the 15.9 miles in about five hours. This included a lunch break, plus shorter breaks when we stopped to talk with other hikers. This speed was amusing, because it felt like we hiked uphill most of the day. Denise is an experienced runner, so we ran part of the Trail today. This undoubtedly contributed to our extraordinary pace. The Trail had been very kind today with only one rock scramble.

Afterwards the three of us enjoyed delicious cheeseburgers at the Wayside concession stand. We are all staying at the Lewis Mountain Campground in Shenandoah tonight. I stored all my food, gear, and backpack in Steve's car because of the high probability of bears in the area. Once our tents were set up, we cleaned up and drove to Big Meadows Lodge for dinner. It was at this lodge that I saw my first bear and took a picture. A life-sized stuffed bear was sitting in the lobby. On the drive back from the restaurant, we saw deer all along the road.

My Achilles tendon hurt today because of the running. I haven't run in a long time. The ball of my left foot hurts, too, probably because of the new boots. I will go slower tomorrow.

DAY 75 MAY 31: LOFT MOUNTAIN STORE TO SKYLINE 66.7.
TODAY'S MILES 16.1
TRIP MILES 902.0

RW means Rising Warrior. Banner day! I made a mileage sign out of large green leaves with white stones on top that read: 900 miles.

Steve and I hiked nearly seventeen miles. We began slackpacking about 7:45 a.m. and finished at 3:30 p.m. The day started cool but quickly warmed up to 80 degrees. We spotted deer, but no other sizeable animals. This section of the Trail was unusual because it had been weed-whacked. It freed us from fighting overgrowth as we hiked down the Trail. The sky was clear and we enjoyed outstanding views of the Shenandoah Valley and surrounding mountains. There were several steep climbs, and by the end of the day, we were both tired.

I met a hiker called Gone Walking today for the first time. He started the Trail on March 18th, the same day as me. Gone Walking is an older man and this is his second thru-hike. Kit and Kat each made their respective walk-by. Kit told me he was no longer bicycling, in addition to hiking the A.T. It was too much doing both. After Steve and I finished hiking, we all went out for a bite to eat. While at the restaurant, we ran into Forester Gump. The last few times I saw him were in the Greyson Highlands and the Baptist Church hostel shortly after I left Damascus. It was a real treat to see him again.

When we returned to camp, I reviewed all my equipment and decided to get rid of some clothing to reduce my weight load. The reduction was minimal, but I wanted to eliminate as much weight as possible, so I removed my extra underwear, shirt, and socks.

I plan to go to bed early tonight, but may not sleep well. Camped next to me is a family with very noisy young children. I must wake up extra early tomorrow, because Denise and I start hiking at 6:30 a.m. We have a very long day planned.

Oh, I forgot to mention that I saw some bears on the roadside while we were driving. My first wild bear sighting...finally!

MONTH FOUR: JUNE
DAY 76 JUNE 01: SKYLINE 66.7 TO BIG MEADOWS LODGE.
TODAY'S MILES: 18.3
TRIP MILES 920.2

RW means Ruining Webs.

Denise and I started slackpacking at 6:45 a.m. The morning was cool, and most of our time was spent climbing. We tunneled through heavy forest all morning. We met several thru-hikers I knew and talked with each one for a short while. Kit and Kat didn't stop when they hiked past us. They were in a hurry. We arrived at Lewis Mountain Campground at 10:30 a.m. after hiking 9.5 miles and stopped for an early lunch. Denise had more blisters on her feet, so she decided to stop here for the day.

I continued on my own and saw a bear, but it was too far away to get a picture. Exhaustion had already set in by the time I reached Big Meadows Lodge at 2:30 p.m. After checking into the lodge, the three of us went to the Wayside stand and ordered sandwiches. While I was checking the contents of my pack, I realized the rain cover was missing. I had lost it. A plastic bag will have to do until I can buy a new one. Steve ran into Isn't Black and Bear Bag. I offered to share my lodge room with them, so we are now back together.

It wasn't long before Steve and Denise had to say their goodbyes. They drive back home to Indiana tomorrow. We shared four great days on the Trail and I will never forget our time hiking together.

Later that night, Isn't Black, Bear Bag, and I enjoyed live music in the lodge bar. We were especially delighted when the band played John Denver's song, "Take Me Home, Country Roads." We had sung this song together on the Trail. Isn't Black was teaching himself how to play it on his harmonica at night. He loved that song and sang it in German and English. Bear Bag added Yiddish lyrics, just for fun.

DAY 77 JUNE 02: BIG MEADOWS LODGE TO PASS MOUNTAIN HUT.
TODAY'S MILES 18.8
TRIP MILES 939.1

RW means Rattlesnake Wrapped.

We got up late and went to a diner for breakfast. Gone Walking joined us. We finally starting hiking on the Trail around 9:45 a.m. During the morning, someone called Bear Bag, "Bear Balls." This provided a running joke all day.

Today's trail section had the best views in the Park, but sharp rocks covered the ground most of the way. My Achilles tendon ached terribly, and I took more ibuprofen than ever just to get through the day. By now, I was mixing a cocktail of anti-inflammatory drugs, ibuprofen and naproxen sodium, over a thousand milligrams a day, just to deal with the pain. I was not the only one hurting. Bear Bag may have stress fractures in the metatarsal bones of both feet. Yet, he still out-hikes me. Oh, to be young and invincible!

We hiked fast and stopped to enjoy a great lunch at the Skyland Resort and Restaurant. My Achilles tendon became more painful by the hour. I stopped to talk to people as often as possible just for the rest. Around 2:30 p.m., we encountered an angry and awesome rattlesnake and were able to get many good photographs. Bear Bag attached his camera to a trekking pole and videotaped the snake striking it. Venom dripped from his pole.

At 7:30 p.m. we finally arrived at the shelter. I was too tired to set up my tent. Gone Walking and Hoops were there. Hoops is a 34-year old woman from Indiana, now living in Washington, D.C. She was hiking the Trail with a Wounded Warrior called Kosmo, who was a 23-year-old ex-soldier suffering from post-traumatic stress.

I came across a new system for hanging food bags. A 12-foot tall iron post had steel ribs extending from the top, in the shape of an open umbrella. There were hooks on each of the ribs. I used the long steel pole which was clipped to the side of the post and raised my food bag onto one of the rib hooks. This is a very convenient way to hang food bags. I like this method much better than the cable and pulley system.

DAY 78 JUNE 03: PASS MOUNTAIN HUT TO COMPTON GAP TRAIL.
TODAY'S MILES: 22.7
TRIP MILES: 961.8

RW means Recklessly Watching bear.

I slept well, but Bear Bag said I snored all night. He even recorded it. I was very tired yesterday. I wear earplugs at night, especially in shelters, because it's hard to sleep in them. Shelters are cold, noisy, uncomfortable, and dirty. Plus, mice are the "special sauce" that adds zip to this unpleasant sleeping situation. Tent camping is better.

We left camp at 6:00 a.m. My legs were weak and my feet heavy. I fell far behind. We reached the Elk Wallow Wayside by 8:30 a.m. and waited for the concession stand to open at 9:00 a.m. We ate breakfast and got back on the Trail by 10:00 a.m. The meal recharged my battery and I hiked strong all day. Maybe my energy was low due to hunger. I can't seem to eat enough anymore. I am always hungry.

Shortly after lunch, we saw a bear on the Trail—everyone except Isn't Black. He had to answer nature's call, and was squatting a hundred yards behind us. The bear ran away, but we did get some pictures, much to Isn't Black's dismay. We joked for a while, wondering what Isn't Black's reaction would have been if the bear had charged toward him. Later on, we walked next to a protected peregrine falcon nest site that was fenced to give the birds privacy. This man-made nesting site was designed to attract falcons and improve their chances for reproduction.

The big news is Bear Bag. His feet are really in trouble. He's probably in more pain than me, but hides it better. We cut our day short and went to Terrapin Station Hostel in Front Royal, Virginia. Tomorrow, we'll take Bear Bag to a hospital where he can get his feet treated. His extreme mileage, frequently over 30 miles a day, combined with minimalist shoes, have taken a toll on his feet.

We ordered Chinese take-out food and went to bed early. Left Turn is the only other person staying at this hostel. I had never met her before. She was waiting for a postal delivery of online purchases, including new hiking shoes. Left Turn is hiking the Trail to find new meaning and direction in her life. She once struggled with substance abuse and has experienced many family sorrows, including the death of her teenage son from heart failure.

I often meet people like Left Turn, who are walking off life's troubles and searching for a new beginning. Left Turn's trail name is an abbreviated version of her favorite motto: "When life is going in the wrong direction, make a left turn, and go a new way." Not many people are staying here at this hostel. I think we are in between hiker bubbles. A hiker bubble is a large group of hikers traveling close together at the same speed along the Trail.

DAY 79 JUNE 04: COMPTON GAP TRAIL TO MANASSAS GAP SHELTER.
TODAYS' MILES: 14.5
TRIP MILES 976.3

RW means Roasted Walnut Hills, renamed by a group of high school kids from Walnut Hills, Ohio.

This was a big day for Bear Bag. The doctor at the hospital said he'd sprained both feet, but could continue hiking if he could tolerate the pain. Bear Bag is elated. We ate breakfast and then bought some food. I got my hair cut and beard trimmed. We hit the Trail at noon and got soaked by rain. We were still dripping wet when we reached the shelter at 7:00 p.m. The rain has forced everyone to sleep in the shelter.

The Trail was more of the same today. I am getting tired of Virginia. Hiking the Trail in this section is like walking through a green tunnel. The impenetrable tree cover constantly blocks out the sunlight. We only see the sun at road crossings, or when walking next to power lines. I am tired of the forest and trees. The eyelet on one of my new boots broke and I spent an hour on the phone trying to get Merrell® to replace them. I purchased new insoles for my boots, and they really help. I still got another blister today.

Isn't Black burned his fingers at dinner, but not badly. Bear Bag burned his leg. Both accidents happened separately, but from the same cause. They spilled boiling water on themselves while making dinner. We will know more tomorrow about the true extent of their injuries.

Spirit Hawk is also in the shelter. I first met him just before Waynesboro, Virginia. He is 51 years old and appears to have lost everything, including his family, during the economic recession. He writes prayers in shelter logbooks and seems to be searching for a new beginning. He said that he chose the trail name Spirit Hawk because God told him to hike the A.T., and an American Indian spirit guide in the form of a hawk was accompanying him on the Trail.

Later that night, a young couple from Alabama called Ginger and Gilligan showed up at the shelter. They are in their late twenties and very strong hikers, often covering 30 miles a day. The only other presence in the shelter is a tent. Inside this tent is an unknown person who is not socializing. We're all wondering if this stranger is sick, maybe even contagious. A voice from inside the tent warned us to leave him alone. None of us could figure out what was going on with him. "Don't mess with people who don't want to be messed with" is pretty much everybody's motto on the Trail. Not everyone you meet in the woods is a hiker or rational person.

DAY 80 JUNE 05: MANASSAS GAP SHELTER TO SAM MOORE SHELTER.
TODAY'S MILES: 19.8
TRIP MILES 996.1

RW means Rollercoaster Warmup.

It rained non-stop last night. We slept late and it was still raining when we reluctantly left camp about 8:00 a.m. The first to leave were Gilligan and Ginger. They planned to hike nearly 25 miles today. The stranger in the tent never came out or spoke. Bear Bag and Isn't Black's burns are minor, and they hiked all day with few problems.

This morning before leaving the shelter, Bear Bag sewed the eyelet back together on my boot. He is good at sewing and was able to fix my boot. I texted the information and photos of my boots to my wife, and she is now trying to get replacements from Merrell.

Morning fog draped the forest with a lovely opaque light and hue. I love the way wet leaves glisten in the forest. Rain brings out a spectrum of different shades of green. I took many spectacular pictures this morning. The forest here is unlike any other I've seen on the Trail. The trees, mostly ash and hickory, are tall and straight, and at least one is 125 to 150 feet tall.

The fog burned off about noon. Despite the deep greens of this forest, I miss sunlight. We hiked all day without incident and met several day hikers. Spirit Hawk hiked close by all day.

We entered a trail section known as the Rollercoaster at 3:00 p.m. The Rollercoaster is approximately 13.5 miles long and very rocky, with steep ups and downs. By the time we got to the shelter, we were halfway through the Rollercoaster.

At the shelter, a 67-year-old grandfather and his two grandchildren were picnicking just for the day. Spirit Hawk had already set up camp, bathed in the stream, and hung his clothes on a line after rinsing them in the stream.

It was a comfortable night, and I copied Spirit Hawk's example by taking a quick bath in my clothes, and then hanging them on a line to dry. During dinner, Isn't Black realized he had left all his spare clothes at the last shelter. His trekking poles had started to fall apart today, and the tip of one of my trekking poles broke, too. After dinner we sat around the campfire with the two children and told them hiking stories. We had a great time.

I originally planned to hike this section with my cousin all the way to Harpers Ferry, but she was still recovering from foot surgery and decided to cancel the trip. A wise decision—this section is hard, too hard for a first-time long distance backpacking trip. Tomorrow, I cross the 1000-mile mark.

DAY 81 JUNE 06: SAM MOORE SHELTER TO BLACKBURN A.T. CENTER.
TODAY'S MILES: 11.0
TRIP MILES 1,007.1

RW means Rollercoaster Wisdom Walk. We solved the world's problems while hiking the Rollercoaster.

I crossed the 1000-mile mark today and entered West Virginia. The mileage sign that I constructed with large sticks covered the entire width of the Trail.

Last night the temperature fell. Woke up at 5:30 a.m., and had to dress myself in wet, chilly clothes. They never dried during the damp, cold night. When we left camp at 7:30 a.m., Bear Bag and Isn't Black hiked much faster than me and soon were out of sight. I hiked with Spirit Hawk and tried to get to the Bears Den Hostel before 9:00 a.m. They close at 9:00 a.m. and hikers must wait until they reopen later in the day to resupply. It was only three miles, but they were three Rollercoaster miles, all rocks and steep climbs.

Once at the hostel, we all ordered pizza, ice cream and Cokes for breakfast. We saw Forester Gump. He was now wearing a kilt and encouraged me to buy one. We ate and hung around the place until 11:30 a.m. Isn't Black and Bear Bag decided to go wine tasting at a local winery near the Trail. I wasn't interested and hiked on with Spirit Hawk and Forester Gump. As we worked our way through the Virginia Rollercoaster section of the Trail, we spent our time solving the problems of the world. Forester Gump, a professional woodsman and educator from northern Michigan, regaled us with facts about the trees and forest.

Listener joined us. I had hiked with Listener near Erwin, Tennessee, during an ice and snow storm. Listener had left the Trail temporarily to spend time with his family and was restarting his hike. Time passed quickly, and by 4:00 p.m. we were at the Blackburn Appalachian Trail Center. It is a beautiful place and hikers stay for free, but the accommodations are limited.

While there, I ran into Buzz and his daughter, Tandem. I had hiked with Buzz and Tandem off and on before Damascus, but they had gotten far ahead of me. After a while, I stopped seeing their names in the shelter logbooks. It turns out Buzz developed serious shin problems and went to a hospital in Atlanta for treatment. He was diagnosed with shin splints, a common and painful muscle stress injury. Rest is the only cure. Buzz and Tandem had been off the Trail for nearly two weeks while he recovered.

More thru-hikers arrived in the evening, including Freeman. For the past nine years Freeman has lived on the Trail as a protest against the United States' invasion in Iraq. He loves life in the woods and is a friendly sort of guy. He never yogies for food and says, for him, living on the Trail is a lifestyle choice, not a matter of money. He receives a pension from his prior job at a weapons manufacturing facility.

Bear Bag brought out a bottle of wine at dinner. He purchased it at the winery to celebrate our 1000-mile mark. He shared the wine with everyone. It was very generous of him. After nightfall, we gazed at the moon through a large telescope, and then were able to locate the Washington Monument visible on the horizon toward Washington, D.C.

That night we also discovered Isn't Black had lost his camp shoes after the trip to the winery. In the past two days, he has lost most of his spare clothes, and now his spare shoes. He is unhappy about losing so many important items two days in a row. All the beds and tent sites had been taken by the time Isn't Black arrived late after his winery stop, so he had to sleep on the porch. We heard him playing his harmonica on the porch. He was starting to get good at John Denver's "Country Roads" song. Before leaving the Blackburn Appalachian Trail Center, I updated my A.T. passport and got my seventeenth stamp.

DAY 82 JUNE 07: BLACKBURN A.T. CENTER TO APPALACHIAN TRAIL CONSERVANCY HEADQUARTERS, HARPERS FERRY, VA.
TODAY'S MILES: 11.9
TRIP MILES: 1,019.9

RW means Roaring Wheels, because of all the car noise at Harpers Ferry.

Last night was a lot of fun. I truly enjoyed the Blackburn A.T. Center and highly recommend it. Bear Bag had slept in his hammock. The next morning, he told us a bear came right up to his hammock during the night and was trying to sniff out what was hanging inside it. Bear Bag woke up, looked the bear straight in the eyes, and yelled at it to go away. The bear ran away.

We got up early and left camp by 7:00 a.m. Without food and with only one liter of water, our packs were light. We hiked fast and steady all morning, but the rocky trail prevented us from making as many miles per hour as hoped. Thank goodness for my new Dr. Scholl's insoles, the best I have used so far!

Bear Bag talked about his campaign work for President Obama's election as we entered Harpers Ferry. We turned off the A.T. and started hiking down a side trail headed toward the Appalachian Trail Conservancy. The side trail ran through the former campus of the historically black Storer College, which operated from 1865 until 1955. While there, we encountered a group of African Americans taking a guided tour. Their guide was a black woman who invited us to stop for a moment so she could briefly explain the purpose of the Appalachian Trail to the group. Then, she asked us to explain our trail names.

Bear Bag went first, then me, and finally, Isn't Black. When Isn't Black announced his trail name with a thick German accent, she got flustered and scurried the tour group away. The guide never gave him a chance to explain that the name had been given to him by other hikers because his poncho wasn't black like the rest of his clothes. Isn't Black was confused and wanted to know why the woman had cut him off. Had he mispronounced or misused a word?

Bear Bag told him Storer College had once been a prominent and historically significant college devoted to the advancement of African Americans and was formed shortly after the American Civil War to educate freed slaves. Isn't Black thought about it, and again, asked, "Why did they leave so fast and not let me finish the story?"

I had my picture taken at the ATC and signed up to join their organization. Last March, when I set out from Springer Mountain, Georgia, I was registered as thru-hiker No. 507. Here, I was thru-hiker No. 453, the four hundred fifty-third thru-hiker to reach this point this year. I searched for My-Way's photo and registration without success. He would have been one of the early ones. I don't think he made it this far, but I can't say for sure.

According to the ATC, approximately 50 percent of all thru hikers make it this far. I am grateful to be one of the top 50 percent. Studying the ATC logbook and journal, I realized that many hikers who started the Trail weeks after me, had already passed me by. I wasn't moving up the pack. The young hikers are so fast and strong. "Oh, to be young!"

This 59-year-old body just can't compete with youth on a physical basis. But the young still break down and fall victim to the Trail. Often, they just don't have the resolve to continue hiking every day. Their minds tire long before their bodies. It is frightening to see how many hikers the Trail has already broken. The Trail feeds on someone every day. It is both generous and terrifying, and takes anyone it chooses, whenever it wants. The

Trail rarely forgives mistakes and is quick to punish the careless and unlucky.

I met so many other thru-hikers at the ATC that it feels like a class reunion. The ATC staff is the best, so helpful, and the other hikers really do feel like family. We happily shared our hiking stories and remembered those who have already left the Trail. We felt confident and full of bravado that we would make it all the way to the end. Mixed into the conversation, though, the hint of apprehension could be heard. What did the Trail have in store for us ahead?

This is almost the halfway point. I am amazed and find it difficult to comprehend that I have backpacked 1,019 miles over some very rough mountains. Would I fall victim to the Trail during the second half of the hike? The ATC predicts at least one-third, and up to half, of all thru-hikers who reach Harpers Ferry will not complete the Trail. The Trail is a hungry animal and uses every opportunity to take down a thru-hiker. Few are spared.

After leaving the ATC we hiked into Harpers Ferry, ate lunch, and then shopped at the outfitters. I wanted new camp shoes, trail soap, fuel, a rain cover for my pack, and repair parts for my trekking poles. The store was out of rain covers and fuel. They couldn't repair my poles and didn't sell trail soap. Isn't Black purchased some clothing and picked up two mismatched Crocs at a bargain price. Bear Bag was able to get his poles repaired, but couldn't find shoes in his size, which is very wide.

Baltimore Jack, a famous lifetime thru-hiker, was working the register. He is a great guy. When I left Springer Mountain last March, he was helping out at the Mountain Crossing outfitter store in Neel Gap. Baltimore Jack moves up the Trail with the NOBOs heading north. Miss Janet is another A.T. trail legend who rides the waves of thru-hikers moving up and down the Trail.

Just as we left the store, Buzz and Tandem pulled up in a free shuttle, so we hopped in and rode to Walmart. I bought soap and shoes, but everything else was sold out. Isn't Black purchased more clothing and will immediately return some of the more expensive clothes that he just bought at the outfitters. I bought some pre-cooked pasta dishes, instead of ramen noodles, for my main course evening meals. Isn't Black had us all laughing hysterically in Walmart. He rode around the store in one of those motorized handicapped grocery carts. Seeing him race up and down the aisles was hilarious. People stared.

A woman began asking questions, and we talked to her at length about the A.T. She was mesmerized by our stories, which we heavily embellished for her benefit. We ran into Forester Gump and Spirit Hawk at the store and gave them a lift. Now the free shuttle car, which was small, held eight people, including their backpacks and food. The scene reminded me of high school days when everybody was always trying to cram into one small car.

We checked into the EconoLodge, ordered take-out food, and watched television. Bear Bag's feet were very sore and he soaked them in ice for a long time. We all were exhausted. My feet hurt, and I prayed this zero day would reduce the pain in my feet, ankles, knees, hands, back, and other joints. My muscles are very stiff. I will take two zero days here. My last day off was May 20, at mile 724. I have hiked 295 miles in eighteen days without a break. I am tired.

We are preparing for the next stage of our adventure. Our plan is to hike four days without a break and reach Pennsylvania. We only need to hike two days to get through Maryland. We are in West Virginia now. Georgia, Tennessee, North Carolina, and Virginia are behind us. Four states finished! Once I start hiking again, West Virginia and Maryland will go by fast.

DAY 83 JUNE 08: ZERO DAY.
TODAY'S MILES: 0.0
TRIP MILES: 1,019.0

RW means Rushing Where? Nowhere.

We are spending three nights at the EconoLodge. Since there are three of us, and only two beds, we rotate every day with one person sleeping on the floor in their sleeping bag. I slept on the floor last night and had the weirdest experience. I woke up during the night, and in my half-waking/half-sleep state, thought the legs of the tables and chairs were trees. The light from the hallway peeped in under the door and seemed like a reflection from a shining object. The beds were giant boulders of stone, and other tents. I couldn't understand how I got out of my tent, and had no idea why I was lying on a carpet.

It was all very disorientating until I turned on my headlamp. (Yes, I turned on my headlamp!) I never thought about flipping the light switch on in the room. They don't exist in the woods. When I realized I was sleeping on the floor of a motel room, I shook my head in amazement and laughed. I have been in the woods too long!

Bugs have become a problem. They are taking a special interest in Isn't Black and Bear Bag. Isn't Black is covered in all kinds of bug bites from chiggers, mites, gnats, and another irritating insect. His sleeping bag is infested with them, and he thinks he picked them up from the porch at the Blackburn Appalachian Trail Center. As for Bear Bag, ticks are especially attracted to him. He is constantly pulling them off his body. Both of these guys spent a good part of the day just spraying insecticides on their sleeping bags and clothes and treating itchy bites and rashes. I'm embarrassed to admit that bugs haven't been overly interested in me, just a few minor mosquito bites and other insect bites. No complaints...yet.

A zero day is so nice! Usually zero days are busy. You come into town after a long hike and eat, buy food, eat, do laundry, search for the AYCE (trail lingo for an all-you-can-eat restaurant), make phone calls, eat, charge your electronics, think about going back to the AYCE, go there again, and then plan the next stage of your hike. Oh, did I mention eat? The day is then topped off by going out for ice cream. Since I finished all that hustle and bustle yesterday, I am doing very little today, just letting my feet recover.

I spent time on the Internet looking for information on numbness in the toes and feet. Everyone has numb toes. Numbness is a frequent topic of discussion in the shelters and camps, after talk of food, equipment, and then more food. Sometimes we talk about bears and rattlesnakes, but mostly food, feet, and equipment. The best I can figure out from the Internet is that numbness is caused by worn out, improperly fitting shoes. This can't be the only reason. Too many hikers complain about numb feet. Surely we all don't have improperly fitting, worn-out shoes.

I did read one article linking foot numbness and shin splints to the rigors of backpacking and the constant pounding of the lower part of the body from hard trails, heavy packs, long miles, and loose, sharp rocks. Every hiker spends a great deal of money and time on shoes and insoles, yet we still have sore toes and numb feet. The new Dr. Scholl's insoles have provided relief and reduced the numbness. My feet feel much better after a day of rest, but numbness still exists, especially in the big toes.

The other very strange thing about zero days is the overwhelming desire to get back on the Trail as soon as possible. Every time I stop to resupply and rest, I feel like I've been taken out of the big game. The Trail is now my life. Life must keep moving ahead, only ahead, all the time, on the Trail. To stop is to hit the pause button on life. Zero days hold me back from moving toward my goal. They are critical and essential for health, but contrary to the daily routine of trail life. Trail life requires hiking, not rest. Getting off the Trail separates you from that life and sets you in an alien environment of speeding cars, noise, the need for money, and the rules of social etiquette. Stopping outside in your tracks to take a pee is no longer acceptable.

Harpers Ferry is an interesting and historic town, and the ATC is wonderful. I went there again today to talk with other thru-hikers. I saw several more that I recognized. They are also staying at the EconoLodge, so the pizza delivery guys will be busy tonight.

DAY 84 JUNE 09: ZERO DAY.
TODAY'S MILES: 0.0
TRIP MILES: 1,019.0

F.W months Reohuping Water.

We all weighed ourselves. I lost twelve pounds. Isn't Black lost about 35 pounds, the same amount of weight as a heavy backpack. Bear Bag hadn't lost any weight.

Clothes are falling off both sexes. Men are losing upper body muscle and belly fat, turning into Tyrannosaurus Rex, all legs and no upper body. Women seem to be replacing fat with lean, heavier muscle. Toned and shapelier, but not losing much weight in the process, much to their dismay. We men were happy to see the belly disappear, but not about losing so much upper body strength.

Trail magic was incredible yesterday and today. Last night, a trail maintainer named Shellie Moubray left a message on my online guest book. She thought she'd found Isn't Black's lost clothing. Isn't Black contacted her and confirmed that they were his belongings. Shellie will mail them to Pine Grove, Pennsylvania, for general delivery. Amazing! The Trail takes and gives back. Thank you, Shellie Moubray! You are a trail angel and a true ambassador for the A.T. and America!

Today my wife contacted Merrell, letting them know I had repaired my boots. Instead of cancelling the replacement order, Merrell promised to give me credit for another pair at a later date. Amazing! I broke the tip of my Black Diamond trekking pole a few days ago on the Trail and called the company's customer service number. They agreed to send a replacement for the entire lower part of the trekking pole, at cost, plus shipping. I will pick up the package at the Pine Grove post office, the same place where Isn't Black will collect his lost clothing. Again, amazing!

My wife's good friend, Maryglenn, lives in Clear Spring, Maryland. Maryglenn and her husband, Bob, met me for lunch in Harpers Ferry. I introduced them to Isn't Black and Bear Bag, and we all had a wonderful time together. Our visit was much too short. In addition to the tremendous trail magic and good fortune with scheduling mail deliveries, being able to see Bob and Maryglenn again was the cherry on the sundae of a perfect zero day!

A very funny incident occurred during the day. Isn't Black was using the bathroom in the motel room, and Bear Bag needed to relieve himself as well. He knocked on the door and Isn't Black responded authoritatively, with a loud, heavy German accent, "The German is occupying the bathroom!" His booming voice ricocheted off the walls of the tiled bathroom. Bear Bag and I rolled on the floor in hysterical convulsions of laughter. The thought of a German occupation in the motel bathroom struck us as hilarious. For the rest of the day, Isn't Black would repeat this phrase at every opportunity, bringing Bear Bag to his knees every time.

Bear Bag has decided to get better shoes, but finding the correct shoe size is difficult for him, especially along the Trail. He ordered an overnight delivery of ten pairs of shoes from Zappos.com. Isn't Black and I are heading out tomorrow. After

Bear Bag finds a pair of shoes that fit, he'll return the rest and catch up to us at a rendezvous site.

Before I went to bed, I mailed my wife a "Missing You" card, and my father a "Happy Father's Day" card.

DAY 85 JUNE 10: APPALACHIAN TRAIL CONSERVANCY HEADQUARTERS TO DAHLGREN BACKPACK CAMPGROUND.
TODAY'S MILES: 17.8
TRIP MILES 1,036.8

RW means Recap Wonder, a name given to me by the Wolf Pack Five Family and the Swiss Family Robinson Four.

Bear Bag stayed behind to wait for shipment from Zappos shoes. Isn't Black and I left for the trail around 8:00 a.m. and quickly entered Maryland after crossing the Potomac River. Another new state; five states down. Crossing the Maryland state line was a disappointment, because there was no border sign to announce our arrival.

We hiked along the C&O Canal and Potomac River for several miles. At one point, railroad tracks ran along the other side of the trail. Sandwiched between water on one side and tracks on the other, we were blasted with noise whenever a train roared by, but the scenery was worth it. Maryland's shelters and campgrounds are the best I've seen so far, and the forest here is different than any other forests I've already hiked through. The trees are younger and shorter, allowing daylight to peek through the tree canopy. We could look up and see sky and clouds on many occasions. The green tunnel is not so dark in Maryland, but the Trail is still a monotonous and confining corridor of green foliage. Not many flowers, but a few scattered patches of mountain laurel were blooming.

One section was very rocky and eroded, and it tortured my Achilles tendon. Morning fog lasted until 10:00 a.m. Rain has lasted for days, and it rained again this morning. My feet were soaked. We learned that Curious George has permanently left the Trail. His heel is still injured and his knees hurt now.

We met nine people who were all members of two families. Each family had started out hiking on their own, but joined up when they met each other on the Trail. They use the collective trail name of SKAGR and post their hiking journals jointly on www.trailjournals.com. The two families began hiking on March 20th, and leapfrogged 400 miles ahead. They planned to continue leapfrogging on the Trail, returning later to complete the sections they skipped. Their goal was to complete the entire Trail by the end of November. The children, all young teenagers, appeared to be doing well and were taking a year off from public school in order to hike the Trail. The parents were home schooling them along the way.

DAY 86 JUNE 11: DAHLGREN BACKPACK CAMPGROUND TO RAVEN ROCK SHELTER.
TODAY'S MILES: 18.8
TRIP MILES 1,055.6

RW means Raven Weather.

It stormed hard last night. A pool of rain water collected under my tent. I managed to stay dry, but had to pack up a wet tent. I got up at 6:00 a.m., right after the rain stopped. We hiked for a while, and by 9:00 a.m. Bear Bag had already caught up to us. Amazing!

We climbed over South Mountain and walked through the Washington Monument State Park. We stopped to look at the 30-foot monument tower built in 1827 in honor of George Washington. Back in school, I had never learned about this monument. I thought the first and only George Washington monument was the famous one built in Washington, D.C. It was hard to give the park the attention it deserved because the weather was foggy and rainy, and I was tired and foot-sore. I just wanted to hike on.

We noticed a hiking couple searching for something around the grounds of the monument tower. I asked them if they needed any help. They said they were fine. They were just looking for a geo-cache. We spent a few minutes talking with the man while the woman kept walking around holding a GPS device. His trail name was Bismarck, and she was called Hopper.

We hiked in rain all day long. It has rained four days straight now, and the Trail and forest are saturated. My feet look like blistery prunes and are very painful. Some hikers have suggested that I coat my feet and socks with Vaseline. I haven't tried it yet, but they swear it prevents blisters on wet and rainy days.

We arrived at the shelter at five o'clock. A beautiful shelter, but unfortunately, drinkable water was located 0.6 miles away at the bottom of a steep hill. I could just scream! My feet did not approve of these extra miles to fetch water, and I am very tired.

Penguinman stayed down at the water source for a long time to soak his feet and filter water. I have met him before on the Trail and like him a lot. He is retired, in his sixties, and started the Trail on February 17th.

At 7:00 p.m., it thundered and the rain started pouring down hard. I was picking up cell service and used my phone to check the weather forecast. A tornado warning had been issued for this area. The humidity is just crushing.

DAY 87 JUNE 12: RAVEN ROCK SHELTER TO ROCKY MOUNTAIN SHELTER.
TODAY'S MILES: 19.8
TRIP MILES 1,075.4

RW means Rocky mountain Wonder.

Not many views today because of the thick fog and rain. Bear Bag and Isn't Black pulled ahead today. I was moving too slowly with my aching feet, and the Trail was very rocky.

I am amazed that there is a four-state challenge on this section of the Trail. To complete this challenge, a hiker must walk 43 miles from the Virginia/West Virginia border to the Maryland/Pennsylvania border in 24 hours or less. Bear Bag had been talking for weeks about attempting the four-state challenge, but decided against it now that his feet were so sore.

Within two miles of the shelter, the rain really let loose again. I hiked alone, focused on getting to the shelter and out of the rain. I buried my head to protect my eyes and nose from the drowning rain, and paid no heed to my surroundings. Everything is wet. I arrived at the shelter at 5:30 p.m. and changed clothes. There are eight of us in the shelter, and I know everybody.

It wasn't long before Jim, a trail and shelter maintainer, stopped by. We had a good conversation, and he mentioned that pizza could be delivered to this shelter. Immediately, we called to order pizza but couldn't get through. Jim walked out in the rain for half a mile, drove into town, and bought us four large pizzas and two liters of pop. Carrying the pizza boxes and large bottles, he walked back in the rain and said we didn't owe him anything.

We forced Jim to take some money, but it was a pittance compared to the real cost and time and effort it took for him to bring it to us. Great trail magic, and what a great guy! Now we no longer needed to get off the Trail and resupply tomorrow. We have enough food to make it to the next hostel.

DAY 88 JUNE 13: ROCKY MOUNTAIN SHELTER TO CALEDONIA STATE PARK.
TODAY'S MILES: 3.4
TRIP MILES: 1,078.8

RW means Rough Walk.

This is Friday the 13th, and it was a disaster. The weather continued to storm most of the night. I woke up thirsty in the middle of the night and tried to drink some water, but ended up spilling most of it inside my sleeping bag. I slept wet and damp for the rest of the night. The clothes that I had hung up to dry were still dripping wet when I put them on this morning.

We all left early today, about 7:00 a.m., but I was the last to leave. I hurried for over an hour trying to catch Bear Bag and Isn't Black. Then, I saw a building at a road crossing that looked familiar. I thought it was odd that it looked just like the one I saw yesterday. And then it struck me like a bolt of lightning. I shouldn't be recognizing landmarks. I was hiking the wrong way!

I was frustrated, astounded, and felt incredibly foolish. How could I have made such an error after hiking over a thousand miles? I decided to hike back slowly because of my sore and blistered feet. The extra hours from the morning's mistake, and the spilled water during the night, left me without drinking water well before reaching the next water source. I hiked without water for about 45 minutes. When I got to Caledonia State Park, Pennsylvania, I stopped for water and took a break. My feet were hurting terribly. I had been hiking hard for hours, only to move forward 3.4 miles on the Trail.

I was demoralized and out of momentum. I had reached the bottom, physically and emotionally. It was the lowest I had ever felt on the Trail. We had intended to hike nearly 22 miles and reach the halfway point today. But now it was clear that I couldn't do it—and worse, I no longer had the desire to even try.

After my despondent break, I talked with two middle-aged couples sitting in their parked SUVs. I asked each couple, separately, if they would drive me three miles to the motel. They both refused, it was out of their way. One couple thought I was homeless and treated me with disdain. I tried to explain my situation, that I was a thru-hiker and my feet were very sore, but they just drove off. I called a shuttle driver and he took me to the Scottish Inn in Fayetteville, Pennsylvania, where I sat dazed and wondering if this was where my great hike was going to end.

After washing my clothes in the sink, I walked to a restaurant near the motel and enjoyed a good meal. Echoing in my head were Tic Toc's words, told to me back in Amicalola at the start of my hike: "Never quit on your worst day!" I called home and talked to my father and wife. I said I may be done and coming home. I will decide tomorrow.

As I sat outside my room, another motel guest named Mike offered to drive me to the Dollar General, where I bought medical stuff for my feet. Mike also agreed to drive me back to the Trail the next morning. Another real trail angel! I decided to keep his phone number in case I couldn't hike anymore and needed someone to pick me up.

I hoped to hike to the halfway point tomorrow only a few miles away, take a picture, and then call Mike for a ride to the next hostel, where a mail delivery of replacement parts for my trekking poles was waiting for me. I would probably have to make arrangements to go home from this location, too.

I described the kind of day I had on my online trail journal and told readers that tomorrow was likely going to be the end of the Trail for me. I also wished Bear Bag and Isn't Black the best and said I hoped to see them again, even though it is doubtful that I will ever be able to catch up to them.

While online, I learned that Guy-on-a-Buffalo was sick with Lyme disease. Hearing this made me feel even worse... a super hiker fallen on the trail. Guy-on-a-Buffalo was already far ahead of me in Connecticut. Ticks are there, too.

It isn't raining now, but more thunderstorms are predicted for tonight. The Trail will be soaking wet again tomorrow. My spirits remain dampened, but at least I'll start off with dry clothes and dry socks.

DAY 89 JUNE 14: CALEDONIA STATE PARK TO A.T. MUSEUM.
TODAY'S MILES 19.1
TRIP MILES: 1,097.9

RW means Reverse brain Wave.

Today took a 180-degree turn in an opposite direction. Yesterday and today could not have been more different. The text messages, emails, and journal entries that I received from friends, family, trail angels, and others encouraging me to continue were overwhelming. I couldn't have even started today, let alone hike a few miles, without their prayers, praise, and encouragement. My feet are still in pain, but the support from so many well-wishers has lifted me up, even though I didn't think I could go on. It is difficult to express how I felt. I knew I had to try.

I called Mike, and he agreed to give me and AZ Cruiser a ride back to the Trail. AZ Cruiser planned to accompany me today. He is a very strong hiker. When Mike pulled up, we struggled to shove our packs into the trunk of his car. Most of the trunk space was already taken up by an old golf bag missing all but one wheel, and four vintage golf clubs.

While getting inside Mike's car, we quickly spied a shotgun lying on the back seat. He said he carried it for protection. I hadn't noticed the gun yesterday; it must have been hidden under a blanket. Scattered around the front seat were several Rambo-style knives. Mike said he liked to keep them close at hand. He drove us to the Trail and charged only five dollars for gas money.

Let me tell you a short story about how much my readers have contributed to making my dream come true. A trail angel called Iceman offered to help me slackpack today. I didn't take him up on his offer, because I figured Mike would pick me up off the Trail.

Iceman's real name is David Martin. He is a regular section hiker who lives in Pennsylvania. Iceman drove to a point on the Trail where he guessed I might be hiking today, and then started walking south in hopes of running into me. He found me at Birch Run Shelter.

We talked for a while, and then he hiked with me when I needed a helping hand and emotional support more than ever before. It was a rare encounter with a true angel. I had never met or heard of this person before today and was unaware that he read my trail journal until he contacted me last night. Iceman said he could provide assistance to help me hike through the state of Pennsylvania. I may take him up on his offer later, but for now his touching generosity and the tremendous encouragement from other readers have recharged me emotionally and restored my determination. I will continue to hike as long as my body holds up. Never before have I experienced such uplifting support from so many people, known and unknown. The renewed strength and energy given to me by this passionate outpouring is overwhelming.

Today the weather was perfect. The sky was beautiful, and the Trail amazingly kind. The ground was mostly dry and soft, with very few rocks all day. The trees are thinning and daylight penetrates all the way to the forest floor in large patches. Could this be the end of the green tunnel?

We crossed the midpoint of the Appalachian Trail at 1:45 p.m. and Penguinman took my picture. The thru-hike is more than halfway finished. As we talked together all day, AZ Cruiser and Penguinman inspired me to keep walking to Pine Grove Furnace State Park, farther than I believed I could hike today. Without the inspiration and support of Iceman, AZ Cruiser, and Penguinman, my hike would have ended here.

I went to the Appalachian Trail Museum and considered taking on the half-gallon challenge. To win, a hiker must eat a half-gallon of ice cream in a half-hour or less. I decided not to accept the challenge because of all the stories about hikers who got miserably sick afterwards.

While there, I ran into Dependable Pete, and Dirt, who I've seen occasionally on the Trail. Dependable Pete is from Rockford, Illinois, and was leaving the Trail for a few days to be with his wife.

At the end of the day, Bear Bag and Isn't Black showed up at the same hostel as me, the Ironmasters Mansion Hostel. I was flabbergasted and became emotional at seeing them again. They are twenty miles ahead of me, but decided to shuttle back and stay another night in hopes of finding me here. I was so glad to see them, and we shared dinner together. They will jump ahead twenty miles tomorrow and continue hiking high-mileage days from where they left off. I hoped to catch up to them, but that seems impossible. A 20-mile lead is too much. It would require several 30-mile days back to back, in order to catch up with hikers I can barely keep up with in the first place.

DAY 90 JUNE 15: A.T. MUSEUM TO BOILING SPRINGS, PA.
TODAY'S MILES 19.6
TRIP MILES 1,117.5

RW means Rock Maze.

I have been hiking for ninety days, an unbelievable three months, and have averaged about 12.4 miles per day. Last night was cold and I was glad to be inside this hostel. Ironmasters Mansion Hostel is great, and I highly recommend it. Cuz, AZ Cruiser, Isn't Black, Bear Bag, Blue Jay, and I were the only hikers staying at this wonderful historic building. After breakfast, Cuz gave me a bandana as a gift to replace the A.T. bandana I had lost two days ago. Starting the day with trail magic was wonderful!

AZ Cruiser and I left the hostel at 7:30 a.m. and quickly passed the 1100-mile mark. I made a sign with large white rocks. The Trail was smooth and flat most of the day and we made great time, arriving in Boiling Springs at 3:30 a.m. The flat, easy trail during the last two days gave my body a break, and I appreciated it, even though my Achilles and feet still hurt. We saw an interesting rock formation known as the Maze. The Maze is a huge pile of giant broken boulders that weaves through, under, and over the Trail. It was fun.

The green tunnel abruptly ended in a farm field at the end of the day. During our last few miles, the mountains behind us receded with every step forward. Ahead of me was open farmland. I ran into Iceman when we got to Boiling Springs, and he provided trail magic again by driving us around. Boiling Springs is a beautiful town and I hope to come back one day just to relax and explore the area.

We checked into the Allenberry Resort Inn and Playhouse, which is normally expensive, but they gave us a hiker-rate of only $20 per person for a double room. No play tonight, which would have been an extra treat. My feet still hurt, so I planned to hike only a few miles for the next several days. Plus, the weather was supposed to heat up into the nineties. AZ Cruiser was gearing up for a 26-miler day to get to Duncannon. Many other hikers hoped to do the same thing in order to reach the next town and avoid carrying extra food. I planned to take two days' worth, and then buy more food later for the next 70 miles on the Trail. AZ and I said our goodbyes.

DAY 91 JUNE 16: BOILING SPRINGS, PA TO PA ROAD 850.
TODAY'S MILES: 16.5
TRIP MILES: 1,134.0

RW means Rotgut Whiskey, according to Pat, the bartender at the Doyle Hotel.

All my plans collapsed today. After breakfast, Hawg Driver and I hit the Trail. The breakfast at the Allenberry Resort Inn was excellent and only cost six dollars. Yesterday, I wrote that most of the Trail was now running through farmland. That is inaccurate. Although there were a few times we hiked through farmland today, we mostly hiked in the trees adjacent to the farmland.

Hawg Driver is a former military A-10 Tank Killer pilot. The military plane he flew was called a Hawg. Hawg Driver is now a Delta Airlines pilot and hikes the Trail in between flights, which can be scheduled weeks apart. Hawg Driver calls himself an executive hiker. He plans his trail days by taking maximum advantage of slackpacking (not carrying a pack), and pays shuttle drivers handsomely to ferry his gear to the next stop, which is usually a motel or hostel. I first met Hawg Driver in Harpers Ferry.

My pack contained two days' worth of food because I wanted to cover less miles and give my feet a break. During the day, Hawg Driver convinced me to hike a little further because he had a shuttle arranged to drive him to Duncannon, Pennsylvania. He planned to slackpack for several days from this town. My aching feet convinced me to slackpack with him. I hoped the absence of the pack would give my feet some time to heal.

After 10.3 miles, we stopped for lunch at Scott Farm Trail Work Center. A ridge runner was there and he agreed to drop off our packs at the Doyle Hotel in Duncannon. This gave me a chance to slackpack the next six miles before getting picked up by the shuttle driver.

Unfortunately, the shuttle driver never showed up because the scheduled pick-up hadn't been confirmed. Hawg Driver tried to confirm, but couldn't get a cell phone connection. At 3:00 p.m., I was without gear or water, and in no condition to walk the remaining 9.1 miles to Duncannon. Hawg Driver was limping, too, but decided to push on to Duncannon. He may be suffering from a common trail injury, like tibialis tendinitis, or shin splints. Both require several days of rest for healing.

Trail magic to the rescue! After a few minutes, I asked a man who was sitting near his parked car for a ride to Duncannon. He was listening to our conversation and agreed to give me a lift. On the way to town, Dennis and I talked about the A.T. It turned out that he was a former trail maintainer who had hiked several sections of the A.T. His goal was to hike all the Trail sections in Pennsylvania. We had a very pleasant drive. I told him about myself and the journey so far. Later that night in Duncannon, I saw him again at the local ice cream stand. He was there with his family and he introduced me to them.

The Doyle Hotel is an ancient four-story hotel located in the old town center of Duncannon. It has no elevators, and I am staying here in a room on the fourth floor. The Doyle hotel/hostel is worn out and in need of repair, but the bar still retains some of its old world charm. The Doyle's main attraction is its bar and grill, offering good food and cheap prices. The upper levels are in dire need of reconstruction. The rooms are tiny, the woodwork is dark and dingy, and the plaster is peeling off the walls. I'm writing this entry on top of a worn-out wooden dresser attached to a mirror missing most of its silver. The only light in the room is a bare bulb on a pull chain hanging from the ceiling.

The place is sold out with thru-hikers tonight. The Appalachian Trail not only cuts through the town of Duncannon, but it runs alongside this historic hotel building. I recognize many of the hikers staying here tonight, and the conversation is fun. Hawg Driver finally walked into the lobby around 7:00 p.m.

My feet hurt so much. The blisters are painful, and my Achilles tendon is damaged. I have limped severely for the last four days and can hardly walk at the moment. Since there's no ice at the Doyle, I plan to soak my feet in cold water tonight and tomorrow.

DAY 93 JUNE 17: PA ROAD 850 TO DUNCANNON.
TODAY'S MILES: 0.0
TRIP MILES: 1,143.1

RW means Rules by Whom?

The weather forecast calls for isolated thunderstorms for the next ten days. I'm moving slowly today and soaking my feet as much as possible. While sitting in the bar downstairs, I read an old photocopied article about this place printed in The Burg, a local magazine published in Harrisburg. The Doyle was originally a three-story wooden hotel built in the 1770s. It burned in 1903, and was replaced with the current four-story brick building. Charles Dickens once stayed here during an American lecture tour

In 1880, Adolphus Busch, the wealthy beer magnate, purchased the property. Later, the hotel was owned by the Budweiser Company, until it was sold during the Prohibition era. In 1944, the hotel was renamed by its new owner, Jim Doyle, who purchased the hotel after winning $444,444.44 in the Irish lottery.

Current owners Pat and Vicky Kelly bought the place in 2001. Today, the hotel/hostel is known for serving good food. Pat Kelly prepares a Southern-inspired menu and half-pound pub burgers. His wife, Vicky, is a Mississippian who goes by the trail name Q.B., short for Queen Bit**. She is friendly and has a colorful personality. The Doyle is an A.T. landmark and worth a stop at the bar for a drink or meal, and its yesteryear atmosphere.

During the morning I met Lamb Chop, an Australian hiker with a strong Aussie accent who moved to the States nine years ago. This is her second A.T. attempt. Her first hike ended quickly because of a serious Achilles tendon injury. Lamp Chop said it took over a year to recover from the injury. I used the Doyles' free shuttle to go to the grocery store today and do some other chores before hiking tomorrow.

DAY 94 JUNE 18: DUNCANNON TO MILE 1,159.2.
TODAY'S MILES: 16.1.
TRIP MILES: 1,159.2

RW means Rocky Woods.

After a poor night's sleep in the Doyle without air conditioning, I left Duncannon about 8:00 a.m. with Left Turn as my hiking companion. The Trail was in the trees and rocky all day. As usual, my feet hurt. Water is difficult to find, and when you do, it's located at the bottom of a steep hill. I hiked with a heavy pack weighed down with four days' worth of food and lots of drinking water. The temperature was 85 degrees today, and humid.

Penguinman, Gone Walking, Left Turn, and I are camped in a small clearing next to the Trail tonight. The ground is flat and we are all too tired to hike to the next shelter. No water here, though. A light rain is sprinkling. Penguinman is concerned about his swollen knee, and Left Turn is chafed badly. We're all over 50 years old, and three of us are in real pain. Gone Walking says he is fine. No healthy young hikers allowed in this camp tonight!

It's been three months on the Trail.

DAY 95 JUNE 19: MILE 1,159.2 TO SWATARA GAP.
TODAY'S MILES: 19.0
TRIP MILES: 1,178.2

RW means Ragged Wrapped feet.

Last night there was a dramatic lightning storm, and of course, it rained. Everything I carried stayed dry except for my tent. No one else has complained about getting wet in the rain storm. Most of us were back on the Trail by 7:30 a.m. Again, this morning was very foggy. Heading out in heavy fog is becoming normal.

At 8:30 a.m., Left Turn and I planned to meet Iceman at a road crossing, so that we could slackpack for the rest of the day. As usual, Iceman came to our rescue. We had texted him to say I needed socks and Left Turn needed a headlamp, plus a few other items. He picked up everything, and let us borrow two daypacks while we slackpacked.

So far, this part of Pennsylvania has been my favorite section of the A.T. Shelters are good and the people friendly. This particular stretch of the Trail was exceptional. The trail maintainers do a very good job of designating and managing water sources. Water was readily available and abundant all day, with far more water locations than listed in the Trail Guide.

It started to rain around 10:30 a.m. and rained steadily until 3:00 p.m. The Trail remained in fairly good condition throughout the storm. We were soaked and the rain was cold. We shivered every time we stopped. That's one reason we hiked so many miles today. Wet and chilled, we decided it was time to get off the Trail and check into a motel for a hot shower and a warm bed. We weren't alone—several other thru-hikers showed up at the motel. The evening gave us a chance to wash our clothes, ourselves, and rest up for tomorrow.

More blisters today. I hope my feet heal soon. The new socks improved my comfort level. Shoes, insoles, and socks are the most important gear on the Trail. I am forever experimenting with new ways to protect my feet, but every time I find a solution, the Trail or the weather forces me to look for another solution. Left Turn said that I needed to change my socks much more often. In her opinion, the problem was dirty wet socks, not the brand or type. She's probably right. I only carried two pair of socks—one for sleeping, and the other for hiking.

DAY 06 JUNE 20. SWATARA GAP TO HARTLINE CAMPSITE.
TODAY'S MILES: 17.0
TRIP MILES 1,195.2

RW means Rethinking Worldly. Sleeping in the motel was wonderful last night.

This morning while eating breakfast, we met Walking North, another hiker who checked into the motel to escape from the rain. A husband and wife from Canada agreed to give us a lift back to the trailhead at 9:30 a.m. The weather was lovely; so different from yesterday. This is the last day of spring and a total joy.

The Trail started with a tough climb, but leveled off, although rather rocky all day. We're back in the green tunnel.

Occasionally, the trees thinned out, allowing us a good view of the valley below. The valley farmland was laid out in a patchwork pattern. We ran into Three Thumbs, an interesting man who lost parts of his fingers in an accident. The result is that several fingers now look more like thumbs.

The three of us crossed a milestone, the 1,183 mile marker. We are now less than one thousand miles from our destination! Pleasant conversation made the day go fast, and my blisters hurt a little less and show no sign of infection. New, clean socks are a big improvement.

We made it to the 501 shelter by 3:30 p.m. and ordered a pizza. This is one of the few shelters close enough to town where you can get a pizza delivered to the Trail. I ordered a medium calzone, and the other hikers ordered pizza. Three Thumbs didn't stop, he kept on hiking. After our enjoyable meal, Hank joined our group as we set out to hike another three miles to a campsite. We never did find the campsite, and after a while, Left Turn decided to stop for the night and camp next to the Trail.

I had counted on finding water by now. I didn't have enough left for the night. Left Turn gave me a little of her water supply, and I kept on hiking for several more miles to a camping area next to a stream. I regret leaving Left Turn alone, but I needed to find water. Now I have a bit of a dilemma. I'm only 9.5 miles from the next shelter and 18 miles from town. Depending on the Trail, I will walk as far as possible tomorrow.

Our camp area could have been nice, but Boy Scouts had taken all the good, level spots. I ended up tenting on a pile of sharp rocks angled over a steep incline. Later that night, Grinder arrived and camped next to me, on another pile of rocks. He was very dehydrated, and I let him have the water I filtered from the nearby stream.

DAY 97 JUNE 21: HARTLINE CAMPSITE TO PORT CLINTON.
TODAY'S MILES: 18.5
TRIP MILES: 1,213.7

RW means Rattlesnake Wrangler.

This first day of summer proved to be remarkably enjoyable. On the A.T., June 21st is known as Naked Hiking Day. I never did see any naked hikers, but I didn't hike naked either.

The weather was wonderful and the Trail easier than expected. In fact, the Trail was far less rocky than the descriptions in other hikers' trail journals would suggest. Still, there were difficult rocky sections.

Ferns covered great wide swatches of the forest floor that went on and on. An unusual filtered light shone down through the trees, making it appear very different from the dark green tunnel in Virginia.

I crossed the 1,200-mile mark, but it was hard to find anything to make my mileage sign. All the rocks were buried in the hard ground, so I ended up using small broken branches on top of a small clearing by the side of the trail.

Just before lunch, I ran into a guy named David. He lives near Allentown, Pennsylvania, and hopes to hike the A.T. someday. As I walked past him, we said hello, and then he asked my name. When I told him I was RW, he was surprised and said he had been reading my trail journal. We had a pleasant conversation, and he said he would email new name ideas for the meaning of RW.

I arrived at a shelter at 11:00 a.m. and stopped to eat lunch. The weather was comfortable and they were good company.

Mid-afternoon, I was struggling to crawl across big boulders when a SOBO told us there was a rattlesnake a few hundred yards ahead on the trail. I had met two other hikers a few miles back, so the three of us approached slowly. Hank was in front, searching for the snake. All of a sudden, in front of Hank, the frightening sound of a rattle came from the bushes. Hank jumped back so fast that he knocked down both Grinder and me. All three of us were tumbled together in a tangle of legs, arms, and backpacks. We frantically pushed and twisted, trying to get back up on our feet. Trekking poles flew everywhere.

After regaining our composure and laughing nervously, we checked for injuries. Then I picked up a trekking pole and used it to clear away the underbrush until I found the rattlesnake. It was a real doozy, at least four feet long, and coiled, ready to strike. We tried to drive it away from the Trail, but it stubbornly resisted. Back in Damascus, Blue Jay told me to take a swallow of water and spit it at the snake. The jet of water will scare it and make it crawl away. She must be fearless! I didn't have the nerve to get that close. I gently placed the tip of my trekking pole under the snake and flipped it into the woods. Afterwards, we found the remaining trekking poles and hustled away. I don't know what it is about rattlesnakes, but the mere sound of their rattle makes me jump as if I had touched a hot stove.

We were in Port Clinton by 4:30 p.m. Just as I stepped off the Trail, Iceman was standing there! He was waiting for Left Turn, who was slackpacking today. Since she wouldn't arrive for several hours, Iceman drove us to Cabela's and Walmart. Tonight I'm sleeping in the Port Clinton Park, which is maintained by a local church. Port Clinton is an old and interesting small town, located far enough off the Trail that hitchhiking or calling for a driver is required. Tomorrow I enter a section of the Trail referred to by hikers as "Rocksylvania." Iceman agreed to help Left Turn and me slackpack through this tough part of the Trail.

Guy-on-a-Buffalo is back on the Trail. He returned June 18th, after taking five days off to recover from Lyme disease. Hikers are starting to leave the Trail for different reasons. Before, it was mostly because of exhaustion and stress injuries. Now disease and injuries from trips and falls are taking people down. Only the strong, fit, and determined hikers remain on the Trail.

DAY 98 JUNE 22: PORT CLINTON TO ECKVILLE SHELTER.
TODAY'S MILES 14.8
TRIP MILES: 1,228.5

RW means Robin Work. A day hiker gave me the name.

This is the second day of summer, and just as nice as the first. We broke camp in the park about 7:00 a.m., had breakfast with Iceman, and then started slackpacking by 8:00 a.m. Slackpacking sure makes my feet heal faster, and the Achilles tendon doesn't hurt so much.

Slackpacking days are ending. I'm back with a full pack tomorrow. We hiked through a beautiful state park called Windsor Furnace and found trail magic. Someone hung a large plastic bag filled with goodies from a tree, next to the Trail. Left Turn and I helped ourselves to a few candy snacks, and then hiked on.

I saw my first copperhead snake curled up next to a rock a few feet away from Pulpit Rock. Many people were sitting and eating their lunch there, distracted by the beautiful view. The copperhead ignored everybody.

Another wild event happened last night. I was awakened by strange lights flashing in my tent. At first I thought the lights were coming from an electronic device, but their color was unusual and appeared only on the surface of my tent ceiling. It took a minute to realize lightning bugs had gotten trapped between the bug screen and tent fly. I watched them flash their distress signals for a few more minutes, and then went back to sleep.

Another unique aspect of the day was that I was surrounded by many thru-hikers in the senior age group. I hiked with Journeymen, who is 64, retired and recently widowed.

I also heard from Rob. He called me today. Rob is the guy I hiked with before Damascus. It turns out Rob is only two days ahead of me. We are both hiking at about the same pace. Maybe, in another two to three hundred miles, I can catch up to him.

I slept in the Eckville Shelter because of the threat of rain. It did rain, off and on, during the night. This shelter is rough and infested with spiders. The area around the shelter, however, has many amenities not usually found at other shelters. There is a shower, flush toilet, electricity for charging devices, a clothesline for drying clothes, and a caretaker who lives in a nearby house. The caretaker gave us watermelon slices, and we all enjoyed spitting the seeds into the grass. The melon tasted delicious.

DAY 99 JUNE 23; ECKVILLE SHELTER TO LEIGH GAP.
TODAY'S MILES: 11.5
TRIP MILES 1,240.0

RW means Remeeting Will, AKA Dad.

After a good night's sleep, I took my time getting started in the morning. It was 7:45 a.m. before I hit the Trail today. All of us senior hikers left around the same time. It looked like it would be a great day. Unfortunately, the gnats pestered me for hours, constantly attacking my eyes and ears and nose. I wore my bug net for the first time today.

Generally the Trail was pretty good, but roughly 40 percent was made up of difficult, rocky terrain. The rocks were tough on my Achilles tendon. The pointed rocks were frequently sharp and set at steep angles to the Trail. Their hard edges penetrated deep into the soles of my feet and often twisted my ankles. I've been told there is a law here in Pennsylvania. If you break a point off a rock, you must re-sharpen it. No one seems to be breaking this law.

By early afternoon the rocks had taken a toll on my Achilles tendon. I started to fall every time my foot landed at an angle, which seemed to be with every step. I was falling all the time and realized that I couldn't go on this way. It was time to take a break. I called Iceman and he agreed to pick me up. I immediately called the Microtel Motel in Hamburg to book a room. The motel manager said a trail angel called Dad could shuttle me to the motel right away for a small charge. I called Iceman back right away and cancelled the pickup. I was feeling guilty about the huge amount of personal time he had given in order to assist me. Iceman has been tremendously generous, more than I could ever repay.

Dad picked me up. I met him on the trail in the Great Smoky Mountains on a very rainy day. Dad had to get off the Trail in Erwin, Tennessee, because his Achilles tendon was in bad shape. He is young, and we had a long talk about remedies for the Achilles tendon. Dad told me his dream is to try and break the non-assisted hiking record for the Trail. I told him about my trail journey since Damascus and the struggles with my Achilles tendon. I tried to assure him that it was possible to achieve his dream, if he took care of his damaged Achilles tendon.

I read Penguinman's trail journal today. He is taking time off because of severe knee and foot pain. I am in Hamburg and will take a few days off to rest before getting back on the rocks.

DAY 100 JUNE 24: ZERO-DAY.
TODAY'S MILES: 0.0
TRIP MILES: 1,240.0

RW means Rather be Walking.

I am sitting in the Microtel resting, icing, and heating my ankle after yesterday's rough hike. It is still very sore. These Pennsylvania rocks have twisted the ankle so much that it's now a struggle to walk. As the day wore on, I decided to get medical treatment. I telephoned my father in Indianapolis and asked him to pick me up and drive me home. My wife had planned to fly to California to visit our grandchildren, so she couldn't help. I was almost exactly on schedule with my original trail plan, putting me at mile 1,258 after one hundred days.

DAY 101 JUNE 25: GOING HOME.
TODAY'S MILES: 0.0
TRIP MILES: 1,240.0

RW means Road Weak.

Hopefully, after taking a few weeks off to heal, I'll draw up a new plan to finish the Trail. I leave this morning for Chicago. While sitting at breakfast, I ran into Blue Jay. She felt weak and began taking antibiotics yesterday after testing positive for Lyme disease. Blue Jay planned to spend another day resting. If she felt well enough in another day, she would try to keep hiking the Trail. Up until recently, loneliness had become a problem for her and she considered quitting. Then, about a week ago, a five-time thru-hiker said he would take her under his wing and hike with her to Mt. Katahdin. They got along, and she preferred hiking with a companion. Blue Jay wished me luck and said she was sorry that I was leaving the Trail.

I thought about Left Turn and wondered how she was doing today. It was the anniversary of the passing of her 17-year-old son. Miss Janet appeared while I sat outside of the lobby waiting for my father. She had been napping in the motel, and was now ready to get back to her trail angel work. We talked for a long time. Miss Janet's compassion and wishes for a speedy recovery made me feel much better. Is this end of my dream? How badly am I injured? Sorry, readers, I hope I am not letting you down, but I may be through.

DAY 104 JUNE 28: ZERO DAYS AT HOME.
TRIP MILES: 1,240.0

RW means Restoration underWay. I am back home in Illinois, wondering what my next step should be.

My father picked me up on Wednesday and drove me to Chicago. The ride home was emotional, since I didn't know if I would finish the Trail. My father and I talked during most of the long drive back to Chicago. We really opened up, and I think it was the closest we have ever felt with each other. On Friday I saw my family doctor. X-rays didn't indicate fractures, so he prescribed a six-day program of Methylprednisolone, a cortisone steroid and strong anti-inflammatory drug. I can already see results; there is less pain. Therapy lasts three hours a day. I soak my feet in cold water for twenty minutes; warm them to room temperature for twenty minutes; and then immerse them in hot water for another twenty minutes. The process is repeated three times a day. The next step will be an MRI to discover if there is soft tissue damage. When the full extent of my injuries is known, the doctor and I will decide on a plan to get me back on the Trail. Even if the MRI results are good, it will take another two to three weeks before I can restart the hike.

Reading trail journals keeps me updated on the progress of other hikers. I noticed Penguinman left the Trail today because of foot plantar fasciitis and osteoarthritis in a knee. He left the Trail only 11.5 miles behind me. This is his third Appalachian Trail thru-hike attempt. His body seems to give out near the same section of the Trail.

There are three alternatives for restarting my hike. It all depends on how long recovery takes and how much time is left before cold weather sets in on the Trail. The first alternative would be to continue hiking north on the trail from the point where I left off, and hope there is enough time to beat winter.

Secondly, I could flip-flop, which means starting where I left off and hiking for as long as possible before getting off the Trail to fly or drive to the north, and then hiking south back to point where the NOBO portion ended. Flip-flopping is logistically more difficult, but provides more time to hike before the cold weather moves in.

A third alternative would be to leapfrog. Leapfrogging means jumping ahead a significant distance on the Trail, and then continuing to hike in the same direction to try and reach Mt. Katahdin before cold weather closes it off. When the summit is completed, I would have to drive back south in order continue hiking the skipped portion of the Trail. This last alternative should allow enough time to complete the hike before winter weather sets in. All three approaches have their own advantages and disadvantages. Avoiding winter weather is the top priority, because winter gear is heavy.

MONTH FIVE: JULY
DAY 109 JULY 04: ZERO-DAYS AT HOME.
TRIP MILES: 1,240.0

RW means Rest does Wonders. The Achilles tendon is responding well to drug and ice treatments.

Yesterday the doctor prescribed a second round of strong steroids to get me back on the Trail. Another six days of Methylprednisolone. I thought I could restart the Trail on the ninth, but the doctor advised waiting at least another week.

I plan to book a flight to Allentown, Pennsylvania, on July 14th and restart hiking the next day from the point where I got off, mile 1,240/Leigh Gap. My health will not be fully recovered. I'll take it slow for a few days to test my physical condition. Since I'm starting from where I left off, it's back to the rocks and the Knife Edge, only three miles away. A YouTube video shows the Knife Edge as a short, but tough, boulder climb near the edge of a cliff.

When I first began thru-hiking from Springer Mountain, I carried a base-winter weight of fifteen pounds (excluding food, water and fuel). This base weight steadily increased as I realized I didn't have enough gear. Over time, an insulated shirt, gaiters, stove, cook set, more socks, water bag, sleeping bag liner, and warmer hat were added to the pack. I don't know exactly how much my weight increased, but it was by several pounds.

With warmer weather, I switched to lighter gear and removed other gear altogether. This summer weight was still about sixteen pounds, excluding food and water. The extra pound of weight was due to the addition of socks, gaiters, and a more robust medical kit, necessary for the increasing injuries and blisters.

I plan to restart hiking with a stripped-down base weight, as light as possible. I replaced my Granite Gear pack with a new Gossamer Gear Mariposa Ultralight backpack. When it arrives, I will reweigh everything to determine the new base weight. I am also thinking of ditching the stove and cook set again. I hiked without a stove and cook set in the beginning. After a month of still-cold weather, I felt deprived and went back to carrying them again. But that was winter, and this is summer, so I shouldn't feel the need for hot food as much.

DAY 116 JULY 11: ZERO DAY AT HOME.
TRIP MILES: 1,240

RW means Rate Weather. I am hoping for good weather on July 14th. That's the day I fly to Allentown, Pennsylvania, and restart the Trail.

It will be exactly three weeks since I left the Trail. My Achilles tendon feels better than it has for a long time, even though it will still take more time to completely recover.

With the new pack and changes in equipment, my base weight dropped from 16 lbs., 8 oz. to 12 lbs., 10 oz.—a substantial reduction, but at a cost to my comfort. I won't carry the 16 oz. alcohol stove and cook set, and switched from a Therma-rest sleeping pad to a three-quarter length foam pad. I also eliminated most emergency equipment and extra clothing, except for spare socks. This is a short-term situation. The abnormally stripped-down pack will likely prove to be too much of a deprivation. Once I am sure of my stamina, I may add some comfort items. But for now, I can make do at this minimal level. If cold weather moves in earlier than expected, extra clothes will have to be added, along with other equipment.

I changed shoes again. I'm starting with a pair of stiff-soled New Balance boots. While breaking them in, I found the stiffness reduced the stress on my Achilles tendon. Tougher soles should help improve my chances for withstanding the Pennsylvania rocks. The Merrell boot soles were just too soft for the Trail.

The heavy luxury items in the pack are: 1) A second phone. I have AT&T as my carrier, but added a second Verizon phone. This should increase the odds for picking up cell service. 2) Camp shoes weighing 9 oz., but I might exclude them at the last minute. 3) A ground footprint weighing 3.5 oz. for my two-man tent, which is also used on shelter floors to keep my sleeping bag clean. 4) Three pair of spare wool socks, and 5) a second pair of insoles.

I am running out of RW names. Any suggestions from readers will help. My only rules are no profanity and no repeats. I like fun and clever names, or names that reflect recent events on the Trail. No promises, though, on using any of the suggested names.

I haven't put together a new Trail plan. My major concerns now are hiking with physical limitations and restarting the Trail without the companionship of fellow thru-hikers who had ridden the same hiker bubble as me on the trail. They are all far ahead of me now. Remembering my conversation with Blue Jay, I realized loneliness would be my new companion on the Trail—but hopefully not for long.

DAY 120 JULY 15: LEIGH GAP TO SUPERFUND TRAILHEAD.
TODAY'S MILES: 13.9
TRIP MILES 1,253.9

RW means Ready to go Walking.

Thanks to everybody who emailed new name suggestions to my blog. I wrote them down for future use. Flight connections went well and I arrived in Allentown without incident. A hard, driving rain pelted down throughout the night and a tornado warning was issued for the area. The tornado missed, so I'm taking it as a good sign for the restart of my thru-hike. I am concerned about my physical condition, though, and the rocks ahead. Today's weather forecast calls for more rain.

Iceman picked me up on time and dropped me off on the Trail at Leigh Gap by 7:15 a.m. I started hiking alone in thick fog, which remained all day. After the first few miles, the legendary rock formation known as the Knife Edge lived up to its namesake. The long, hard boulder field climaxed with a steep-sloped ledge that was half a mile long and perched along the edge of a cliff. The rocks were lichen-covered and slippery, forcing me to crawl on my hands and knees for hundreds of yards. My fear was that I would slip and fall if I stood up. After the scary and dangerous Knife Edge, the next six miles were filled with boulders and big rocks and an occasional island of soil. The trees here are small and struggling to sink their roots into the rock. There is no tree cover to shield me from the drizzling rain.

Just before noon, I met and hiked with Mighty Blue. I hiked with him for an hour until he got off the Trail to dry out in a motel.

Trail magic appeared at lunch time. A trail angel left plenty of water and food at an intersection where the Trail crosses a road. It was so welcomed and enjoyed! There are not many places to find drinking water in this section of the Trail. Except for the lack of water, the tenting campsites were well arranged and easy to find. I moved slowly and babied my Achilles tendon all day. It worked. I came out of the woods next to a stoplight and asked a driver for a ride to Palmerton. He said yes. My first successful—and fast—hitchhike! Maybe I am figuring out how to hitchhike.

By 2:30 p.m. I was already in Palmerton at the Jail House Hostel. This is a free hostel run by the city. No jail bars, just wooden bunk beds minus mattresses set up in a smelly basement of an old municipal building. According to the story, it was once the city jail. The place is crowded with young hikers all in their twenties. I have never met them before and I don't have much in common with them, except for the fact that we are all thru-hikers. After a hot shower, I called my wife and father to tell them I was okay. I sent my wife a nice postcard. The weather forecast calls for more slippery rocks and rain.

DAY 121 JULY 16: SUPERFUND TRAILHEAD TO WIND GAP.
TODAY'S MILES: 20.1
TRIP MILES: 1,274.0

RW means Really Worked.

Today was long, but interesting. At 5:00 a.m. I got up, packed, and was ready to go. After a quick breakfast at Dunkin Donuts, I met Andrew Hollywood. Andrew is taking pictures of all the hikers who come into Palmerton as an art project. He took my picture and then drove me, along with two other hikers, to the trailhead. Andrew Hollywood's artwork can be seen on Facebook and other social media.

I started hiking at 7:00 a.m., and right from the start, it was brutal with a nearly vertical, hand-over-hand climb up a cliff. It took an hour, and we covered less than three-quarters of a mile. It was a very good thing the weatherman was wrong about rain. This cliff would've been extremely dangerous if the rocks had been wet.

After I made it to the top of the cliff, I walked by the Palmerton Zinc Pile, a Superfund site controlled by the Environmental Protection Agency. The EPA's Superfund program is responsible for cleaning up some of the nation's most contaminated land. Only a few stunted trees grew in the area, and KEEP OUT signs were posted everywhere. Flowers, wild sumac, and raspberries, however, grew in abundance. I wasn't about to taste the berries, in case of zinc contamination. I hiked several miles alongside this polluted area. Here the Trail was almost flat, but rocky.

After the initial hard climb, the Trail eased up for several miles, but then the rocks started again. My new boots were working in the rocks. Today's rocks were especially frustrating because, just a few hundred yards away and parallel to the Trail, was a soft, grass-covered service road. I thought about walking on it but wasn't sure where it led, so we stayed on the Trail. I stumbled my way over the rocks for miles within sight of that tempting road before it finally veered off.

I didn't understand the purpose of placing a tortuous Trail path next to a smooth, unused forest service road. There were no water sources on today's portion of the Trail because of contamination. I carried three liters of water, enough to get me through the day.

I hiked more miles today than I thought I would. My legs felt good all day. I ran into trail magic around two o'clock. A couple from Fort Wayne, Indiana, was handing out water, soda pop, and snacks to thru-hikers as they waited for their son to show up. He was hiking about an hour behind me. They were anxious and excited to see him again. Their son started the Trail on March 19th, one day after me.

As I neared the Leroy A. Smith Shelter, I changed my mind about staying there. It was 0.2 miles off the Trail, and the closest water source was even farther. If I was going to walk that far for shelter and water, I may as well walk 0.6 miles to the next road and hitchhike into town. When I got to the road, a guy in a pickup truck stopped immediately and gave me a ride into town. He dropped me off at the Beer Stein Bar and Grill in Wind Gap, located about one mile from the Trail. My luck with hitchhiking has changed since returning to the Trail!

The bar and grill allowed tent camping on their property. After setting up the tent, I ate in the bar. A guy rode up on a bicycle and said he was a thru-hiker. I asked him about the bike; he said Pennsylvania was too rocky to walk, so he was cycling across it. Then he finished by giving me a look, and saying, "Man, hike your own hike!"

I found this confusing. Nowhere in that phrase is a bicycle mentioned. He wasn't the first thru-hiker I met who wasn't strictly hiking the entire trail. I had met a few hikers who were aqua-blazing a portion of the Trail, and others who chose to walk along the paved road in Shenandoah because of the panoramic views. Aqua-blazing means floating or boating down a river near the Trail. Bicycling, aqua-blazing, and paved road walking are all called yellow-blazing. Yellow-blazing may be fun and efficient, but these modes of travel, and the routes they follow, don't meet the criteria set down by the ATC for the Two Thousand Miler award.

The award application states: "The Appalachian Trail Conservancy (ATC) recognizes anyone who reports completion of the entire Trail as a "2,000-miler." The term is a matter of tradition and convenience based upon the original estimated length of the Trail. Conservancy policy is to operate on an honor system, assuming that those who apply for 2000-miler status have hiked all of the Appalachian Trail between Katahdin and Springer Mountain, either as a thru-hiker or in sections. In the event of an emergency, such as a flood, a forest fire, or an impending storm, blue-blazed trails or officially required road walks are viable substitutes for the white-blazed route. Issues of sequence, direction, speed, length of time, or whether one carries a pack are not considered. ATC assumes that those who apply have made an honest effort to walk the entire Trail, even if they did not walk past every white blaze."

Riding in a boat, on a bicycle, or walking along roads doesn't count unless the above official criteria are met. The bicyclist didn't appreciate hearing my explanation. To him, I was just an extreme purist. To me, I was just following the rules and making an honest effort to white-blaze the entire A.T. I wondered how many hikers who apply for the certificate hadn't made an honest effort to follow the white-blazed trails. Maybe I'm hypocritical. Earlier today I was tempted to violate the rule, and didn't simply because I wasn't sure where that tantalizing service road might lead me. Here's a question: "If I had known, would I have violated the rules?" I don't know.

DAY 122 JULY 17: WIND GAP TO DELAWARE WATER GAP.
TODAY'S MILES: 15.6
TRIP MILES: 1,289.6

RW means Real Watermelon!

More than a dozen hikers camped on the grassy lawn next to the Beer Stein Bar and Grill last night. It was a great camping location! I got up early, had some coffee, and dried out my tent. I tried hitchhiking back to the Trail without success, so I walked for a mile to get to the trailhead and started hiking at 7:40 a.m. I took a pass on the Beer Stein's free thru-hiker breakfast. The bar allows thru-hikers access to their kitchen and food supplies, and lets them cook up the breakfast of their dreams, for free! I skipped the offer because I knew everybody would be hiking to the next hostel, and I wanted to make sure I got a bed. If I had stayed to partake in the free breakfast offer, I would have gotten far behind these fast, young hikers. I now seem to be the old man.

I hiked alone, rarely seeing anyone all day. The Trail was extremely rocky for the first seven miles. After that, the rocks eased up and reappeared in a few bad patches. A few unusual incidents happened. First, while focusing my eyes on my feet to avoid tripping over the rocks, I walked straight into a low-hanging branch and bashed my head. Stunned by the collision, I fell to the ground and sat in disbelief at what I had just done.

This was the second time since my return to the Trail that I had done something like this. The first time was on the morning of the first day back. But now, as I sat on the ground, I could feel warm liquid pooling on the top of my head. My fingers were red with blood when I touched it. Seconds later, blood dripped down my face. I compressed toilet paper on the wound for a few minutes. When the bleeding slowed down, I wrapped a dirty handkerchief around my head and used my hat to hold it in place. I poured water on top of my head and started hiking, satisfied for the moment that I had things under control.

Ticks attacked all day long, but I managed to sweep them off before they could bite. They seemed to be working in league with a bee, which stung me on the leg. What a day! At least the temperature was in the low eighties, not too hot, but the bloody handkerchief on my head was still soaked with sweat.

A mile before town, Braveheart, a young woman thru-hiker, caught up to me at a place where Sug, a trail angel, was grilling hot dogs and hamburgers. She had tables set out filled with food. Sug's daughter had almost completed a thru-hike in 2012, but partway up Mt. Katahdin, bad weather drove her back, keeping her away from summiting the finish line. Sug said her daughter didn't want to risk her own life or the lives of potential rescuers, so she turned back at the last moment. The weather stayed bad that year, and her daughter couldn't finish the thru-hike. She hasn't gone back to complete the final summit and was still inconsolable about being turned back within hours of reaching the finish line.

Shortly after arriving at Sug's tables full of trail magic, a young thru-hiker named Flint asked me if I had lost my trail Guide. I checked... and I had. He found it! Another great trail magic moment!

I made it to the Church of the Mountain Hostel run by the local Presbyterian Church by 3:30 p.m. It was a good thing, too, because the beds were nearly all taken. After staking out beds, Braveheart and I went to the local outfitter. The tip of my left hiking pole had broken off today, and Braveheart needed a new water bag for her water filter. The bag had sprung a leak two days ago. Once again, I was lucky and the outfitter let me rummage through a pile of broken trekking poles. I found the bottom half of a trekking pole that fit my pole perfectly. He let me have it for free!

Braveheart needed food, so she caught a ride to the Walmart, where she also found a replacement water filter bag. I walked to the local convenience store and bought some protein bars to supplement my food bag. I had plenty of food left from grocery shopping in Palmerton. Lately I was starting to eat ramen noodles dry, like crackers. Not the tastiest, but lightweight, and available everywhere. I was taking a page from Merlin's food handbook

At 6:00 p.m. the church provided a meal for all the thru-hikers, and it was a feast. There were at least fifteen of us seated at the tables. Cold watermelon, homemade ice cream, plus all the food thru-hikers could ever want, as well as great company. Many church members were helping out, and we chatted for an hour.

DAY 123 JULY 18: DELAWARE WATER GAP TO MILE 1,311.8.
TODAY'S MILES: 22.2
TRIP MILES: 1,311.8

RW means Radio Waves.

I was back on the Trail by 7:40 a.m. this morning. Hiking alone, I finally walked out of the state of Pennsylvania, and crossed the 1300-mile mark, as well. Someone had written "1300 Miles" on the wooden steps of a bridge crossing, so I didn't have to make my own mileage sign. Another banner day!

The biggest bear I have ever seen so far was rummaging in a dumpster close to the hostel this morning on the way out of town. Minutes later, I left Pennsylvania and entered New Jersey. I was hoping to see a PA/NJ state border sign, but none appeared. It was disappointing.

New Jersey is very different than Pennsylvania. Here, the Trail section is relatively flat with occasional rocky stretches. I made it to the Mohican Outdoor Center in short time and bought the most expensive (but lousiest) sandwich I have ever eaten on the Trail. I had planned on buying two sandwiches, another one for my evening meal, but quickly changed my mind.

During the day I passed two female forest rangers who were hanging posters announcing a Poconos photo contest. We talked for a while and they allowed me to take their picture, providing I didn't enter it into the contest. They were the first forest rangers I have met on the Trail so far, even though the Trail ranges primarily through federal forests and park land.

Water was a concern today, so I carried more than usual. Many of the places I had planned to stay were unmarked, and I passed them before realizing my mistake. I wasn't too upset about it because most of those campsites didn't have water, and I never like to camp without nearby water. I kept on hiking until I forced myself to stop at a point less than four miles from a shelter. I just didn't feel like camping at a shelter. Right now, I am camping alone on a beautiful flat area with water next to the Trail. I had hoped other thru-hikers would stop here to camp tonight, but it is already late. Being alone is risky if a bear enters your campsite.

My tent was pitched between a rock wall and a creek flowing with excellent water. I built a warm campfire and sat beside it, just listening to the sounds of the forest. Suddenly, I heard a baby crying. I called out several times but didn't get a response. Maybe it was a hiker with an infant. The baby kept crying, so I started walking up the Trail and calling out, but no one answered. What was this eerie cry? The screaming stopped by the time I returned to my campfire.

DAY 124 JULY 19: MILE 1,311.8 TO MASHIPACONG SHELTER. TODAY'S MILES: 15.0 TRIP MILES: 1,326.8

RW means Ryegrass Waving.

Other than the sound of a crying baby, the night passed safely. I hiked alone again all day. Near the town of Branchville, around 10:00 a.m., I heard a crashing sound on my right. A bear was running away from me as fast as it could. It ran so fast that I couldn't get a picture in time. When I got to the road, a coffee stand was set up at the corner, so I stopped to enjoy a hot cup of coffee before hitchhiking into town. The owner of the coffee stand came out and yelled at me for disturbing his business. He told me to leave immediately or he would call a cop. I walked toward town for a quarter mile and then tried to hitchhike without success. I ended up walking the rest of the 1.5 miles into town and bought enough food to last three days.

I did catch a ride back out of town, and then stopped for lunch at a bar and grill located a quarter mile from the Trail. At 4:30 p.m. I passed the Mashipacong Shelter and met a ridge runner named Zedd. I thought about hiking on, because this shelter had no privy and the closest water source was 0.6 miles away. This shelter did have a beautiful lawn, though, and Zedd had brought lots of water and potato chips to share with hikers. The next shelter was only 2.9 miles ahead and had a privy, but was situated almost half a mile from the Trail. Plus, the trail Guide listed its water sources as unreliable. This shelter was starting to look like a better place to stop for the night. Later in the evening, I told Zedd about last night's strange encounter with the sounds of a baby crying in the forest. He said it was probably the screeching of a fisher cat, a type of weasel.

Trail magic was plentiful today and I had good luck catching a ride out of town. When I got back on the Trail, several people shared their fresh fruit with me. And today's final magic was Zedd's generosity at the shelter tonight. The shelter was crowded with people I've met since my return to the Trail. They are all young, strong, capable, and pleasant. Braveheart, Rambler, and a trio of hikers called Flint, Gunpowder, and Survivor are among this group tonight.

DAY 125 JULY 20: MASHIPACONG SHELTER TO POCHUCK SHELTER.
TODAY'S MILES: 19.6
TRIP MILES: 1,346.4

RW means Rest Wanted.

Today turned out to be an easy hike. New Jersey is much better for hiking, far more beautiful and scenic than I imagined it would be. Braveheart and I started the day early and hiked out together. By 9:00 a.m., I was standing in the High Point State Park visitor center, signing the guestbook as the 342nd thru-hiker. I thumbed through the pages. Isn't Black and Bear Bag had signed in already and were somewhere far ahead of me. Every thru-hiker gets a free can of pop. We stayed at the visitor center to recharge our cell phones and dry out our wet tents on the grass. I only stayed long enough to dry my tent. My phone wasn't low on power, but Braveheart's phone was dead.

As I was leaving, I ran into Flint, Gunpowder, and Survivor, who were hitchhiking into town. They took every Sunday off to go to church. I headed back to the Trail alone and thought about walking down to the park beach for a swim, and then eating at the concession stand, but decided against it. I wanted to make a lot of miles today.

The Trail offered many great scenic views, and wildlife refuges and farms bordered along the Trail. This section is a popular destination for the general public, so the Trail here is often flat and well-maintained. Today's white-blazed route included paved roads for long distances. The easy walking surface helped to increase my daily mileage.

Braveheart is a 36-year-old single mother from Washington State. She has multiple sclerosis and is hiking the Trail now, before the disease progresses. Braveheart began her hike on May 1st, and intends to keep hiking on the Long Trail this season after completing the A.T. We have been passing each other, or hiking together, ever since Palmerton.

I met many nice people on the Trail today, and spent a long time hiking and talking with a couple from New Jersey named Lou and Jean. They have hiked most of the A.T. sections in New Jersey and love to meet thru-hikers. We talked for a while and they took my picture.

Because water was readily available today, I didn't have to carry water. I drank nearly two liters of water first thing in the morning, and later forced myself at every stop to drink until I was filled to the gills. I walked by the Wallkill Nature Preserve, and later, up a steep hill. The Guidebook said to stop for water at a house near the base of the hill before heading to the next shelter. While filling up with four liters of water at the house, I talked to Ireland, an international thru-hiker from Ireland. I had seen him on the Trail a few days earlier.

I climbed the half mile up the hill to the shelter and pitched my tent around 5:30 p.m. Bugs were horrible, so I ate fast, stowed my food in a bear box, and hid inside my tent. Every New Jersey shelter is equipped with a bear box, a sturdy steel box built to withstand bear attacks. Every hiker is expected to use them.

Braveheart got to the shelter at 8:30 p.m. and complained that it took over three hours to recharge her phone at the visitor center. She planned to hike 26 miles tomorrow, in addition to running into town to buy food. That was more than I could hike, so we said our goodbyes. Rambler showed up an hour later; he had been swimming at Highland State Park.

DAY 126 JULY 21: POCHUCK SHELTER TO WAWAYANDA SHELTER.
TODAY'S MILES: 11.5
TRIP MILES: 1,357.9

RW means Rock Wall, a name given to me by a local hiker.

Before leaving the shelter, I shoved a bandana between the pack belt and my chafed hip for extra cushioning, and rubbed Vaseline on the damaged skin in an effort to help reduce the chafing. I got up early, said goodbye to Braveheart again, and ate breakfast with Rambler. It had been a high-mileage week, 117 miles, so I decided to keep the miles short today. Rambler and I hiked out together and spent a pleasant morning strolling through picturesque New Jersey farmland.

I had hoped to stop for lunch at The Haven Hill Farm & Deli. When we got there, the deli was closed. The grocery portion of the store was open, so I bought a cup of coffee, donuts, and a few pieces of fruit, and rested for an hour while recharging my phone. The Trail had been wonderful this morning, with easy walks through marshes and wetlands. In the afternoon, though, the Trail changed, becoming rocky and difficult with many steep climbs. I hiked with Rambler until I got to the shelter about 2:00 p.m. He planned on hiking for another eight miles to a point where his brother was waiting to pick him up. Rambler was taking a week off to attend a wedding in Texas. After saying our goodbyes, I walked a half mile to the Wawayanda State Park and filled up with four liters of water. While there, I washed up in a park bathroom, relaxed in the air-conditioned lobby of the visitor center, recharged my cell phone, and then called my wife and father. Refreshed, I headed back to the shelter and ate dinner. The shelter here was okay, but the mosquitoes were terrible, driving me into my tent.

The first week back on the Trail has been hard on many parts of my body. The heat and humidity aggravated the chafing on my shoulders and hips caused by the constant rubbing of the pack. I will sleep on this new medical problem, and hopefully, woke up with a solution. Even with new boots, I have two blisters on my feet. The weather forecast called for more heat and humidity. Constant sweating had left my clothes completely drenched. They will still be wet in the morning.

DAY 127 JULY 22: WAWAYANDA SHELTER TO FITZGERALD FALLS.
TODAY'S MILES: 13.9
TRIP MILES: 1,371.8

RW means Ruckus at Wawayanda Shelter.

A bear tried to get into the bear box last night, making a ruckus in the process. We chased it away.

I left camp early and hiked into the state of New York by 9:00 a.m. The mosquitoes and gnats were terrible. I had to use Deet for the first time and wear a mosquito-net hat. New York's first four miles were rough and rocky. At one point, the trail was vertical. An aluminum ladder installed on the cliff face had to be climbed in order to go up or down. After this, the Trail smoothed out and became an easy walk. The forest is slightly different. The trees are small and thin, and there is grass on the forest floor.

Water was scarce for most of the morning. When I got to a roadside, I saw that the many gallon water jugs left by a trail angel were all empty. By noon, I needed water. I got off the Trail and stopped for lunch at a nearby hot dog stand, and then walked over to the Creamery, an ice cream shop, where I had three helpings of delicious homemade ice cream. While there, I talked to a young couple of SOBOs, southbound thru-hikers, who started from Maine on May 31st.

I refilled my water bottles at the Creamery and hit the Trail again on a very hot afternoon. The Trail seemed deserted as I hiked alone all day. At four o'clock I stopped at Fitzgerald Falls to solo camp tonight. This is a pleasant spot with good water, but the Guide doesn't list it as a designated campsite. It had been another hot day, so I took a quick bath in the waterfall and built a small campfire next to it. Only one hiker walked by my campsite that evening. The sound of the falling water was soothing, and I felt clean, cool, and relaxed after spending three-quarters of an hour soaking at the base of the waterfall. I fell asleep earlier than usual.

DAY 128 JULY 23: FITZGERALD FALLS TO WILLIAM BRIEN MEMORIAL SHELTER.
TODAY'S MILES: 17.8
TRIP MILES: 1,389.6

RW means Repelling Washboard.

I started hiking early this morning at 5:30 a.m., because I suspected the Trail would be tough today. My suspicions proved to be true right away. In the first eight miles, many steep bluffs had to be scaled, and it felt more like mountain climbing than hiking. It took six hours to get through this stretch, and all the while, mosquitoes and gnats hounded me mercilessly. This part of the Trail is aptly called Agony Grind.

After Agony Grind, the Trail became manageable, so my hourly mileage increased. I had hoped to hike at least three more miles, but I stopped early. I was beat. Again I hiked alone today. After the bluffs, grass-covered stretches of ground gave the Trail a park-like appearance, albeit a very rocky park.

One reason I was so tired was the tough trail, but another was the heat and humidity. According to the Weather Station App on my phone, it had been 91 degrees with a heat index of 100 degrees today. Drenched in sweat all day, it was a struggle to keep skin chafing down to a minimum. For the past three days, my hips have been raw from the constant chafing caused by the hip belt. Besides covering the skin with a bandana, I started applying Vaseline and lip balm on my hips to protect the skin. The combination worked and my hips were starting to heal. The pain was easing.

A youth group was camping in and around the shelter tonight, as well as two other thru-hikers—Ireland, a NOBO, and a SOBO named Conner. Ireland is about my age. We have been passing each other for the last 30 miles. This is his second attempt to thru-hike the A.T. The first time he tried, his six-month visa expired before he was able to finish his thru-hike. Ireland was concerned once again about the new visa expiring before he reached Mt. Katahdin. Conner is young and he hiked 30 miles today. There was also a homeless man here with his dog, plus two locals out for a few days of hiking. I'm staying in the shelter tonight, as are most of the hikers, because of an 80 percent chance of thunderstorms tonight.

DAY 129 JULY 24: WILLIAM DRICN MEMORIAL SHELTER TO TRAILSIDE MUSEUM.
TODAY'S MILES: 9.6
TRIP MILES 1,399.2

RW means Reeking and Washing clothes.

The forecasted thunderstorm never materialized, but it did rain a little, and there was an impressive lightning display. I didn't sleep much because a female hiker from New York City on an overnight trip was nervous about sleeping in the shelter. She woke everyone up several times during the night. Everybody, that is, except her boyfriend, who slept through everything! She was convinced there was an animal in the shelter. No animals were found.

In the morning, I placed the bandana against my hip again and greased up with Vaseline. This was working and the chafing was healing. I left the shelter early, uncertain of the day's destination. I hiked past Ireland, who had also left early to beat the heat. He was hoping to stop at the Palisades Parkway visitor center where, he'd heard, there was a payphone. He didn't have a cell phone and wanted to call his family in Ireland. He was finding it difficult to locate payphones along or near the Trail.

When I got to the Palisades Parkway, I had to cross a busy four-lane divided highway. It was just after rush hour, so it took five minutes just to cross traffic going one direction, and then three minutes from the other direction. If it had been rush hour, who knows how long it would have taken to cross each of the expressway lanes? Without access to a foot overpass or cross walk, this was one very scary, run-for-your-life, and by far the most dangerous road crossing yet on the Trail.

From there it was up to Bear Mountain, the oldest and most deceptive section of the A.T. From the top, we could see New York City in the distance. I had been to NYC many times and, being from Chicago, wasn't awestruck by the view. I was impressed, however, by the fact that we were hiking next to this huge metropolis without leaving the wilderness experience of the Trail. A dense tree canopy camouflaged the fact that the largest city in the United States was just a few miles east of the Trail.

I met Stan Goldblatt at the Trailside Museum near the base of Bear Mountain in Ft. Montgomery. Stan is a professional photographer working on a portrait book about thru-hikers. He asked if he could photograph me at his studio. I was hesitant, but he showed me photos of other thru-hikers who had agreed to be subjects for his book, and I recognized several of them. So I took a chance; the guy seemed legitimate. Plus, he promised a bowl of chili! Food easily buys a thru-hiker's trust. The photo session and lunch was pleasant, and I think Stan will publish an interesting photo-book. In the studio, I made a prop by writing "1400 miles" on a large piece of cardboard. I hope he chooses this shot of me holding the mileage sign for his book.

Even though it was only 1:30 p.m. when I got back to the Trail, I asked Stan if he would drive me to the Holiday Inn

Express, and then pick me up the next morning. He agreed, so I stopped early for the day to wash clothes and other chores before getting a good night's rest. Tomorrow, I will pass the 1400-mile mark and visit the Trailside Museum, a museum devoted to local animals no longer surviving in the wild.

I called my daughter today and discussed the idea of leaving the Trail. I just didn't have the same drive anymore, and I was hiking alone all the time now. I had hoped to meet more hikers like Bear Bag and Isn't Black during my return, but everyone was so young, strong and fast. I was the slow-moving turtle constantly being passed by all these hikers. My daughter said I was an inspiration, and many of her friends were following my trail journal. She was exercising again because of me and kept saying how proud she was of me. A father doesn't hear praise like this very often from his children.

DAY 130 JULY 25: TRAILSIDE MUSEUM TO FAHNESTOCK STATE PARK.
TODAY'S MILES: 20.7
TRIP MILES: 1,419.9

RW means Reaching Where?

I left early and hiked many miles today, despite a poor night's sleep. I hiked across the Hudson River Bridge and crossed the 1400-mile mark as soon as I got back on the Trail. I met Flint, Gunpowder, and Survivor, who had just started hiking after breaking camp. I hiked with them all morning. Flint and Gunpowder were husband and wife. Flint was a missionary in China, and Gunpowder worked in China as a trail guide. That's where they met, fell in love, and hoped to return someday. Devoutly religious, they got off the Trail every Sunday to attend church, yet still hiked more miles in a week than me. Flint is tall and handsome; a strong hiker who frequently must stop to wait for the rest to catch up. He never seems to get tired. Gunpowder wears ultralight running shoes without insoles or socks. This is as close to barefoot as you can get. Survivor is about their age and also religious. He sported an orange Mohawk haircut and hung back all day, preferring to hike alone.

The Trail was fairly level and bordered with many stone walls. It reminded me of New England countryside. We had fun hiking together. At one point, Flint tucked large ferns into the back of his pack to make his own angel wings. He hiked for about an hour looking angelic while they sang hymns and other Sunday school songs.

I had planned to stay the night at the Graymoor Spiritual Life Center, a monastery where hikers are allowed to camp on their property. At the last minute, I passed on the opportunity and continued hiking. The weather was great and I felt good until the end of the day. And then, I was very tired.

During the day's hike we stopped at the Appalachian Market. It was still early, so I didn't buy a deli sandwich, just a few groceries. I had hoped to have dinner at the state park concession stand, but we arrived late, and it was already closed. We ordered a pizza after finding a take-out menu posted at the campground.

We all decided to camp in the state park because thru-hikers could stay for free in a specially-designated campsite area. Once we got there, though, I was a bit shocked by the noisy and never-ending sound of car traffic. Survivor and Ireland joined us later. Ireland's thick Irish accent and easygoing nature added to the camaraderie of our little band of hikers. I hadn't enjoyed this much trail companionship since my earlier days hiking with Bear Bag and Isn't Black. It was comforting to be able to hike with such pleasant people.

A section hiker walked into the campsite carrying an incredible amount of gear—so much stuff that he couldn't possibly qualify as a thru-hiker. He told the park ranger he was anyway. This section hiker said he had reduced his pack weight down to eighty pounds after getting advice from Miss Janet. Miss Janet told him he could either hike comfortably or camp comfortably, but couldn't do both on the Trail. He chose to camp comfortably.

DAY 131 JULY 26: CLARENCE FAHNESTOCK STATE PARK TO MORGAN STEWART SHELTER.
TODAY'S MILES: 14.0
TRIP MILES: 1,433.9

RW means Ron Weasley, because we talked about Harry Potter today.

After a noisy night at the state park campground, we hit the Trail by 7:40 a.m. The day was cool, but humid, and I was soaked in no time. The Trail was fairly easy, but I was still tired and sore after the long miles yesterday. Signs along the trail warned that the water in the springs, streams, and wells was polluted with coliform bacteria, a strain of E.coli. I had gotten a little careless while hiking and badly scratched my arm across a raspberry bush. On top of this, mosquito bites aggravated the scratches, making me look like I'd been beaten up.

For lunch I walked a half mile off trail to a deli and enjoyed a very tasty sandwich. This section of the Trail has many nearby deli shops. It's possible to get freshly-made sandwiches practically every day. Just didn't feel like making another long hike today, so I stopped at 3:00 p.m. after fourteen miles. Flint, Gunpowder, and Survivor decided to camp with me for the night.

Mosquitoes are ravenous, so I am hiding inside my tent that is set up inside the shelter. Later, my tent caused problems in the night when a couple of hikers arrived at 11:00 p.m. They were upset that my tent was taking up so much shelter space. I paid them no mind, because there were only three other people in the shelter when they showed up. There was plenty of room for two more latecomers, so I didn't budge.

DAY 132 JULY 27: MORGAN STEWART SHELTER TO TEN MILE SHELTER.
TODAY'S MILES: 20.6
TRIP MILES: 1,454.5

RW means Race Walker.

It rained last night. I was very glad that I had been inside my tent inside the shelter. We all left early because we wanted to get to the Appalachian Trail Railroad Station before 11:00 a.m. The station was eleven miles away. On the way there, we passed the largest living tree on the Appalachian Trail.

I ran into Ireland near Nuclear Lake. He didn't know it was called Nuclear Lake, and that it had once been the site of an experimental nuclear research center. In 1972, a large chemical explosion spread bomb-grade plutonium around this entire area.

We joked with Ireland and asked him if he saw any three-eyed fish. He said no, but he had swum in the lake last night and drank the water. After letting him stew for a little while, I told him the area had been tested and was reported to be safe. He was still skeptical and said he wouldn't have camped there, and definitely wouldn't have swum in the lake or drank the water, if he had known.

During most of our hike together in the intermittent rain, Gunpowder felt weak and needed to stop occasionally because of lightheadedness. As we neared the Appalachian Trail train station and metro stop for New York City, she told me she might be pregnant. If it proved to be true, she said they would still, most likely, return to the Trail. We made it to the Appalachian train station on time, and I said my goodbyes to Flint, Gunpowder, and Survivor. They were headed to the Big Apple for a couple of days off the Trail.

I went to the Outdoor Center near the station to dry off and buy some lunch. All they had was candy and protein bars, so I made a meal out of them. I met two hikers there called Racewalker and Obsidian. Obsidian's first question for me was, "Do you know what obsidian is?" I told him, "Yes, black volcanic glass." My college geology courses had finally paid off! At one time, I had wanted to be a geologist. Obsidian told me he was happy that I knew what it meant, because almost everybody on the Trail had no clue.

Racewalker is 64 years old and a race walker. Shorter than me, Racewalker carried an immense backpack, weighing close to 45 pounds.

Obsidian is a well-mannered, bespectacled medical doctor from Germany. His trail name was given to him because he always wears black clothing, much like the other German hiker I met, Isn't Black. Racewalker and Obsidian were well rested after a week off from hiking, and just getting back on the Trail.

Obsidian had spent a week in New York City with his girlfriend. He said she was appalled by his haggard appearance when she first saw him. Obsidian had lost a lot of weight and was exhausted. His girlfriend fed him often during his week in NYC. His "hiker hunger" helped him happily eat as much food as she could give him. Racewalker had used his time off the Trail to compete in a race.

I decided to hike with them and ended up going further than planned because of their good company. The rain intensified all the colors; greens were especially vibrant. We walked through fields blooming with flowers. Ripened raspberry and blueberry bushes grew in places alongside the Trail, and we sometimes stopped to taste the berries. When the rain stopped, we were able to make great time in the afternoon. By four o'clock, we crossed into the state of Connecticut.

We had a hard time locating the shelter. The Guide mentioned a side trail, but we couldn't find it. We took a chance on a small road, finally spotted the shelter on the other side of the woods, and cut through the trees to get to it. At the shelter we saw the side trail mentioned in the Guide and realized we hadn't walked far enough in our quest to find it. If we had gone just another two hundred yards, we would have been able to walk right up to the shelter.

This was an unusual shelter. A large gap existed between the outside wall and the sleeping platform. The structure's design was intended to prevent porcupines from gnawing on the wood inside the shelter. The animals were attracted to the wood because it was saturated with the salty sweat of sleeping hikers. We drew water from a pump in the ground next to a large sign warning that the water may be contaminated with coliform bacteria. I hung my clothes on a clothesline. Everything is wet.

DAY 133 JULY 28: TEN MILE SHELTER TO STEWART HOLLOW BROOK SHELTER.
TODAY'S MILES: 15.7
TRIP MILES: 1,470.2

RW means Riddle Without solution, a name suggested by Obsidian.

It was a good thing that I took extra care in staking out my tent last night, because it had been a stormy night, or so I'm told. I slept through the whole thing. I was so tired that I probably snored louder than the thunder. I like to think I'm a light snorer.

I packed in the rain this morning. Hardly anything had dried from yesterday. All my clothes and gear were wet, except for the sleeping bag, which was damp and clammy.

After breaking camp, we took a minor detour and hiked down Bulls Bridge Road to get to a gas station, where we bought hot coffee and breakfast. On the way there, we had to walk through a covered bridge. Obsidian had never seen a covered bridge before. As we hiked, I told Obsidian that I thought the shelter design was a poor attempt at preventing porcupine damage, because the animals are such good climbers. I asked him if he noticed the chewed edges of the shelter floor last night.

He said, "What! They climb trees? How amazing! How big are they?" I said, "Porcupines can weigh maybe 25 pounds and are two or three feet long with thousands of quills that can stab you if you touch them." Then Obsidian asked me to explain the meaning of the word quill.

He said I must be joking. Pigs don't climb trees or have pointy spears on their backs, just big tusks. It took me a second to realize that Obsidian thought I said, "porkypine." He thought a porcupine was a wild pig named after a pine tree. When I finally stopped laughing and was able to get cell reception, I searched for an Internet picture of a porcupine. Obsidian was amazed that such an animal existed.

It rained off and on all morning. We hiked for a short distance across Schaghticoke, the only Native American tribal land on the Appalachian Trail. No sign or marker was posted. If I hadn't read about it in the Guidebook last night, I wouldn't have known.

We had to climb down a steep and demanding cliff in the afternoon. The rocks were slick from the rain and lichens, and our boots were muddy. As soon as we finished scaling down the cliff, a heavy thunderstorm hit. We were thankful to be off the cliff before the storm hit and rushed to put on our raingear. The storm didn't last long but dumped enough rain to thoroughly soak the ground and trail. In a matter of minutes, an already dangerous and difficult climb would have been that much more treacherous.

The terrain was getting more difficult, with lots of ups and downs. The forest remained damp and wet all the time now, and the forest floor was covered with mushrooms. Sometimes the ground was soft and squishy. The forest is changing. Pine trees appear regularly now, and I saw birch trees for the first time. No flowers, though.

We're camped again in a wet, wooded area next to a river with very little sunlight and no breeze. I doubt my clothes will dry out tonight. They're hanging on a tree branch next to my tent. We had all hoped to camp in a sunny area where our clothes and equipment could dry out, but no luck.

I was zipped inside my tent by 7:00 p.m. because of mosquitoes. This would be a beautiful spot in dryer times without insects. But now, the forest thrums all around us with the drone of flying mosquitoes. I am buried inside my sleeping bag, praying that body heat will dry out the dampness of the bag.

It has been two weeks of hiking since returning to the Trail. In that time, I covered 230 miles and walked out of Pennsylvania, New Jersey and New York, and entered Connecticut. Nine states done!

DAY 134 JULY 29: STEWART HOLLOW BROOK SHELTER TO WEST CORNWALL.
TODAY'S MILES: 8.9
TRIP MILES: 1,479.1

RW means Ruptured Waist.

Another hard storm hit last night. That makes it three days and two nights of rain. We packed up early and headed to West Cornwall, Connecticut, this morning, hiking fast to catch the noon shuttle to the Bearded Woods Bunk & Dine Hostel. This hostel has one of the best reputations on the Trail. The place is run by Hudson and Big Lu. Hudson is a past thru-hiker, currently attempting his second thru-hike. If successful, he will become a 4,000 miler.

The Trail was moderately difficult today with no particular problems, except for a long detour around a flooded section of the Trail. Racewalker didn't like to take bypasses and, like me, only wanted to hike on white blazed trails. Only after hiking down to check the depth of the flooded trail did he grudgingly follow the alternate trail around the hazard.

After checking into the hostel, Frankie the Sleeper showed up. I was surprised to see him. I thought he was far ahead of me. He said he took ten days off due to tibialis anterior tendinitis, an inflammation in the front and just above the ankle. Many thru-hikers have gone home for short periods during their hike.

I dried out all my gear and tent today. This hostel is beautiful, the crown jewel of hostels on the entire Trail. Bearded Woods is so nice that I decided to spend another night and slackpack tomorrow. Dinner was outstanding!

Just before retiring, I took my usual dosage of vitamin "I", two ibuprofen tablets, and went to bed. This is the cleanest hostel I have ever stayed at so far.

DAY 135 JULY 30: WEST CORNWALL TO SALISBURY.
TODAY'S MILES: 16.6
TRIP MILES: 1,495.7

RW means Reverse in the Wash.

Obsidian and I slackpacked, and Racewalker carried his pack with all his gear.

I laughed harder today than I can remember laughing in a very long time. This morning after getting up and dressing, I noticed my pants were really tight. I told everybody that my pants had gotten tight overnight from last night's great feast. As the day wore on, my pants felt tighter and tighter and began pinching my crotch. At lunch time, I looked at Racewalker and realized his pants were the same design and color as mine. We looked closely at our pants and discovered they had been mixed up in the wash. He was wearing mine, and I was wearing his! I laughed for nearly ten minutes, and tears came to my eyes. I still laugh, even as I write this entry.

The Trail was beautiful today with very few rocks. We walked through stands of pine trees where the ground was blanketed with soft pine needles. We hiked on roads and trails with beautiful waterfalls next to the Housatonic River. Open areas of fields were covered in wildflowers, and houses proudly displayed their colorful flower gardens. The weather was lovely all day long and doubly appreciated after three days of rain. The day felt like a sweet reward as we hiked to Salisbury.

I enjoyed Bearded Woods Hostel so much that I am staying another night, along with Racewalker, Obsidian, and Frankie the Sleeper. During the evening I looked through the hiker logbook and noticed Wrecking Ball's name. I recalled a text from Wrecking Ball that said she had Lyme disease and was staying here during her recovery. Big Lu said Wrecking Ball had been very sick when she arrived, but after visiting a local clinic and starting treatment, she resumed hiking. I texted Wrecking Ball to tell her that I saw her name in the hostel logbook and had talked to Big Lu. Wrecking Ball texted me back and said she was back home, too sick with Lyme disease to finish her thru-hike.

DAY 136 JULY 31: SALISBURY TO GLEN BROOK SHELTER.
TODAY'S MILES: 13.5
TRIP MILES: 1,509.2

RW means Run Witch, just because I like the word combination.

Yesterday we purchased food and weighed our food bags for the next few days of hiking. Obsidian's bag and my food bag both weighed about nine pounds. Racewalker's food bag weighed eleven pounds. He clearly didn't mind carrying extra food weight, and didn't get as hungry as we did either.

Another great day! Rain sprinkled in the morning, but the rest of the day was dry and comfortable. The Trail was a bit rough with several steep climbs, but we discovered spectacular views while walking across the cliffs. Just before Bear Mountain, Obsidian and Racewalker helped me assemble a 1500-mile sign. Soon after that, we climbed Bear Mountain, the highest mountain in Connecticut with an elevation of 2,316 feet. On the way down the other side, we entered the state of Massachusetts.

Not many miles were covered today, due to the terrain and the inconvenient spacing of campgrounds and shelters. Another reason for the slow pace was that we just wanted to take it easy today. There was one instance of trail magic—someone had left many bottles of clean drinking water next to the side of the Trail.

While talking to Hudson at the hostel, I learned that he didn't consider any of us to be thru-hikers. He defined a thru-hiker as someone who has already completed the hike. In his opinion, I was a LASH until I completed the hike: a Long Ass Section Hiker. And if I didn't make it all the way, then I was just a section hiker who'd hiked a long way. He said anyone who hikes 273 miles or more at one time is a LASH. He came up with this figure because the Long Trail is officially 273 miles long. Since the Long Trail was considered long, the same mileage could be applied to a LASH on the Appalachian Trail, in his opinion.

I stopped to read a shelter logbook during the day and found an entry written by Gone Walking. He said he was giving up. He was too sick with Lyme disease.

MONTH SIX: AUGUST
DAY 137 AUGUST 01: GLEN BROOK SHELTER TO MT. WILCOX SOUTH SHELTER.
TODAY'S MILES: 19.6
TRIP MILES: 1,528.8

RW means Red Welts.

Hikers are calling Massachusetts the Mosquito and Mud State. It rained last night and this afternoon. Mud and swamps dominate the Trail, with thousand-foot climbs spaced in between. It was a long, exhausting day of climbing hills and fighting mosquitoes. In the swamps, our raingear and bug nets were of little use. The mosquitoes were voracious and ignored all insect repellent.

During a three-quarter mile hike through a swamp, swarming mosquitos forced Obsidian and me to stop and put on raingear. I was too slow in digging out the raingear from my pack. Mosquitoes covered my entire body, and I howled in pain from their bites. The raingear, once it was on, became another torture. Its waterproof fabric trapped body heat and sweat, causing me to become miserably overheated. Stopping for water was another torment—we were dive-bombed from every direction by these flying monsters.

When we finally got out of the swamp, we found an historical marker stating this was the location where Shays' Rebellion took place. The rebellion was a bloody battle fought by a group of farmers against the United States militia in protest of taxes, soon after the Revolutionary War. This was just one of many historical markers posted along the Trail. I enjoyed finding and reading them.

We had to take an alternate route today, much to Racewalker's dismay, because the white blazed trail section was flooded by an overflowing river. Unfortunately, this bypass added even more unofficial miles to the hike.

Eventually we climbed to the peak of a mountain, where the views were spectacular. For long distances, we walked along the cliff edges completely enjoying the view... and the mosquito-free zone!

We're staying in a shelter area with our tents pitched in a grove of pine trees and our food stowed in a bear box. A lot of hikers are here, including the one who grumbled about the rules for the 2,000 miler award and the Trail in general. He believed that hiking any route from Springer Mountain to Mt. Katahdin should qualify, especially if it was longer, which he said his was because he often hiked unofficial miles just to explore other places far off the Trail, such as historic sites, and other more interesting trails besides the A.T. He didn't care about the rule, and when he made it to Mt. Katahdin, he planned to apply for the 2,000 mile award. He hiked his own hike, and it didn't matter how he got there.

Racewalker and I told the hiker, rules are rules. We felt he couldn't just make up new ones to suit his preference.

I partly sympathized with him. I was getting tired of the green tunnel and preferred open spaces, any open space, even under a high tension power line. I wished the ATC would move the Trail out of the trees occasionally and use forest service roads more often. It seemed ridiculous to ignore them. I sympathize with the ATC's position that the Trail is a wilderness experience, but building a Trail less than a few hundred yards from a forest service road seems to be at odds with the ATC's stand on wilderness protection. The wilderness experience would hardly be diminished by occasionally walking on a forest service road, and would likely reduce the impact on the surrounding forest.

DAY 138 AUGUST 02: MT. WILCOX COUTH SHELTER TO UPPER GOOSE POND CABIN.
TODAY'S MILES: 15.8
TRIP MILES: 1,544.6

RW means Rambunctious Walker.

It did not rain last night. Cell phone communication is poor, forcing me to postpone uploading entries to my trail journal by several days. We started hiking at 8:00 a.m. because we wanted to reach Upper Goose Pond Cabin before nightfall. It's one of the rare shelters with an on-site shelter maintainer, and the only one that serves pancakes in the morning. Unfortunately, this shelter is also located a half mile off the Trail. The weather was good all day and the Trail mostly dry, with very few swampy areas. The forest is thick with maples and oak trees, and an occasional stand of pine. Not many views, but the mosquitoes were minimal today because of the cool weather.

The four of us did not have much to say. We just hiked and enjoyed the Trail. Racewalker carried a fancy stopwatch/altimeter around his neck and dutifully informed us how fast we were walking, and how far we were from the summit, at every hundred-foot interval.

Upper Goose Pond Cabin is beautifully situated on a lake. The cabin was totally enclosed and two stories high, staffed by three caretakers. There was also a swimming beach and free canoes, but the temperature was in the low sixties; too cold for me to go swimming. Many hikers were already canoeing all over the lake, or waiting to use them, so I gave up on that idea. The cabin is overflowing with hikers, and many are camping close to the cabin. I may try to get my winter gear back early. The past few nights have been cold.

DAY 139 AUGUST 03: UPPER GOOSE POND CABIN TO DALTON.
TODAY'S MILES 20.6
TRIP MILES: 1,565.2

RW means Ring Worm, so says Frankie the Sleeper.

Last night, 38 thru-hikers filled up the Upper Goose Pond cabin and camping area. I got up early for a pancake and coffee breakfast. Racewalker and Frankie the Sleeper left at 7:30 a.m., and I was ten minutes behind them. Frankie loved giving Racewalker a hard time about the stopwatch and his constant measuring and tracking of speed and hourly mileage. Frankie reminded him, over and over again, "IT'S NOT A RACE!"

But Racewalker was in a hurry and wanted to make high mileage for the next several days. He hoped to rendezvous with a racing companion and get off the Trail for a few days to compete in another race. Obsidian was hungry and stayed for a second helping of pancakes and conversation with other Germans. He left the shelter an hour after me.

During the morning I walked with different hikers and enjoyed many pleasant conversations. I remember one particular conversation with Genesis, a devoutly religious woman, about my age. As we hiked, I told her I had started the hike last March with an audio recording of the Book of Proverbs loaded on my cell phone, and listened to them every night. The proverbs were insightful, but I stopped listening after I realized how much the audio recording was draining the cell phone battery. Genesis had a portable MP3 player with headphones that she used to listen to gospel music while she hiked. We talked about religion for about an hour and shared our beliefs about how we found God's work all around us every day.

Many hikers used these portable devises on the trail. Music helps pass the time, plus the rhythm and beat bolsters their energy while climbing. I preferred not to listen to music, especially with headphones, for several reasons. Mostly, I liked listening to the sounds of nature, but I also considered headphones to be a safety hazard. If a bear or hiker approached from behind, I wanted to be alerted to their presence as soon as possible. I startled many hikers who wore headphones by walking up from behind and tapping them on the shoulder to ask if I could pass by.

I stopped at the Cookie Lady's house around lunchtime. She is a well-known trail angel who offers cookies to hikers. I ate a few cookies, and then another trail angel named Dave gave me a can of soda pop, which I guzzled gratefully. Dave was waiting to pick up a group of slackpackers. I took his trail card in case I needed a trail angel with a van in the future.

The Trail was mostly flat and mud-free. Rain sprinkled in the morning, but was short-lived. The sun came out and made it a beautiful hiking day. The forest was changing again. Birch trees were starting to appear more often. Maple and oak predominated, but they were gradually giving way to birch and other species.

I had planned to stay at a shelter just before town, but when I arrived at the side trail for the shelter, I found a note addressed to me. It was from Racewalker and Frankie, encouraging me to join them in town for the night. I hurried down the Trail, and in about an hour I caught up to them. They were just about to enter Dalton, one of the few places where the Trail actually runs through town.

The motel is full of thru-hikers. Many are getting drunk. The rest just want a good night's sleep. Tomorrow, four of us will eat a hearty breakfast together and then resupply for the Trail. I wanted to upload photos, but the Internet connection is poor.

DAY 140 AUGUST 04: DALTON TO CHESHIRE.
TODAY'S MILES: 8.8
TRIP MILES: 1,574.0

RW means Running to Williamstown.

We enjoyed a hot breakfast in town before hitting the Trail at 9:30 a.m. Along the way, I talked to Racewalker about the sport of race walking. At the start of the conversation, I made the mistake of calling it speed walking. He quickly corrected me by saying speed walking is what old ladies do inside shopping malls. He is a race walker, and there is a big difference. For the next hour, he explained the differences in detail.

We walked by several beaver ponds in the morning and arrived at Cheshire, Massachusetts, around 1:00 p.m., where we joined other thru-hikers at a deli/ice cream shop for lunch. Obsidian needed to pick up mail in Williamstown tomorrow, so we planned to head there for the night. Unfortunately, all the lodging in Williamstown was booked because of a festival. Obsidian and I decided to stay in Cheshire and get a bunk at the Catholic Church Hostel. Racewalker and Frankie the Sleeper continued on the Trail, so we said our goodbyes.

Racewalker had to keep moving—he had a rendezvous to catch a ride for his next race. There was another reason that he was in such a hurry. His 65th birthday was less than a month away, and he needed to be in Maine by then to stay in compliance with his trail slogan: "Maine before Medicare."

While we were explaining our post office dilemma to Father David, the priest who runs the church and hostel, a van pulled up next to us. It was Dave, the shuttle driver I'd met yesterday. He gave us a free round trip ride to Williamstown. Two hours later, after waiting around while he shuttled other hikers, we had accomplished our goal. St. Mary's Catholic Church and hostel is a good place and there are ten other hikers staying here, including Mad Jack. I met him at Bearded Woods. We slept on a carpeted floor.

Obsidian echoed the same reaction that other German hikers had expressed regarding the amazing generosity of American churches, especially towards hikers. Obsidian was surprised to see so many churches providing free or nearly free lodging to hikers, as well as significant amounts of trail magic. He found it remarkable that American churches are completely funded by congregation members who willingly choose to give money to the church. He figured the reason American churches gave back so freely and generously was because they practiced what they preached: "As you give, so shall you receive."

Obsidian went on to say that German churches were not supported with freewill offerings, but by forced income taxes on their church members. As a result, in his opinion, churches in Germany were not as generous with the money they received. He also thought that clergymen in general enjoyed a very high standard of living in his country.

DAY 141 AUGUST 05: CHESHIRE TO WILLIAMSTOWN.
TODAY'S MILES: 14.2
TRIP MILES 1,588.2

RW means Righteous Wonderer, a name given to me by a lady at the church.

We slept late and awoke this morning in heavy fog. We attended the church service, and then went to the post office and Dunkin Donuts for breakfast. The fog burned off and we hit the Trail about 10:00 a.m.

We climbed Mt. Greylock today, the highest peak in Massachusetts, and the highest mountain since Virginia. The climb was strenuous, but worth it because of the panoramic views of the Green, Catskill, and Taconic mountain ranges. I toyed with the idea of staying at the mountain top hostel, but decided I needed to make more miles today. I called Dave, the trail angel, from the top of the mountain to ask if we could stay at his place tonight. All the accommodations in town were sold out due to the festival. After Dave picked us up, he collected his slackpackers—who were all very young, barely 21—and drove us all to a campground where he leased a trailer.

We took hot showers, and after a good scrubbing, piled back into his van, headed for a grocery store and a restaurant for dinner. Two of the slackpackers in our group were pink blazers.

Pink blazing refers to people hiking together as a romantic couple on the Trail.

Severe thunderstorms started at 6:00 p.m. and lasted for four hours. Obsidian and I pitched our tents in a downpour, while the others found floor space in Dave's trailer. It has rained in Massachusetts almost every day. I'm fed up with rain.

DAY 142 AUGUST 06: WILLIAMSTOWN TO CONGDON SHELTER.
TODAY'S MILES: 14.6
TRIP MILES: 1,602.8

RW means Rising Water.

Two milestones today! I crossed the 1600-mile mark and entered the state of Vermont. Eleven states down, three to go! Obsidian found a bunch of yellow leaves, and we used them to create a 1600 mileage sign on top of a moss-covered rock. The Long Trail starts in Vermont and merges with the Appalachian Trail for about 105 miles of its 273-mile length before veering off and heading toward Canada.

It rained hard until 3:00 a.m. last night, but I stayed dry in my tent. It took forever for the young slackpackers to get moving this morning. We finally left camp around 10:00 a.m. All the young slackpackers, including the girl, now sported haircuts just like Dave. They went from long hair to shaved heads, with the exception of a circular two-inch topknot sprouting from the tops of their heads. I should mention here that Dave was a bit of a character. Besides his very distinctive hairstyle, he was overweight, in his mid-fifties, and claimed to be part Native American.

We all started hiking together from the Hoosic River Bridge crossing in Williamstown. We met a police officer on patrol while we were still on the bridge. He stopped to talk to us for a long time and said he admired thru-hikers. He wanted to take a picture with each of us, and made a point of saying that he tries to speak with every hiker he meets while on duty. The officer told us that he would like to hike the entire A.T. someday.

The Trail was tough today. I am exhausted. This mud is unbelievable! I hiked in mud all day long, sometimes ankle deep. The Trail was a muddy stream up and down both sides of the mountains, some of which were 3,000 feet high. I am in the

Green Mountains now and keep climbing higher every day. There were several expansive views today. The sun came out during lunch, so I laid my tent out to dry. By the end of the day, I was covered in mud.

The shelter is crowded tonight with at least 24 hikers. Most of them are northbound on the A.T., but a few are hiking on the Long Trail. Only one young 19-year-old was new to trail life. At this point, A.T. NOBOs were now expert at a lot of hiking skills, including how to hang food from a tree. We used fifty feet of lightweight 3/32 or 5/32 inch water-resistant poly rope to hang food bags.

We all watched the 19-year-old newbie make many attempts to tie a hundred-foot, 3/8 inch cotton rope around a big, heavy rock. As expected, after heaving the large rock, it slipped free of the rope and sailed through the air like a shot-put. We started to laugh, and he became even more determined to show us up. After several attempts, he finally secured his rope to the rock, but wasn't strong enough to heave it over the tree limb fifteen feet in the air. Next he tried using little rocks, which to our amusement kept getting untied and bouncing off the tree.

No one came to his aid; we didn't want the show to end. Then the kid got an idea. He tied his water bottle to the rope and threw the bottle in the air. Unfortunately, he was standing on one end of the rope, so it jerked back as it flew over the limb and kept wrapping itself, like Indiana Jones' whip. The rope and water bottle were now hanging in mid-air, ten feet off the ground. We were rolling on the ground and howling with laughter. He tried to climb the tree without success, and ended up trying to untangle his line with a large broken branch. He could barely lift the heavy branch, though, making his desperate attempts to swat at the water bottle futile.

Finally, when the laughter subsided, several thru-hikers grabbed a more manageable branch and retrieved his rope and water bottle off the limb. Another thru-hiker then tied the rope to a more appropriately-sized rock and made the throw on the first try.

DAY 143 AUGUST 07: CONGDON SHELTER TO BENNINGTON.
TODAY'S MILES: 4.3
TRIP MILES: 1,607.1

RW means Rascally Weasels.

The night was very chilly and the ground is soaked. A cold wetness crept up from the bottom of the tent and into my sleeping bag. I ended up sleeping in a mud puddle. I need to get my Therma-rest pad back as soon as possible. Around 5:30 a.m., it started to rain again for another hour. We slept late till 7:30 a.m. and did not leave camp until 9:30 a.m.

When we took our food bags down from the tree, we discovered mice had gotten into them. The mice must have climbed up the tree, crawled out onto the branch, and then jumped or climbed down into the hanging food bags. Mice had chewed three holes in my food bag and ate most of my breakfast. They also chewed a hole in Obsidian's food bag and ate most of his breakfast. We talked to the other hikers about it, and Cat told us mice had eaten holes in his food bag, too. He had hung his food bag from the ropes in the shelter that were attached with aluminum cans and plastic pop bottles as a mouse deterrent. Clearly, the mice were outsmarting the rope protection system here in Vermont. Cat is my age, and his trail name reflects the fact that he is a Chinese-American from Taiwan. Another unfortunate hiker was a young Canadian girl called Bliss who had stashed all her food inside her tent. Mice ended up chewing holes in her tent and backpack and got into all of her food.

More mud today. The last mile down to Bennington was a real knee-buster, a steep descent over mossy rocks. My knee is killing me, and I have already taken three vitamin "I" tablets. When we arrived at the road to Bennington about 11:30 a.m., a family we had spoken with earlier on the Trail was hiking nearby and offered to give us a ride into town, over five miles away. We are staying at the Autumn Inn tonight, a typical low-budget hiker motel.

We cleaned up and went out for lunch in Bennington, glad to be off the Trail. This is a nice, relaxing town. Another rainy day, so we sat at the motel, drying out our tents, Obsidian told me he plans to catch a bus tomorrow for Manchester Center. He doesn't think he can finish the Trail before his visa expires and wants to leap ahead and hike with a group of Germans who are closer to the end of the Trail. He had hoped to complete a thru-hike, but no longer thought it was possible.

DAY 144 AUGUST 08: ZERO DAY.
TRIP MILES: 1,607.1

RW means Resting Well. This is the first zero day since returning to the Trail.

I have hiked for 24 days without taking a day off and covered 367 miles. During that time, I finished hiking through Pennsylvania, walked across New Jersey, New York, Connecticut, and Massachusetts, and have now entered Vermont.

Obsidian and I went to the bus station this morning, and I said goodbye to him. I will miss him. I was slowing him down. Afterwards, I rested and purchased food. My hiking boots are falling apart. There are holes in the heels and the toes are separating. Many hikers use duct tape to seal the front of their hiking boots and shoes until replacements can be found. Most manufacturers, even the best, can't make shoes sturdy enough to withstand the demands of hiking at this level. I will hike with these boots for as long as possible, but they will probably fall apart before Mt. Katahdin. This is my fourth pair of boots.

DAY 145 AUGUST 09: BENNINGTON TO STORY SPRINGS SHELTER.
TODAY'S MILES: 19.0
TRIP MILES: 1,626.1

RW means Rainbow Warrior, a name given to me by a trail maintainer.

I ran into Ireland on the way back from dinner, and he agreed to share a motel room with me. Ireland and I got back on the Trail this morning at 6:30 a.m. I quickly got ahead and didn't see him again for the rest of the day. For ten miles, in cold weather, I hiked an uphill distance of 2,381 feet to reach the top of Glastenbury Mountain. I am back to climbing mountains again, because Glastenbury Mountain stands at an elevation of 3,748 feet.

The Trail, while steep and hilly, was drier and in better condition than it has been for a while. Muddy in parts, it was basically good walking over a lot of soft ground. Birch, spruce, oak, and maple trees dominate the forest. The trees are shorter here and spaced far enough apart to allow for a soft, shaded light to filter through. Ferns cover the forest floor, and rocks are green with moss.

There were fewer hikers on the Trail today. I saw four NOBOs and four SOBOs. When I got to the shelter, I discovered it was crowded with trail maintainers who were here for a long weekend of cutting and clearing the Trail. I was the only hiker staying in the shelter for the night, and had a great time talking with the trail maintainers and learning about what they do and how they do it. On this trip, they were using weed whackers to cut away encroaching plants on the Trail.

I noticed signs of their work miles back, along with plenty of moose droppings. At the time, I thought maybe the moose had chewed up all the greenery. Moose droppings continued to show up today on or near the trail. They look like big, roundish clumps of compacted plant material, much larger than deer droppings, and brown instead of black. Trail maintainers told me that if I walked south on the Trail about a mile to the pond above South Alder Brook, I could see moose at sunset. I was too tired— nineteen miles was enough for today.

One of the trail maintainers was a man in his early 20s and very overweight. He told me that he once weighed nearly 550 pounds. When he was 21 years old, he decided to change his lifestyle and started working for the Appalachian Trail. Three years later, he now spends most of his time on the Trail, and has dropped more than 250 pounds. In the beginning, he said, he couldn't walk more than a mile, but he now hikes six to ten miles a day. He figures he has walked at least a thousand miles so far. His plan is to continue hiking, and hopefully complete the Trail within the next three years. By then he expects to shed another 100 to 125 pounds.

DAY 146 AUGUST 10: STORY SPRINGS SHELTER TO SPRUCE PEAK SHELTER.
TODAY'S MILES: 18.3
TRIP MILES: 1,644.4

RW means Running Whipped.

It was cold last night, but today warmed up, becoming sunny and clear. I climbed Stratton Mountain at 3,936 feet. This is the same mountain that inspired Benton MacKaye to envision his plan for the Appalachian Trail. The climb was steep, but I charged right up the mountain, feeling energized after a good night's sleep. At the top of the mountain, I sat next to the fire tower, eating my lunch and basking in the sunshine.

A side trail led to a ski lift and several ski slopes, but I wasn't interested in seeing them. There is also a cabin, staffed by a caretaker, where hikers can pay to stay the night. I passed on this, too. Why pay when camping is free everywhere else?

I met a SOBO at the top of Stratton Mountain called Skookums. His trail name refers to a legendary race of giants who lived in the mountains near Spokane, Washington. I rarely get the chance to speak for any length of time with SOBOs, or southbounders. On the Trail, we pass each other, exchange greetings, and maybe chat for a minute or two, then hurry on our way in opposite directions. Talking to other hikers heading in the same direction is much easier. We can keep moving while we talk. Nobody really wants to stop for more than a short break when hiking.

On this occasion, though, Skookums and I were taking a break after climbing up the mountain from our respective directions, and just happened to meet at the summit. He said he was in a quandary. He had just spoken with his wife and kids on the phone, and they wanted him to come home. He still wanted to pursue his dream of a thru-hike, but missed his family, and realized his absence was taking a toll on all of them. Skookums was about the same age as my son, and his two kids were the same age as my grandkids.

I showed him pictures of my grandkids, especially our three year-old grandson wearing his little backpack and carrying a hiking stick. I told him that I had talked to my son on the phone while in Bennington. He told me that he was backyard camping with my grandkids and telling them about their grandpa's hike. My grandkids wanted to hike with me. I told him that this chapter of my life is about providing inspiration for my family and finding meaning in my life as a grandpa. Skookums got up, asked if I needed some of his food, and then said his family needed him.

Another long day, and I am tired. I didn't take any pictures today because I spent most of my time in the green tunnel, trudging through the forest. Near the end of the day, around five o'clock, I came to a side trail with a sign that said "Look Up" with an arrow pointing straight up. I looked up, and another sign about fifteen feet above my head said "Prospect Rock Overlook." I was amused, but didn't follow the trail to see the view. I had a few more miles to finish before stopping for the day.

DAY 147 AUGUST 11: SPRUCE PEAK SHELTER TO LOST POND SHELTER.
TODAY'S MILES: 17.6
TRIP MILES: 1,662.0

RW means Repellent Wings. Too many mosquitoes tonight!

Last night, three young Jewish boys hiked into camp. I say boys, but they were young men, 18 to 22 years old, I guess. Judging by their backpacking skills, though, they were just babes in the woods. They were on a three-day hike and had never backpacked before. As rookies, they were easy to spot. Their clothing was heavy cotton and they wore running shoes. Nice kids, and I enjoyed their company. Their leader had been to Israel, where he had once gone on an overnight camping adventure. He was their expert. They offered me some of their canned beans. I passed on the offer, which was hard because my hiker hunger was in full swing. I don't really like canned beans. They carried about five pounds of canned beans, along with other canned goods.

After I went to bed, they started to sing in Hebrew and sang for almost two hours. They slept under the stars with only their sleeping bags. Thru-hikers call this cowboy camping. The moon was bright and nearly full. Tree branches were casting strange shadows on my tent walls, and moonlight filled the tent. The roof glowed.

The cowboy camping trio had left all their food on the ground during the night. The next morning, I was curious to know if the mice had a field day with the easy pickings. But they were still sleeping, so I left them alone and kept on moving.

A beautiful day for hiking, but there were too many PUDs (Pointless Ups and Downs). I hiked over some knife-edge cliffs today that offered brief, but glorious, views of the surrounding mountains. I hiked over Mt. Bromley by climbing straight up a ski slope. On top of the 3,260-foot summit stood a well-built ski lift and ski patrol cabin. The cabin was open and several hikers who had spent the night were inside. I took a little break and enjoyed the view.

I ran into Hey Everybody and Appaloosa. I first met Hey Everybody back in Virginia, just before Waynesboro, but I had never met Appaloosa. We hit it off immediately and planned to hike together until Hanover, and talked about hiking the White Mountains together, maybe even all the way to the top of Mt. Katahdin.

We got to the shelter early, set up our tents, filtered water, and washed in the stream. The shelter was overrun with mice, so Hey Everybody used the Pacific Crest method for hanging all our food bags. I had never seen this method before, and it is complicated, so I won't explain it. When he was finished, there were no lines on the ground.

The water was clear and tasted good for a change. Over the last few weeks, water has been stained with tannin. My water filter was not working well and kept clogging up with the tannin and thick silt from the streams. I cleaned it out every day by back-flushing, but the flow was becoming slower and slower.

The campsite was crowded with many day hikers and thru-hikers, a few I knew. Everyone was talking about the White Mountains. They were coming up soon in New Hampshire. We had all read or heard stories describing the difficulties of this tough stretch ahead. Mostly we groused about how much it would cost to hike that section of the Trail, which is maintained by the Appalachian Mountain Club, also known in Trail lingo as the Appalachian Money Club. The AMC apparently charged for everything and provided little in return for thru-hikers.

Many hikers felt the AMC shouldn't be considered a non-profit organization, because their focus seemed to be on money-making projects and finding new ways to charge hikers. I will see if this is true or not. I am not familiar with the club's money-making ventures. This isn't the first time I have heard hikers complaining about the AMC's expensive fees and charges.

DAY 148 AUGUST 12: LOST POND SHELTER TO MINERVA HINCKLEY SHELTER.
TODAY'S MILES: 14.9
TRIP MILES 1,676.9

RW means Rear Window.

Last night was the first time I have heard owls since returning to the Trail, and they were noisy. Up till now, the Vermont forests have been eerily quiet at night.

We were all up early because everyone planned to hike a big day. The scenery was so distracting, however, that we ended up not covering nearly as many miles as hoped. The threat of rain increased throughout the day, so we decided to stop early and stay in a shelter, rather than set up our tents. For most of the day, the three of us hiked together, but at 2:00 p.m. Appaloosa got off the Trail with a trail angel who is going to help her slackpack all the way to Hanover. Now it is just Hey Everybody and me.

The Trail was very rocky with many ups and downs, but lovely to look at as we walked by several beautiful ponds and lakes. We discovered an interesting cairn site on White Mountain. It was the biggest grouping of rock cairns I have ever seen, and quite beautiful. There must have been two hundred of them. Every loose rock for hundreds of yards had to have been collected by hikers in order to build these imaginative creations.

The forest remains mostly paper birch and spruce trees. Frequently, a deep layer of fallen spruce needles created a soft and comfortable hiking surface. Most of the other thru-hikers passed us by today because we were stopping regularly to enjoy the scenery. I'm moving so slowly.

We stopped early at Minerva Hinckley Shelter because of the threat of rain. Everybody else was trying to get into the shelters before the rain started, too. We were lucky and made it into the shelter in time to claim spots. Many hikers arrived after us, including a troop of Boy Scouts, and were not so lucky. They all had to tent.

Flint and Gunpowder caught up to me at this shelter. I had left them just before the New York/Massachusetts border when they boarded a train for New York City. Somehow, I believed they had already passed me by the time I entered Vermont. Flint said

Survivor was ahead of them because he needed to pick up a mail drop. Gunpowder didn't come out of their tent because she was tired, foot-sore, and needed to sleep.

Rain is expected to start early this evening, and the forecast calls for more rain and thunderstorms all day tomorrow. We may decide to cut the day short tomorrow because of some treacherous sections.

DAY 149 AUGUST 13: MINERVA HINCKLEY SHELTER TO COOPER LODGE SHELTER.
TODAY'S MILES: 13.8
TRIP MILES: 1,690.7

RW means Rain and Wind and Rude Weather.

I texted this message to my wife at mid-day: "I am on top of Killington Peak and already in for the night. Terrible rain storm all day and I am huddled in my cold and wet sleeping bag. Not many miles today due to poor weather. Cooper Lodge Shelter tonight on the summit of Killington Peak."

Last night the shelter was packed because of the predicted rain, which thankfully, never took place. Hey Everybody and I left early to get a good start before today's rain. Rain sprinkled for the first three hours, and the Trail was steep. We had underestimated the trail difficulty, and our progress was slow. We climbed only 800 feet and worked hard for every foot. There was a trail detour in the morning due to the still-unrepaired damage caused by tropical storm Irene in 2012.

We finally made it to Clarendon Shelter by noon and just before our arrival, a heavy rainstorm started pouring down. We took a long lunch, hoping the deluge would pass, but it only got worse. We had to get back on the Trail anyway.

Rain flooded the trail and turned it into a river. I was soaked. We were trying to climb up a steep, washed-out hillside in the cold, blinding rain. Then the Trail fell apart where downed trees from tropical storm Irene were scattered. As we crawled over and under and around the fallen trees, we could hear other trees crashing, ripped loose by the gale force winds.

We climbed to the top of Killington Peak and took a steep uphill side trail for 0.2 miles before reaching the shelter. God was with us, because this was a completely enclosed building, instead of the usual three-sided structures. Several hikers were already huddled inside.

We called it quits early, only 13.8 miles. The mountain rises to 3,928 feet, making it the highest mountain on the A.T. in Vermont. We expected the temperature to plunge during the night. Violent winds were driving rain through cracks in the shelter walls, and the roof leaked. We will not hike anymore today, which means I need to get to town tomorrow to pick up enough food to make it to my scheduled resupply point. I haven't been caught in a rain storm like this since Virginia.

Flint and Gunpowder arrived as evening approached. The third member of their trio, Survivor, was still a day ahead, waiting for them in town. They quickly changed clothes and climbed into their sleeping bags. I found a bunk above Gunpowder and talked to her for a minute. She whispered to me that she wasn't pregnant, just exhausted and malnourished and needed to eat more, but hated carrying food. Food was just too heavy. She rolled over and went to sleep.

DAY 150 AUGUST 14: COOPER LODGE SHELTER TO US ROUTE 4.
TODAY'S MILES: 6.3
TRIP MILES: 1,697.0

RW means Rewritable.

Last night was brutal. The storm continued into the evening and howled for hours. It was cold and wet all night. The shelter was only half-full, which was good since the roof leaked and people kept moving to try and find a dryer spot on the floor. I figured most of the other hikers had better sense and went directly to town.

Hey Everybody and I hit the wet Trail in our wet clothes. Nothing had dried last night. From the Trail we could see the Rutland airport, and decided to go to Rutland for supplies. Around 10:30 a.m. we emerged from the forest and walked a quarter mile to a ski resort, where we caught a bus to Rutland.

In town we saw the Yellow Deli Hostel and stopped in. It was good, so we decided to stay, rest, and clean up. The hostel is run by the Twelve Tribes, a commune of people trying to live like the early Jewish Christians around the time of Christ's crucifixion. This hostel is unusual because it provides separate sleeping quarters for men and women that include very comfortable mattresses. It was also one of the cleanest hostels I'd ever stayed in.

Cat showed up, and we talked for a while. I met him earlier at Congdon Shelter on August 7th. He was concerned about his weight loss and thought he looked like an inmate from a concentration camp. While we talked, Cat ate two whole roasted chickens that he had bought at the grocery store.

He said his dream was to be the first Chinese-American from Taiwan to thru-hike the Appalachian Trail. I knew this already from reading shelter logbooks. Cat wrote about his dream in both English and Chinese in every shelter logbook where he stayed or stopped, so that there would be a record of his thru-hike.

He also hiked with a golf club instead of trekking poles. Cat said it fit him perfectly, and also, he just might be the first person on record to hike the entire A.T. carrying a golf club. He smoked, which is not uncommon for younger hikers, but rare for the older ones. Cat, like the other smoking hikers, rolled his own cigarettes. He said he tried for a while to grow a beard like the other hikers, but ended up with a very thin, straggly chin beard, which he didn't like.

I walked over to the local grocery store with some younger hikers to buy food. As we walked through the parking lot, a teenage girl came over and asked if we were thru-hikers. One of the younger hikers said yes, so she opened her grocery bag and said she had pot, mojo, H, glass, and smack. My first drug dealer! I had only heard of a few of the drugs she was selling.

The young guys told me glass was crystal meth, and mojo was cocaine. They were looking for a certain type of pot, which was great for hiking because it gave energy, pain relief, and helped them sleep. She didn't have it with her, but said she could get it and bring it back in an hour. We went into the store and bought groceries. When we came out, she was already waiting for us in the parking lot.

I tried to fix my hiking boots. The soles are falling off. I will see how well this repair works when the glue dries. My wife arranged to have a new pair of boots mailed to me at the Lincoln post office in the White Mountains. I had used all my duct tape trying to patch the mouse holes in my food bag, so Hey Everybody let me use his Tenacious Tape®.

DAY 151 AUGUST 15: US ROUTE 4 TO THE LOOKOUT CABIN.
TODAY'S MILES: 17.3
TRIP MILES: 1,714.3

RW means Restful Words, a name suggested by an employee of the Yellow Deli Hostel.

Enjoyed a good night's rest at this well-run hostel, but hiker hunger got the best of me last night. At midnight I went into the deli and asked them to make me a sandwich. The Yellow Deli is a 24-hour delicatessen. This morning, the hostel provided us with a good breakfast. For a two-dollar fare, Hey Everybody and I boarded a city bus and rode back to the Trail where we had left off. We were hiking by 8:40 a.m. Cat had gotten off the Trail several miles ahead of us, and he stayed on the bus until he reached that drop-off point.

It took me a long time to warm up today. The weather was cold and rainy all morning. We passed the 1,700-mile mark while hiking through Gifford Woods State Park. Hey Everybody helped me make a mileage sign out of big sticks. At 10:00 a.m. we passed a lodge and stopped to warm up and drink hot coffee. What happened to August? This is more like October. We hiked in heavy woods all day. At one point the Trail was so steep that someone had installed an aluminum ladder for hikers to climb up and over the rock face.

Hey Everybody and I planned to stealth camp near a stream after fourteen miles of hiking, but the rain started up again. We decided to push ahead to a cabin known as The Lookout and hope it wasn't locked. The Lookout got its name from the large platform built on the rooftop. According to Cat, who was planning to stay there, it is privately owned, but open to hikers. The Lookout is not specifically mentioned in the Guide and wasn't locked when we got there, but a sign posted on the outside read, "Use of the cabin is at your own risk."

Fourteen thru-hikers were already inside seeking protection from the weather. Pot smoke billowed out when I opened the door. This was the first time since my return that I was engulfed in pot smoke, and I had convinced myself that only a few pot smokers remained on the Trail. We built a small fire in the fireplace, but with little wood, the fire soon went out. It was raining and getting very cold. I hoped there wasn't any repercussion from building a fire in the cabin, despite a sign that clearly stated, "No Fires." Cat showed up a little later and rolled out his sleeping bag next to me. We chatted about the usual things: food, the trail, food, equipment, and food.

There is a girl here named Joe Cool. I first met her in Dahlonega, Georgia, on March 17th, and then two days later on March 19th at the Wolf Pen Gap hostel. This was the first time I saw her on the Trail since last March. She said she was staying toasty warm because she had picked up her winter gear in Rutland and sent her summer gear home. Oddly, she remembered me, but I didn't recognize her. This was happening so often that it was becoming a problem for me. I had met so many hikers along the way that I just couldn't remember them all, especially after not seeing them for weeks or months at a time. Everybody was slimmer now, and the men sported grand beards. I don't know why, but they always remembered me. I hoped it was because of my sparkling personality, but it was probably because of my all-white beard.

The boot repair with Gorilla glue was partly successful, but will need to be reglued again.

DAY 152 AUGUST 16: THE LOOKOUT CABIN TO THISTLE HILL SHELTER.
TODAY'S MILES: 14.2
TRIP MILES 1,728.5

RW means Right Wish, because I make wishes every day.

A beautiful sunrise was very welcomed after a cold and blustery night. The Lookout Cabin proved to be a great decision. We left about 7:40 a.m. and climbed up and down 300- to 800-foot inclines that went on and on all day long. This portion of the Trail is similar to North Carolina, with mostly straight up and down paths and very few switchbacks. We hiked in pine forests throughout the day, so at least the Trail was soft, not rocky.

A large haystack stopped me in my tracks, so I followed a downhill side trail. It led directly to a small store, so we took the opportunity to buy sweet rolls and coffee, but we were no longer on the white-blazed trail. After returning to find the Trail, I wondered if the hay had been deliberately set up as a decoy to lead hikers onto the false side trail headed toward the little store.

Later on, we got off the Trail and hiked to a market mentioned in the Guide. This was the place where I had originally planned to resupply. However, the market wasn't actually a market; it was instead the name of an expensive restaurant. When we got there, the Market wasn't even open for business. It's a good thing we had changed our plans two days ago and bought food in Rutland.

Tonight I am tenting and hoping the weather forecast is wrong. Rain is predicted for tonight. I got a cell phone connection and called my wife and father to let them know all is well, and to tell them about the storms and the rain.

DAY 153 AUGUST 17: THISTLE HILL SHELTER TO HANOVER.
TODAY'S MILES: 14.7
TRIP MILES: 1,743.2

RW means Rocky Walk.

It drizzled most of the night and this morning. We left early to try to reach West Hartford, where we heard there was a trail magic house that provides free breakfasts for all thru-hikers. The stories were true. In 2012, Randy and Linda lost their home in a flood caused by tropical storm Irene. They were uninsured and are still slowly rebuilding their home with little financial help. Despite their loss, they still find the resources to help hikers. They have fed 800 hikers so far this year, for free. We had a wonderful egg, toast, and sausage breakfast. Hey Everybody and I each left ten dollars, which they said was too much. We told them to use the money to help feed other hikers. Later in the day, I hiked into New Hampshire. Twelve states down, two states to go!

When we arrived in Hanover, we called nearly twenty trail angels to ask for a free hiker room, but they were all taken. We called Appaloosa because she had agreed to reserve a motel room and pick up enough food to get us through the next few days. When we contacted her, she had forgotten about our request and was staying at the hostel. I called the hostel, plus every other motel, until I finally found a vacant room located miles outside of town. We ended up walking to the motel after every attempt to hitch a ride failed. When we finally got there, we ordered pizza, washed up, watched TV, and went to bed. I am beat. I will zero tomorrow, and still work hard to get to the post office and stores.

DAY 154 AUGUST 18: HANOVER TO VELVET ROCKS SHELTER.
TODAY'S MILES: 1.4
TRIP MILES: 1,744.6

RW means Radiant Winter gear.

I decided to take it very easy today, making it a nearly-zero day. I bought new supplies, picked up my winter gear from the post office, and mailed back my summer gear. My pack hasn't been this heavy since early spring in Georgia. I am carrying five days of food and winter gear.

I ran into Surefoot. I hadn't seen her since Damascus and thought she was about 132 miles, or roughly eleven days, ahead of me. I was shocked to see her. Surefoot had been getting off and on the Trail because of cellulitis. Now I had caught up to her. The rain and soggy Trail was doing her in. Her shoes and socks were soaked for days, and the deep blisters that developed on her feet were now infected.

I was surprised to see Geo. He said he had gotten off the Trail for a few weeks, but was back and hiking slowly due to pains and injuries. While reading trail journals last night, I saw that Penguinman never returned to the Trail after leaving on June 28. Hiking injuries had driven him to seek medical attention, and the doctors discovered he had cancer. Now, he has to thru-hike on the long road to recovery.

We decided to hike to the next shelter because this town was still overbooked with hikers. Just before leaving town, we stopped for groceries and discovered dehydrated peanut butter. What a fantastic idea! I bought some lunch and sat at a picnic table near the grocery store. While Hey Everybody and I were eating, Miss Janet pulled up with her van full of hikers. I wanted to talk to her, but she was busy dropping hikers off and loading up with new hikers.

Hey Everybody and I got to Velvet Rocks and discovered that water was 0.4 miles downhill, so we hiked past the shelter for 0.6 miles and camped next to a beautiful spring about 0.3 miles from the Trail. It was a peaceful, quiet night. I threw my bear line expertly over a limb on the first try and went to bed after eating my first hot trail meal since July 15. Dinner was a noodle dish and half of a subway sandwich that I picked up just before leaving town.

DAY 155 AUGUST 19: VELVET ROCKS SHELTER TO TRAPPER JOHN SHELTER.
TODAY'S MILES: 15.2
TRIP MILES: 1,759.8

RW means Rejoicing With friends.

Another cold night, and I was thrilled to have my winter gear. I stayed toasty warm for the first time in a while. I started the morning early, long before Hey Everybody was ready. In a dense fog that cast an eerie glow around the forest, I soon met Surefoot, and we hiked together off and on. There were two very rugged climbs today, both over a thousand feet high, and the steepest ascent didn't take place until the end of the day.

The forest is mostly pine now, and many fallen trees are lying across the trail, blown over in the recent storms. On the plus side, there were many great views today.

Hey Everybody and I have been hiking together for a while now. He is 58 years old and a retired Navy COB, or Chief of the Boat, who served 28 years on fast attack submarines. Since retiring, he has primarily worked odd jobs and enjoyed retirement. This is his second time on the A.T. His first attempt was in 2013, when he made it to Erwin, Tennessee, before Achilles tendon problems ended his hike. This year, he started at Erwin in late March and will get his 2,000 miler, although not as a thru-hiker because it took him two years. He said he will try again, maybe next year, to hike the entire A.T. in less than a year and achieve his dream of becoming a thru-hiker.

I hiked fast, and Hey Everybody arrived at the shelter about two hours behind Surefoot and me. Shoes also showed up. The shelter was crowded with thru-hikers and I recognized half of them. One thru-hiker was running around with almost no clothes on. He calls himself Wildman. Wildman is about 24 years old, five feet four inches tall, and very hairy, with long black hair and a full beard. At this point I was wearing my jacket because of the cold, but he strutted around all evening clad only in a mini-kilt. He carried an upside-down seven-foot sapling with a large root ball as a hiking staff. I hadn't seen anyone acting like a fantasy character since mid-Virginia. I thought they were either off the Trail by now, or had given up such whims.

DAY 156 AUGUST 20: TRAPPER JOHN SHELTER TO HEXACUBE SHELTER.
TODAY'S MILES: 12.0
TRIP MILES: 1,771.8

RW means Rusty Warden's fire tower.

Winter gear provided enough insulation last night and enabled me to sleep, despite very cold temperatures. Surefoot and I left camp early, and Hey Everybody followed later. We climbed 2,100 feet in four miles to reach the top of Smart Mountain, an elevation of 3,237 feet. We also climbed several smaller elevations, and I am tired. I haven't worked this hard in a long time. I start the White Mountains on Friday.

The Trail was dry and we walked through pine and birch trees most of the day. We stopped for lunch at a fire warden's tower. While at the top, I tried calling my son and hoped to talk to my grandson because it was his fourth birthday. I really wanted to wish him a happy birthday, but couldn't get a signal. It was the first time I missed his birthday.

Surefoot and I caught up with events since we last saw each other in Damascus. Friends were meeting her with food so she didn't need to hike into town anymore. Cellulitis and chronic foot pain had forced her into a supported hike, assisted by friends. Surefoot is strong and keeps walking through the pain.

We didn't see Hey Everybody on the Trail all day. Again, the Trail was covered with many fallen trees from the recent storms. Some had been very large, mature trees. Surefoot and I arrived at Hexacube Shelter about 4:15 p.m., and Hey Everybody finally showed up an hour later.

This shelter is built in a hexagon shape and located near Hexacube Mountain. A 74-year-old hiker called Shoes is staying in the shelter. He is a remarkably strong section hiker who has been hiking the same distances as me since Hanover. I have seen him three nights in a row now. Shoes is hiking through the states of New Hampshire and Maine this year, and will finish the A.T. next year by hiking all of Virginia. We get along well.

Not a good equipment day. The zipper on the hip belt of my new pack broke; the dirty water bag for my water system broke; and I spilled half my fuel while cooking. Good news, though. According to my wife, new boots should arrive at the Lincoln post office tomorrow. All I need to do is figure out how to pick them up. I will pass by Lincoln during the weekend. The soles of my current boots are falling apart. I poured nearly an entire tube of Shoe Goop® between the outer sole and inner sole, trying to keep them together. That was back in Hanover. Now the boots are lumpy and uncomfortable, but holding together.

A group of college freshman arrived late at the shelter this evening from Harvard University. They were here on a weeklong backpacking course. Most of them had never backpacked before, and their leaders were noisy. They either didn't realize, or respect, the fact that hiker midnight is 8:00 p.m.

The freshmen carried so much gear, you would think they planned to stay in the woods for a year. Shoes slept in the shelter along with the students, who kept rudely waking him up. He finally talked to their sophomore leader about it. The student leader admitted that the group was way behind schedule, and most of them were struggling or just goofing off.

I was glad to be inside my tent. The freshmen wandered around the area looking for sticks to build a fire, but kept tripping over everybody's tents. By the end of the night, all the thru-hikers were hoping for a bear to finish off these smart but outdoor-stupid college students.

DAY 157 AUGUST 21: HEXACUBE SHELTER TO NH ROAD 25, GLENCLIFF.
TODAY'S MILES 14.8
TRIP MILES: 1,786.6

RW means Revolting Way.

Once again, Surefoot and I left early and Hey Everybody followed. The Harvard kids and their leaders were fast asleep at 7:30 a.m., burning daylight. It was warm last night, but cold today.

Shoes, Surefoot, Hey Everybody, and I hiked hard today. During a steep downhill, I fell in the rain and really compressed my left knee. My shin got banged up, too. I limped for a mile, and eventually the pain eased off. Surefoot and I decided to go to a hostel instead of the next shelter like Hey Everybody. I needed a shower.

Later that evening, Shoes showed up at the hostel and stayed. Cat refused to sleep overnight at this dirty place, but stayed long enough to use their shower. Afterwards, he went into town to buy food and then headed back to the Trail, where he planned to sleep in his tent. Surefoot and I both considered following Cat's lead, but it was raining. As the rain poured, Surefoot kept looking out the window. She was struggling between the urge to head out, and the desire to stay dry.

I had hoped to call the post office and check on my boots but got no reception. I also hoped to have the hostel pick up my shoes but couldn't connect with them, either. My plan is to get to town Saturday. If not, I will have to zero someplace and wait till Monday.

Trail legend Baltimore Jack is here helping to run this hostel. He tried to talk Surefoot and me into slackpacking southbound over Mt. Moosilauke tomorrow. He said the weather on the mountain might be too dangerous to hike northbound. I didn't listen to him, but Surefoot was concerned for her safety. I thought it was just a ploy to get more customers for their slackpacking business. The mountain would prove me wrong.

DAY 158 AUGUST 22: NH ROAD 25, GLENCLIFF TO BEAVER BROOKS SHELTER.
TODAY'S MILES: 7.8
TRIP MILES 1,794.4

RW means Rain and Wishing it would stop.

Since it rained hard most of the night, I guess I am not unhappy that I stayed in the hostel. The breakfast was reasonable. Before leaving, I got my A.T. passport stamped for the 29th time.

Surefoot, Shoes, and I left about 7:45 a.m. and caught up to Hey Everybody about 8:15 a.m. It was cold all day. We officially entered the White Mountains by climbing Mt. Moosilauke. It was a long, hard, steep, rocky climb. We climbed 3,747 feet, and the mountain is only 4,802 feet high. It took us five hours to hike the six and a half miles to the top.

The clouds were so thick on the summit, we could barely see. The wind was blowing about forty miles an hour. During the approach, I had to keep stopping to dig clothes out of my pack. I need the extra layers of clothing for protection from the rain and cold, I didn't expect it to be so cold in August. Still, we had fun, but didn't hang around after taking a few pictures. Not many people up there today. It was my first summit above the tree line. We had hoped for a great view, but visibility was limited to only a few hundred feet.

When we got to the top of Mt. Moosilauke, the three of us clung to the summit sign for a photograph. It was all we could do, and Hey Everybody's huge external frame backpack caught the wind like a sail. We dug our heads down into our chests and staggered to the tree line on the northern slope, where we stopped for lunch. We talked about setting up camp halfway down the mountain because of the poor weather and the northern slope's reputation for being steep and treacherous. Surefoot and I began to question our decision to hike today and wondered if we should have taken Baltimore Jack's advice. Shoes arrived, and we all decided to make for the shelter partway down the mountain.

We arrived at the 3,749-foot high Beaver Brooks Shelter after a rugged 1,000-foot partial descent in bone-chilling rain and clouds. We called it quits around 2:30 p.m. The rocky trail was just too dangerous, steep, and slippery. Only 7.8 miles were covered today, and every step required my full attention.

The four of us huddled inside the shelter, trying to stay out of the weather. Hey Everybody hung his hammock while we slept on the floor. Earlier, during one exceptionally high step up onto a rock, my pants split down the front, right up the crotch. I sewed it back together with fishing line as best I could, but I don't know how to sew. My wife brought me these zip-off cargo pants just before hiking with my son in early May. I had needed new pants at the time because I had lost so much weight. Now they were just worn out.

I planned to leave the shelter as early as possible and climb down the steep 1.5-mile descent trail, hitch a ride for the six miles into Lincoln, pick up my boots at the post office before they closed, buy supplies, and then get back on the Trail. Hey

Everybody also planned to go to Lincoln, but was in no hurry. The White Mountains, so far, are unfriendly.

We hoped to meet up at the Eliza Brook Shelter tonight. Hey Everybody read that the Kinsman Pond Shelter charged eight dollars per night and didn't want to pay. Shoes and Surefoot don't need to stop. Shoes has plenty of food, and Surefoot's friends were meeting her with food supplies at the bottom of the mountain. They hoped to make Kinsman Pond Shelter tonight.

DAY 159 AUGUST 23: BEAVER BROOK SHELTER TO KINSMAN POND SHELTER.
TODAY'S MILES: 13.0
TRIP MILES 1,807.4

RW means Remarkably Wretched Water.

Text message sent to my wife at 5:00 p.m. on 8/23/2014: "Hardest day on the Trail. I am still hiking. I should have been a mountain goat. Brutal and I am exhausted. Still have miles to campsite."

The shelter got very crowded last night. There were fourteen of us in a shelter designed for ten. Everybody was escaping from the rain, which didn't stop until 8:00 p.m. During the rain, a group of ten Tuft University incoming freshman showed up with their instructor. Two joined us in the shelter, and the rest had to tent camp.

Unlike the Harvard University crowd, this group was organized and hiked in at a reasonable hour. They were also respectful, even though they were understandably disappointed in not being able to get into the shelter. The next day, we all woke early because the shelter faced east, and we silently watched the sun rise. It was going to be a glorious day.

I packed up very early, said goodbye to everyone while they were still eating breakfast, and left at 6:45 a.m. The Trail was amazingly steep. Iron handholds and foot rungs were installed in many places. The downhill trail ran alongside a beautiful stream and waterfalls, but the Trail was slick. I fell three times in less than a mile. Fortunately I didn't get hurt, just scraped and bruised, and a small rip in a backpack pocket. Hiking down the mountain, I was glad we stopped when we did yesterday. This was just as treacherous as everybody had warned. Is it necessary to build a trail like this?

When I got to the road, I quickly hitched a ride into Lincoln with a young man named Anthony. He bought me breakfast, drove me to the post office where I was able to pick up my new boots, waited while I bought food for the Trail, and then drove me back. I was in and out of town in less than two hours! By 10:15 a.m., I was back on the Trail.

I figured I was back from town before Hey Everybody even made it down the mountain. I ran into Shoes, and he said Hey Everybody was still drinking coffee and looking at the view when he left the shelter this morning, but Surefoot was ahead of him.

About mid-afternoon, Shoes and I passed the 1800-mile mark, and he helped me make a sign. A little while later, I passed the Eliza Brook Shelter, our designated meeting point with Hey Everybody. Hey Everybody and I had gotten along well enough, but it was standard practice on the Trail for hiking partners to break up at some point.

I continued on with Shoes, and we kept falling over the rugged trail, getting bruised but uninjured. During the last four miles, Shoes and I got separated. I was hiking faster and ended up climbing Kinsman Mountain alone, which was scary, but the views were spectacular.

The Trail was brutal today. I only covered thirteen miles and didn't arrive at Kinsman Pond Shelter until 7:15 p.m. at sunset. I barely made one mile per hour because the Trail was so hard. Climbing Kinsman Mountain is as close to true mountain climbing as I have ever experienced. It was nearly a perpendicular cliff, and I had to climb for hours. My hands and feet ached at one point, and I had to stop to let them rest. There was a boulder climb on a poorly marked section of trail, nearly 2,000 feet in only 2.5 miles. I made several wrong turns in the process.

When I got to the shelter, I told the caretaker about Shoes. I was concerned about him climbing up those boulders in the dark. After I paid him eight dollars to stay there, he promised to keep a lookout for Shoes and said I would have to stay in the shelter because the campground was full. The shelter was packed with day hikers, but Surefoot was there. She had saved a spot on the floor for Shoes. I squeezed into the last vacant bit of floor space and waited for him. Much to my relief, Shoes showed up an hour and a half later, exhausted. I asked the other hikers what the caretaker did for eight dollars, but nobody knew. Most felt as I did—that there is nothing here that isn't free everywhere else on the Trail. This started the usual round of bad-mouthing the Appalachian Money Club.

There was a beautiful lake next to the shelter, filled with dark tannin-stained water. Even after filtering, the water in my water bottle looked black and disgusting. When I walked down to the water's edge, the night sky was already dark and the reflection of stars on the lake looked like a thousand twinkling Christmas lights. The forest was black and silent, and it felt sinister standing next to this beautiful image of heaven.

DAY 160 AUGUST 24: KINSMAN POND SHELTER TO LIBERTY SPRINGS CAMPSITE.
TODAY'S MILES: 7.5
TRIP MILES: 1,814.9

RW means Rays Wonderful. It was a great hiking day with a beautiful sunset.

Surefoot left early because she was meeting friends and resupplying. In the morning, the Trail was tough, but not as bad as yesterday. On the way I stopped at Lonesome Lake Hut, the first AMC hut I had visited. It was well-built and situated on a beautiful spot next to a lake. Someone told me it cost $120 to stay for the night and sleep on a wooden bunk without hot water or lights. The meals were reportedly good, but all sold out.

I yogied a breakfast of cold oatmeal from the caretaker. The oatmeal was worse than the prepackaged oatmeal I ate most mornings. Shoes and Cat walked in shortly after I arrived. Cat had stealth camped in the woods near Kinsman Pond Shelter last night and avoided paying the eight-dollar fee. For the rest of the morning, Shoes and I hiked together on an easy downhill path. At noon, Shoes met his son, who drove us both into Lincoln where we ate lunch at Subway. By 2:00 p.m. I was hiking alone again, and by 4:00 p.m. had already set up my tent at the Liberty Springs Campsite.

I ran into Cat while filtering water. He planned to continue climbing up the mountain a little ways in order to stealth camp again. He wasn't going to give the AMC eight dollars for anything. Soon, Surefoot came in and set up on the same wooden tent platform as me. Instead of a shelter, the AMC had built rectangular wooden tent platforms. I didn't have a freestanding tent and had to struggle to secure the corners with rocks.

Later on, Shoes and his son, Richard, arrived and set up on a platform across from us. They planned to hike together for the next 50 miles. This is the first time Richard has ever backpacked. Camped next to the four of us was an older thru-hiker named Hobbit. He planned to hike with us tomorrow. There were no seats or tables in the eating area that was located about one hundred yards away near the water and bear box. You would think for all the money the AMC collects, they could provide hikers with a picnic table to sit on. No, we sat on rocks or the ground.

The sunset was beautiful, the first truly nice, only partially obstructed view of the setting sun I have seen so far. During the evening a woman thru-hiker told me a shocking animal story. She had been cowboy camping in New York when she was awakened by a sharp pain in the left side of her face. Just before getting ready to sleep that night, she had applied a fragrant coconut-scented lotion on her face and hands. While she was sleeping under the stars, a skunk, attracted by the aroma of the coconut lotion, bit her on the cheek. Bite marks were still visible on her cheek, which was distressing, but certainly a badge of courage. She missed a week of hiking afterwards and had to get rabies shots, which she administered herself.

It looked to be a nice night, so I took the rainfly off my tent and watched the stars through the trees until falling asleep.

DAY 161 AUGUST 25: LIBERTY SPRINGS CAMPSITE TO GALEHEAD HUT.
TODAY'S MILES: 10.3
TRIP MILES: 1,825.2

RW means Rowdy Wakes the dead, because the campsite was noisy.

Even though the night air was warm, I didn't sleep well because of all the commotion around me. Surefoot said I was the one who kept her awake all night with my snoring. As a result, she was moving slow. Neither of us cared for the tent platforms. I got up early and ate breakfast with Hobbit, who shared his coffee with me.

The climb up from the campsite was very steep, but not long. Most of the elevation had been scaled yesterday. From the top of Franconia Ridge, I could see for miles and gazed back at the three mountain tops I had just climbed: Haystack, Lincoln, and Lafayette. The day was beautiful, and I enjoyed staying up there admiring the views for over two hours.

This was the first time in my thru-hike that I sat this long on a summit break, just for the sake of the stunning views. I saw my first view of Mt. Washington and the cog-tourist train puffing up the mountain. The weather was cold, but bright and sunny, and the Trail followed along a knife-edge ridgeline with steep cliffs plummeting down both sides. Surefoot eventually caught up to me on the ridgeline.

We started climbing down a treacherous descent at 11:00 a.m. that took hours. Eventually we climbed over Mt. Garfield and continued in a downward direction. The Trail was brutally hard. We reached the campsite where we had originally planned to stay, but decided to keep hiking an extra three miles on the chance that the Galehead Hut employees would let us work for our stay. Galehead is a beautiful hut on top of a mountain. We arrived about 5:00 p.m. and Hobbit was already there. The gamble paid off, but only because we walked into the hut and acted like a couple when asking to work for our stay. Hut rules allow only two thru-hikers at a time to work for their stay, and Hobbit had already been selected for the evening work crew. They bent the rules. We waited for our dinner until 8:00 p.m., and then feasted on leftover chicken and potato soup.

After dinner we washed dishes and did other chores for about an hour and a half. As we worked, the hut's employees performed skits for the paying guests. Afterwards, everyone went out to stargaze with a telescope. The night was clear and the Milky Way gorgeous. One of the employees gave a short astronomical lecture. When all the paying guests had gone to bed, the three of us were allowed to unroll our sleeping bags on the dining room floor. We were happy—it was better than sleeping on the floor of a shelter.

It had been an extremely physical day, and only 10.3 miles to show for it. I barely stayed awake to eat and finish my work chores. I saw Appaloosa and Hawg Driver at the Galehead Hut. I had hiked with Appaloosa in Vermont, and Hawg Driver in

Pennsylvania. Appaloosa and Hawg Driver were slackpacking through the White Mountains and staying in AMC huts, as paying guests. Not surprising for an executive hiker like Hawg Driver.

Just before dark, the hut employees had to turn away a father and son who were section hiking the Trail. The two were forced to leave and climb the very steep South Twin Mountain, a grueling 0.8 mile trail up a 1,100-foot boulder climb. Section hikers do not get to stay in the huts, unlike the lucky few thru-hikers. A perk, I guess, for us.

DAY 162 AUGUST 26: GALEHEAD HUT TO ETHAN POND SHELTER AND CAMPSITE.
TODAY'S MILES: 11.8
TRIP MILES: 1,837.0

RW means Rising Way.

Hobbit, Surefoot, and I left the hut at sunrise. We skipped breakfast at the hut because we did not want to wait till nine o'clock to work for our meal. We had a big day ahead of us. The day was cool and we hiked hard. We climbed South Twin Mountain and hiked above tree line much of the day. As we hiked, we kept looking back at the spectacular views of the Trail section we had covered the day before.

From breakfast to lunch, the Trail was both hard and easy. The mountains were tough in the morning, and we were barely able to make one mile per hour. At lunch time we stopped at the Zealand Hut and bought some soup and protein bars. After the Zealand Hut, the Trail became easy, since it had once been an old railroad bed. Being able to hike at a normal pace was a real treat, and it felt good to stretch my legs. We got to Ethan Pond before 4:00 p.m. and everyone soaked in the pond. The black pond water was surprisingly warm, probably because the tannin helped to absorb heat.

While there, a caretaker collected our eight dollars and invited us to join her for dinner. She prepared the meal and we shared stories. The caretaker wanted to get rid of food because she was leaving that weekend and didn't want to pack it out. She also gave me a lot of oatmeal to help supplement my food bag.

I have been purposely leaving off the rainfly lately, in order to gaze out at the starry night from my sleeping bag. The White

Mountains have been very strenuous, but more beautiful than I imagined. I really like the Whites; they remind me of high Rocky Mountain meadows. I understand why some hikers think the White Mountains should become a national park.

Hobbit is jumping three days ahead of us on the trail and will head north from there. He has already climbed Mt. Washington in past years. This is his fourth section hike of the Appalachian Trail, and hopefully his last.

DAY 163 AUGUST 27: ETHAN POND SHELTER AND CAMPSITE TO LAKE IN THE CLOUDS HUT. TODAY'S MILES: 14.1 TRIP MILES: 1,851.1

RW means Running to Washington.

Last night was warm and the stars bright. Surefoot, Hobbit, and I left at 7:00 a.m. and then said our goodbyes to Hobbit an hour later at the Crawford Notch roadside. We would be crossing and hiking the Crawford Path for miles to get to Mt. Washington. The Crawford Path dates back to 1819 and is the oldest continuously-used trail in the northeastern United States.

Surefoot and I tackled the nearly 1,500-foot high Webster Cliffs. It was a brutal climb that ended up taking hours. At the top, winds gusted to 30 miles per hour, but the views were outstanding.

Afterwards, we climbed Mt. Webster and Mt. Jackson. Many of the mountains here are named after presidents and other famous people, and are known as the Presidential Range. It was a gorgeous, cloud-free day. We could see Mt. Washington most of the time as we hiked toward it. Unfortunately, the weather was humid and hot, and I was completely drenched in sweat.

It was nearly impossible to hike more than one mile per hour here, but we hit a nice, flat stretch today and made it to Mizpah Springs Hut in time for lunch. I bought two bowls of mushroom soup and some candy. Cat was inside the hut, eating pancakes and working for his meal. Surefoot and I had thought this hut would be as far as we could hike today and planned to camp near it this evening, but we were doing well and it was early, so we pushed on. We climbed Mt. Pierce and Mt. Franklin, and part of Mt. Eisenhower and Mt. Monroe in the afternoon.

As evening approached, the temperature plummeted just as we arrived at Lake-in-the-Clouds Hut, where we were able to work for our dinner and stay. There were a lot of other thru-hikers staying at this hut, and the staff was generous and accommodating. Cat joined us later. I learned later that this hut must take in all hikers because of its dangerous location near the summit of Mt. Washington. The hut is situated at an elevation of 5,106 feet and built on top of exposed, fragile tundra.

Mt. Washington, home to the world's worst weather, is also called the "rock pile" because the summit is covered in large blocks of quartzite and mica schist. We found out Mt. Washington has some very scary stats. At an elevation of 6,288 feet, it is considered the most dangerous small mountain in the world, and the most dangerous place in the lower 48 states of the United States. Mt. Washington holds the record for the highest recorded wind speed in the northern and western hemispheres: 231 miles per hour, a wind speed stronger than a Category Five hurricane, which is only 157 mph, and comparable to an F-4 tornado. As of 2010, 137 people have died on this mountain.

Again we slept on the hut floor after finishing our chores, and the employees performed skits for the paying customers. I thought about Mt. Washington and hoped for good weather tomorrow, but the forecast was ugly: high winds, thick clouds, cold temperatures, and rain. Maybe I should wait for a better day.

DAY 164 AUGUST 28: LAKE IN THE CLOUDS HUT TO MADISON SPRINGS HUT.
TODAY'S MILES: 7.0
TRIP MILES: 1,858.1

RW means Raw Weather.

The stars were especially beautiful last night at Lake-in-the-Clouds Hut, and I slept well. I enjoyed staring out the window and looking down at the valley, watching the lights from the different towns. This morning Cat, Surefoot, and I worked for our breakfast. Cat wants to hike Mt. Washington in good weather, so he decided to stay another day at the hut. The staff wouldn't let him stay inside the hut any longer, so he is forced to stay in the dungeon. After looking at the dungeon, I'd rather sleep outside in my tent than in that dark hole. Located in the solid stone basement and accessible only from the outside by a large steel door, the dungeon is a windowless, unheated, one-room emergency shelter with stark wooden bunks.

Surefoot and I left about 9:30 a.m. and headed for the summit of Mt. Washington. Visibility was no more than one hundred feet; and the wind was blowing at 40 miles per hour, with a temperature of about 40 degrees. A hundred yards away from the hut, we encountered a forest service sign that read: "STOP! The area ahead has the worst weather in America. Many have died there from exposure. Even in the summer. Turn back now if the weather is bad."

We decided that we would try to climb to the summit and if the weather was dangerously bad, we could always take the cog train down to safety, or hitch a ride, or something. It took almost 1.5 hours to climb the last 1.6 miles of the "rock pile." At the top, the wind gusted to 60 miles per hour, and thick clouds obstructed our vision. Surefoot and I sat in the Mt. Washington visitor center for 1.5 hours, eating pizza and recharging my cell phone. We decided to hike about 5.4 miles ahead to Madison Hut, where we hoped to work for our stay again. When we left the visitor center at 12:30 p.m. and started down Mt. Washington, the weather was worse than when we had climbed up. We hoped the weather would improve once we got off the summit, and started descending down the mountain.

The Trail was tough, piled with solid rocks and boulders, and we worked hard to cover one mile per hour. On the way down, we climbed over the cog train tracks and barely saw the train pass by through the clouds and rain. Some trail hikers like to moon the train, but it was too cold for us to drop our pants. The wind was terrific.

On the way down we partially climbed two huge "rock piles" called Mt. Clay and Mt. Jefferson. I called them rock piles because that's what they looked like. Most of the Whites appear to be the most beautiful and spectacular rock piles I have ever seen.

Today wins my vote as the worst trail I have hiked so far on the A.T. The wind blew 40 to 50 miles per hour all day, nearly knocking me down, and always throwing me off balance. Besides the wind, clouds frequently obscured the Trail. Surefoot and I struggled from cairn to cairn for hours in limited visibility that was less than one hundred yards at times. This section of the Appalachian Trial is a spectacular, once-in-a-lifetime experience, but one that I am in no hurry to repeat.

We hiked above the tree line all day. As night started to fall, Madison Springs Hut finally appeared at the bottom of a deep valley. We were glad to be so close, but were cold and tired, and moving slowly at less than one mile per hour.

When we finally reached the Madison Springs Hut, they refused to let us work for food, but allowed us to sleep on the floor for two hours of work. We couldn't eat because they were too busy checking in all thru-hikers who were seeking shelter from the weather. Later that night, the caretaker took pity on Surefoot and me, and gave us leftover food from the paying guests. I had a lengthy conversation with two teenage boys from Canada who were on a camping trip with their father. They found my stories exciting and hoped to hike the A.T. in 2015 after their high school graduation.

DAY 165 AUGUST 29: MADISON SPRINGS HUT TO PINKHAM NOTCH.
TODAY'S MILES: 7.8
TRIP MILES: 1,865.9

RW means Rock Walls.

It was a very cold night when I walked out of the hut at 2:00 a.m. to look at the stars. Within seconds, I was engulfed inside a cloud. A blinding white light from my headlamp reflected off the impenetrable cloud walls. I felt like I was floating in the clouds, anchored only by the shadow of ground under my feet. It reminded me of the television series Ghost Whisperer, when Jennifer Love Hewitt says, "Go to the light!" Fearing to get lost in the all-encompassing whiteness, I quickly turned around and grasped for the door handle of the hut.

Surefoot and I left the next morning at 8:00 a.m. in 40-degree weather, thick clouds, and gusty winds. We were starting the climb up to Mt. Madison. Mt. Madison is a steep basalt rock formation located nearly six hundred feet above the hut. The climb was tough, but by 10:00 a.m. the weather began to clear up. Scrambling over the broken rocks was fairly doable for me, but Surefoot had a hard time. Getting far ahead of her, I hiked alone along a treacherous rock and boulder trail, until I eventually got below the tree line. I waited for Surefoot, and then we hiked together down the mountain. As we descended into the trees, the weather warmed up, and by the time we got to the Pinkham Notch trailhead, I was sweating again and stripped down to my tee shirt and shorts.

We arrived at the trailhead around noon and I said goodbye to Surefoot. She was staying with friends. I wanted to stay at the AMC's Joe Dodge Lodge, but it was full. A nice group of hikers from Canada gave me a ride to Gorham, where I checked into a motel. Afterwards, the Canadians and I went for pizza and they paid for my lunch. Trail angels! Their two younger boys, Jukebox and Sour Cream, were enthusiastic listeners who hoped to hike the Trail someday.

DAY 166 AUGUST 30: PINKHAM NOTCH TO IMP CAMPSITE.
TODAY'S MILES: 13.1
TRIP MILES: 1,879.0

RW means Running Wildcats.

I slept poorly at the Colonial Fort Inn last night, just couldn't get to sleep. At 6:30 a.m. the owner drove me to the Trail for a charge of fifteen dollars. After a quick breakfast at the Pinkham Notch Visitor Center, I talked about my thru-hike with some Labor Day weekend tourists who were making the most of a bus trip to the White Mountains.

As I was leaving the visitor center, I ran into a young thru-hiker eating his way through a large pile of potato chips. He told me that he was out of money and secretly camped behind the visitor center. He had tried to work for food, but the manager turned him down. As he was leaving, he noticed a kitchen worker dumping boxes of potato chips into the trash. Mice had gotten into the boxes, so the bags couldn't be sold anymore. The starving young hiker asked if he could have them, but was advised against it. He fished them out of the dumpster anyway, thrilled at the thought of having something to eat. It was trail magic for him and he planned to eat them all. Some would be crushed and carried as trail food for the days ahead.

I started climbing up a renowned ski area called the Wildcats at 7:30 a.m. and hiked alone all day. Surefoot stayed with friends last night and texted to say she planned to make a late start today.

I am in a series of five mountains named A through E. The Appalachian Trail runs over four of them: A, C, D and E. I have no idea what happened to B. Today's hiking was extremely rugged and steep, with many rapid up and downs through ever-increasing gullies and ravines. I lost count of the many vertical ups and downs, but in a matter of hours I was 2,408 feet higher than where I started. From there, it was a nearly vertical drop of 1,200 feet down to Carter Notch Hut.

Carter Notch Hut is small and well-maintained, but it was empty when I arrived. Later on, as more people showed up, I washed dishes in exchange for a lunch. The lunch was a serving of cold leftover eggs from breakfast and a small bowl of soup. I supplemented the meal with some purchased candy bars.

After lunch, I climbed the Carter Mountains, which include Dome, South, Middle, and North Mountains. Dome Mountain is a 1,600-foot climb in just 1.4 miles. Brutal! Each mountain is a difficult up-and-down climb that leads directly to the next one. At the end of the day, I climbed down a cliff to get to the shelter. I wanted to go farther but decided against it. There was plenty of clear water here, so I stopped. It served no purpose to knock myself out. I was only going to Gorham tomorrow, where I planned to buy food and take a zero day.

Since this was a holiday weekend, most of the shelter space and tent platforms were already taken. Of the 30 or more campers, only four were thru-hikers.

DAY 167 AUGUST 31: IMP CAMPSITE TO GORHAM.
TODAY'S MILES: 8.0
TRIP MILES: 1,887.0

RW means Relieved from Whites.

It got very warm in the crowded IMP shelter last night. I slept late and did not get back on the Trail until nearly 8:00 a.m. No need to hurry today. I was worn out after hiking the Wildcats yesterday. Today will be the last eight miles of the White Mountains.

The hiking went fast and the Trail scenery was the best so far in the White Mountains. I climbed Mount Moriah. After that, the Trail became quite normal by A.T. standards, and by noon I was already standing at the trailhead.

Autumn was already setting in at the higher elevations. Trees were turning colors and leaves were starting to fall on the trail path. I didn't take any pictures today, and I hiked in woods all day long.

When I got off the Trail I hitchhiked into Gorham. A Franciscan monk named Father Terry picked me up and drove me into town. God was surely watching over me yesterday, but it wasn't the first time I had felt the presence of an invisible guardian throughout the Trail. Oftentimes, it seemed like an invisible hand was holding me in place and keeping me from falling or getting seriously injured.

I am staying at a hostel called The Barn. It is primitive, but conveniently located in downtown Gorham. The owner, Doc, is a kind gentleman. I swept up the place and in return he drove me four miles to the Walmart, where I bought five days' worth of food. Several other thru-hikers were staying at the hostel, some southbound, most northbound, and I had never met any of them before. The SOBOs gave me good information about the Trail to the north. Many of the hikers planned to hike the entire Wildcats in one day and return here tomorrow night. Too much for me; I wish them luck.

I am beat, unusually tired, congested, and lightheaded. Is this fatigue caused by Lyme disease? I checked for the symptoms and the red bulls eye that usually accompanies an infected tick bite, but found no evidence. Hiking the Whites and the Wildcats must have taken a lot more out of me than I realized. I planned to take a zero day tomorrow before starting the next leg into Maine.

I kept busy this afternoon by repairing rips and tears in my pants and replacing the Sawyer Mini water filter and bag with the purchase of a larger version. It filters water faster than the Mini can handle.

MONTH SEVEN: SEPTEMBER
DAY 168 LABOR DAY, SEPTEMBER 01: ZERO DAY.
TRIP MILES: 1,887.0

RW means Recalculating Walk.

I just learned that Bear Bag and Isn't Black summited Mt. Katahdin on August 29th, and Guy-on-a-Buffalo summited on August 1st. I also learned that Achin' restarted his hike for the third time. I admire anyone who gets knocked down by the Trail and can get back up. Achin' has done just that, more than once. He knows he can't thru-hike anymore this year, but will make as many miles as possible.

Today my body hurt when I woke up. I think I am catching something. Glad I decided to take a zero day and rest. My hips, knees, ankles, feet, and Achilles tendons in both feet are all tired. I am worn out. The White Mountains were really tough. They are spectacular and beautiful, but the Trail is steep and treacherous and badly eroded by years of human impact. Unfortunately, the cost of trail maintenance is expensive, and fixing them all is out of the question.

However, it looks like the Appalachian Mountain Club is more interested in building revenue-generating huts than in maintaining the trails. They won't put picnic tables at shelter sites, but will spend two million dollars to renovate a hut and use helicopters for the project. Overall, the Whites are the most poorly blazed and marked trails on the Appalachian Trail so far.

While reading Isn't Black's blog, I found out that he shaved off his beard. Someone told him about another hiker who went to sleep with peanut butter stuck in his beard. Mice gnawed on his face and beard during the night. After hearing this, Isn't Black started shaving in hopes of preventing this situation. I am trying to avoid shelters.

DAY 169 SEPTEMBER 02: GORHAM TO CARLO COL SHELTER.
TODAY'S MILES: 17.0
TRIP MILES: 1,904.0

RW means Riding with Waldo.

After an early breakfast, a trail angel called Golden Waldo picked me up at no charge and drove me to the Trail. Golden Waldo is a former thru-hiker, and we ended up having an interesting conversation about the Trail.

It was already hot at 7:00 a.m. when I got back on the Trail. The morning hike started with a steep 1,500-foot climb up to the cloud-covered summit of Mt. Hayes. I was soaked with sweat and remained drenched all day. The weather kept getting hotter and hotter. Skies threatened to thunderstorm in the afternoon and evening, but the rain never materialized, just a crushing humidity.

The day was full of steep ups and downs, but I felt good after a zero day and pushed on despite fighting off flu-like symptoms. There were signs of autumn on the Trail. I saw a beautiful maple tree in full color. The forest trees are mostly maple, oak, spruce, and birch here. I hiked at the best pace so far in weeks, 1.75 miles per hour until 2:00 p.m.

Just before starting a difficult climb up Mt. Success, I passed the 1900-mile mark and came up with the idea of making a mileage sign out of red berries. Red berries had been hanging from bushes alongside the Trail for miles, and I wondered what they were. I made the sign out of berries by arranging them on a large moss-covered rock next to the Trail. The red berries on the green moss looked like a Christmas holiday decoration. Twenty yards later, I walked by another 1900-mile sign made out of nuts.

After crossing Mt. Success, I entered Maine. Thirteen states done! The Trail had been so tough here that it felt like New Hampshire was holding me back, not wanting me to leave. Maine didn't seem to want me to enter, either. Bogs and cliffs slowed my pace down to one mile per hour, right up until the last few miles. The last half mile before the first shelter in Maine was a boulder scramble. I had to take my pack off in order to squeeze through some tight spaces on the Trail. I anticipated arriving at the shelter by 4:30 p.m., but didn't arrive until 6:00 p.m.

The shelter was large, and located 0.3 miles off the Trail on a steep and rocky downhill. I thought I was going to have the place to myself, but just as night fell, another hiker arrived. It was Naked Paul, a thru-hiker who used to be called Just Paul until June 21st, the traditional nude hiking day on the A.T. From then on he was known as Naked Paul. He is a chef from Colorado. We talked about food, and he said he started off by cooking good meals on the Trail, but quickly ended up eating the same ramen noodles and pack food as everybody else. Well-prepared, nutritious meals were just too much work and weight.

DAY 170 SEPTEMBER 03: CARLO COL SHELTER TO SPECK POND SHELTER AND CAMPSITE. TODAY'S MILES 9.5
TRIP MILES: 1,913.5

RW means Rumble Water.

I was grateful to be sleeping in the shelter last night. Thunderstorms rumbled and rain poured throughout the night. When I got up at dawn, the humidity had gone down, but the clouds were thick and the forest was soaked. Streams had flooded their banks and roared as they funneled water down into the valley below. Yesterday all the water sources listed in the guidebook had been dry.

The Trail is wet and dangerous. It was only 4.4 miles to the next shelter, but it took four hours of hard climbing with many slippery descents. This is an incredibly hard Trail, much harder than the Whites. Every step had to be thought out in advance, or risk a fall.

While the Trail is just as hard, or harder, than the Whites, Maine has added an extra hazard: bogs. Bogs blocked the path, and the bog-board walkways were frequently underwater. Stepping off the bog-boards, which were located somewhere below my feet in the murky water, was disaster, so I methodically slogged along in the ankle-deep water and mud. Much too often, my trekking poles never touched bottom in the bogs. A hiker just ahead of me made a misstep and sank up to his waist. He used a lot of colorful language that nobody else but me could hear!

Winds howled at 40 miles per hour or more all morning, and until 11:00 a.m. the clouds were so thick that I couldn't see three hundred feet. It was a cold, wet, and windy hiking morning. I planned to hike only 4.4 miles if the weather didn't improve. Up ahead, just past the next shelter is Mahoosuc Notch, considered by many to be the hardest and/or most fun one-mile stretch on the entire Appalachian Trail. It is also recommended that the Notch should only be crossed in reasonable weather.

At 11:30 a.m. I arrived at the Full Goose Shelter and Campsite, still undecided whether I would go through the Notch today. A young Japanese thru-hiker who had camped at this shelter was still trying to decide what to do as well. As I ate my lunch, the sun came out and Naked Paul arrived. The three of us talked about the Notch. Naked Paul and I decided to hike it together, but the Japanese hiker decided to wait and see if the recent good weather would hold.

Naked Paul and I arrived at Mahoosuc Notch about 1:00 p.m. and started in. The Notch is a small river valley between two 1,500-foot high towering cliffs. Over time, monster-sized boulders had fallen into this valley, covering up the floor of the Notch. The boulders are as big as a four-room house, and many are much larger. To get through it, you must figure out how to get by each boulder, or group of boulders. You must decide whether to go over, under, left or right. At selected spots in the maze, blazes mark the Trail, but appear to be placed only at the especially treacherous locations.

Naked Paul and I worked together. We each scouted a potential path, and then selected one. After two hours of struggling through this one-mile stretch, we had gone over, under, left, and right of countless boulders. Some boulders were unstable and unnerving, yet still had to be passed. The Mahoosuc Notch was the greatest two hours of fun I have had on the Trail yet! It was incredibly difficult and tiring, but playful and challenging at the same time. I wish there had been more time just to play in the Notch, but I needed to make miles, and the miles ahead were difficult. I loved the Notch!

After the Notch, we had a steep elevation rise of 1,607 feet in only 1.5 miles. It was a brutal and terrible hand-over-hand climb up Mahoosuc Arm. The Trail went straight up without one switchback that I can recall. It took two hours to make the climb, and I was beat.

At 6:30 p.m., I stopped for the night at Speck Pond Shelter and Campsite, where the caretaker charged me eight dollars. I was happy to pay because I was so tired. Bismarck, Hopper, and Journeymen were already set up for the night. Journeymen and I had hiked together in Pennsylvania just before I got off the Trail in June. He had also gotten off the Trail for eleven days with Lyme disease. I had also briefly met Bismarck and Hopper before, at the Washington Monument in Maryland.

The shelter was situated next to a beautiful lake, but I was too tired to go for a swim. I just ate and went to sleep by 7:00 p.m. Journeymen was already soundly asleep. During the night I got up and looked at the pond. The moon, hanging low in the night sky just above the mountains, reflected brightly on the surface of the clear, clean lake. I sat for twenty minutes marveling at the night's beauty. No sounds of wildlife, though. The northern forests are so quiet, so different from the southern forests. Not even the hoot of an owl or the howl of a coyote punctuates the night.

DAY 171 SEPTEMBER 04: SPECK POND SHELTER AND CAMPSITE TO GRAFTON NOTCH.
TODAY'S MILES: 4.6
TRIP MILES: 1,918.1

RW means Rascally Wabbit.

Last night I was tired and still fighting off what I decided was a head cold, my first illness on the Trail. This morning I talked with the other hikers in the shelter. They are all getting off the Trail today to slackpack. I was so beat that I decided to join them.

The morning's Trail was straight up again for an hour. My legs felt like lead, and I struggled to climb. The views of the Presidential Mountains were great, but I was tired, my energy gone. The downhill was nice, but again, I struggled with sore knees and moved slowly.

At 11:00 a.m. the shuttle picked the four of us up and drove us to The Cabin in East Andover. Originally, I had planned to stop in Andover to buy food, so this worked out well. We ate lunch and made plans. We decided to go to Walmart and buy food for the Hundred Mile Wilderness, and then mail it to Monson. Bismarck said there wasn't a good place to buy groceries between Andover and the Hundred Mile Wilderness. What a stroke of luck, I didn't know this. I also bought food for the next few days after slackpacking. I will get my slackpack food from the hostel. We are in the Grafton Mountains right now, reportedly the toughest on the Trail. So far, I can't disagree.

The Cabin is a nice hostel in its last year of operation. Many other hikers are staying here with us tonight. For fifteen dollars a day, the hostel provides breakfast, lunch, and dinner, and the meals are hearty and delicious. A real deal. I ate until I couldn't eat another bite. I felt recharged, but still congested. I did my laundry, and showered, which also helped to make me feel like a new person.

DAY 172 SEPTEMBER 05: GRAFTON NOTCH TO EAST B HILL ROAD.
TODAY'S MILES: 10.3
TRIP MILES: 1,928.4

RW means Rheumatoid-Wrapped knees.

Last night at The Cabin we dined on a great lasagna meal with all kinds of other tasty side dishes and ice cream. After dinner, many of us watched the Packers football game. Bismarck was a huge Packers fan. He said he had grown up in Wisconsin. In the morning, we woke up to a breakfast of eggs, pancakes, bread, potatoes, sausage, and other good food.

We hit the Trail without our gear or backpacks around 8:40 a.m. on a warm and clear day. It felt great to hike with only a lightweight borrowed daypack. I started out sluggish because of the lingering head cold, but perked up as the day progressed.

I hiked with Bismarck, Hopper, and Journeymen all day and enjoyed many pleasant conversations with them. Bismarck is about five foot seven inches tall, stocky, with the biggest, fullest beard I have ever seen on the Trail. His beard dangles down to his belly. I told Bismarck about the hiker whose face and beard had been chewed by mice. Bismarck said he woke up once with mice in his beard, but hadn't gotten bitten. He thought his beard was too thick to permit mice to get to his skin, but just in case, he wears a polyester beard cover on cold nights or when sleeping in shelters.

The hike was hard as we climbed Baldpate, a 2,400-foot climb up to a 3,810-foot elevation. The views were spectacular all day, and we often turned around to look at the Whites. Then down a steep trail to Frye Notch for lunch, a descent of 1,500 feet in 1.7 miles. I wore knee braces on both knees today, which helped to reduce the knee pain.

After lunch the Trail smoothed out and we were able to hike steadily at a rate of two miles per hour. In the afternoon, the Trail was fantastic. We passed by several beautiful waterfalls and ended the day's hike at 4:00 p.m. Now I am back at The Cabin deciding if I want to take a zero day tomorrow. I am tired and the mountains in Maine are tough. It depends on the weather. Tomorrow's forecast is calling for rain in the afternoon.

DAY 173 SEPTEMBER 06: ZERO DAY.
TRIP MILES: 1928.4

RW means Relaxing at Window, Rested and Well-fed.

I didn't hike today because heavy thunderstorms were predicted. The thunderstorms held off until 5:00 p.m., but I am still glad for the zero. I feel weak. I weighed myself and discovered I had lost another two pounds, which is surprising since I feel like I am eating non-stop. My head is still congested and I napped most of the day.

In the afternoon, I used the hostel's computer to order flowers for my wife. Our 35th wedding anniversary will be in two days, on September 8th. According to my original Trail plan, I should have completed the thru-hike yesterday. Instead, I am 257 miles short and still have to cross a large section of Maine. She understands and wants me to complete my A.T. dream.

After ordering the flowers, Bismarck, Hopper, Journeymen and I went to attend a worship service at the local Catholic church. Bismarck and Hopper are both devout Catholics who plan each week's hike around a zero day in a town with a Catholic church. Their trail plans are quite an undertaking, requiring research and careful scheduling, since many of the small towns along the Trail don't have Catholic churches. They prefer to slow down, if necessary, to attend a mass, rather than increase their mileage. They aim to hike 90 miles a week or less. Bismarck and Hopper left Springer Mountain in February. Journeymen is a theologian, now retired and widowed, who once taught interfaith studies at a seminary.

After church we stopped at the all-you-can-eat pizza place in Andover and met many thru-hikers who are catching up to me. I have slowed down so much. I need to get back to hiking—two zeros and a nearo in seven days! I saw Cat and Nubbins again at the pizza place. Cat complained that he is weak from hunger and fears he will be too weak to finish the Trail at this rate. He ate nonstop, though; we all did.

While in town, I found time to mail nine days of food to Monson for the Hundred Mile Wilderness before heading back to The Cabin.

DAY 174 SEPTEMBER 07: EAST B HILL ROAD TO SOUTH ARM ROAD.
TODAY'S MILES: 10.1
TRIP MILES: 1,938.5

RW means Racing Wyman Mountain.

The past few days have been very hot and humid, but last night's storms brought cool weather and clear skies. Today is a beautiful day to hike. My knees appreciated yesterday's rest, but the Achilles tendon is still sore. I am finally getting over the congestion in my head. Eating large meals these last few days has boosted my energy level.

Last night, The Cabin was packed with thru-hikers. Most I knew, and I greatly enjoyed seeing them again. There was Racewalker, and Bliss, the Canadian girl whose tent, pack, and food sacks had all been damaged by mice in Vermont.

After breakfast, we headed out for another day of slackpacking. Bismarck, Hopper, Nubbins, Journeymen, and I started with a hike up a steady, but gentle, five-mile climb of nearly 1,500 feet. We passed several beautiful beaver ponds. On one occasion I must have startled a beaver, because it slapped the water with its tail to send a warning to the other beavers. I looked for moose, but didn't see any. Darn, would I ever see a moose? Hopper looked everywhere, sometimes venturing from the Trail to look for moose in ponds and marshes, but no luck. After several hours of hiking in a forest carpeted with soft moss, we reached the summit of Wyman Mountain, and then stopped for an early lunch at the Hall Mountain Lean-to.

After our lunch break, the Trail became much more difficult, although the forest floor remained heavily moss-covered. We went down a steep 1,600-foot drop in 1.4 miles to Sawyer Notch, then immediately back up a very steep climb to the top of Moody

Mountain. We rose 1,400 feet in elevation in only 0.8 miles. Not a high mountain at 2,440 feet, but like all the mountains in this stretch, it's separated and stands alone without ridge lines to connect it. The Trail was so steep in this section that ladders, iron foot-rungs and handrails were installed in the particularly steep sections.

We made great time, and by 3:00 p.m. we were finished for the day and heading back to The Cabin. Tonight we were having a great feast. The Cabin was serving surf and turf (lobster and steak). Incredible! Too bad this is their last year of operation. The owners are elderly and decided to shut down the business after this season. They will remain open a few more weeks, and then close their doors for good.

I forgot to mention that my attempts to repair the ripped crotch of my pants didn't hold today. I was hiking commando-style when the entire crotch ripped open while straining to scramble up a ten-foot cliff face. Hopper, who wore a long skirt and preferred to hike at the rear of the group, was an unfortunate witness. My "private" fanny pack was exposed. The Cabin has a sewing machine, and Hopper volunteered to sew my pants back together. Using brilliant white thread, she stitched many seams to piece together the tattered green fabric in the crotch area of my pants. I have my very own "white blaze" now that really draws the attention of other hikers to the fly of my pants. Laughter usually ensues when they become self-conscious about staring at my "white blaze."

DAY 175 SEPTEMBER 08: SOUTH ARM ROAD TO ME 17.
TODAY'S MILES: 13.2
TRIP MILES: 1,951.7

RW means Right Way, some, a name given to me by Bliss, the Canadian girl.

I feel better today. Maybe I have finally shaken off the sniffles and cold. I hiked with the same group today: Bliss, Nubbins, Journeymen, Bismarck, and Hopper. We hiked up Old Blue Mountain first thing, and later Bemis Mountain. Both were hard climbs, but not the hardest part of the day. The weather was perfect for hiking, but the constant rocks and roots on the trail made every step slow. It took nine hours to hike 13.2 miles. Roots snagged and grabbed at my feet all day, trying to trip me and take me down. We all managed to get through without a tumble.

Hopper told me about the time when she was cowboy camping and woke up in the middle of the night with a great weight on her feet. Mustering her courage, she beamed a flashlight at the end of her sleeping bag. A porcupine was curled up and sleeping on the foot of her bag. The flashlight startled the sleeping porcupine, and Hopper froze as they both stared at each other. Slowly, the porcupine got up and walked away. Hopper thought there might have been quill pricks in her sleeping bag, but there wasn't, not even one hole.

I saw my first moose today while driving in the shuttle car back to the hostel. Not an encounter in the wild as I had hoped, but at least I saw a moose. The hostel is packed with hikers; some are sleeping in their tents on the lawn because the beds are filled. I recognized a few, but most were young hikers who started in May, months after me. I talked to them briefly but wasn't in the mood for conversation. It was my wedding anniversary and I had planned to be finished by now. I wanted to be home and done with the hike. I called my wife, and she cheered me up. We made plans to meet at the end of the Hundred Mile Wilderness, just before climbing Mt. Katahdin.

In the evening, eight of us watched the movie "The Last of the Mohicans." Throughout the movie, side comments and snide remarks erupted at nearly every outdoor scene. We were shocked by the lack of roots and rocks, and the actors never carried food and water. They seemed to run everywhere they went; never got cold at night; didn't run out of ammunition; and generally made outdoor living look like a breeze. We all wanted to hike like that!

DAY 176 SEPTEMBER 09: ME 17 TO PIAZZA ROCK LEAN-TO.
TODAY'S MILES: 15.0
TRIP MILES: 1,966.7

RW means Rangeley Walk by, because I didn't stop at Rangeley, Maine, today.

Journeymen, Bismarck, Nubbins, and I hit the Trail late at 9:30 a.m. because of the many booked shuttle trips. We had to wait for a car to return before we could leave the hostel. Hopper didn't join us because she stayed to help the elderly owners. She would catch up to us in a few days in Stratton, and then come back to finish the section she missed after climbing Mt. Katahdin. I learned that Hopper and Bismarck have hiked the Appalachian Trail many times, as much as seven hikes between the two of them. They are good friends with the owners of The Cabin hostel and usually spend a month or more every year working for their stay at The Cabin. The elderly owners really appreciated their volunteer efforts.

Several years ago, Bismarck decided to give up the rat race after his wife died. He sold everything he owned, including a successful business, and hit the Appalachian Trail. He works briefly during the cold winter months, and then hikes the Trail for the rest of the year. When Hopper's husband died, she walked the Trail with his ashes as a memorial and celebration of his life. Bismarck and Hopper met afterwards on the Trail and continue to enjoy the A.T. lifestyle together. They both have the resources to live a comfortable urban life, but prefer the active outdoor life of a hiker.

The Trail was kind today, with fewer ups and downs, and less rocks and roots. Scenic ponds full of clear, clean water kept coming into view. Just before lunch, the three of us were hiking, stretched out, in a long single file. Bismarck was in the lead, Journeymen in the middle, followed by me in last place.

I heard Bismarck yell, "Something just ran between my legs!" Then I heard Journeymen say, "Me, too!" Suddenly, a terrified rabbit ran between my legs and dashed off. A movie scene from Monty Python and the Holy Grail instantly came to mind, the one with the crazed Killer Rabbit of Caerbannog.

Something had been chasing it, and when I turned, I heard Bismarck yell again, "WHAT IS THAT?" After finally meeting up with Bismarck, he told me that the weasel-like creature chasing the rabbit had almost crashed into his legs. He didn't know what it was. Once the creature realized we were staying on the Trail, it gave Bismarck a frustrated look and dashed off into the woods. We took a quick break and decided to ask around town when we got to Stratton. Maybe someone could help us figure out what type of animal it was.

I covered more than two miles per hour and still took an hour off for lunch. I haven't moved this fast since Vermont!

Starting tomorrow, though, I enter the most difficult part of Maine.

DAY 177 SEPTEMBER 10: PIAZZA ROCK LEAN-TO TO POPLAR RIDGE LEAN-TO.
TODAY'S MILES: 8.9
TRIP MILES: 1,975.6

RW means Rock Whacker.

The morning was cold and dark, and I could see my breath. Days are getting shorter already.

Our hike started with a 2,500-foot climb up Mt. Saddleback. Halfway up, I crossed the tree line and enjoyed fantastic views of the surrounding mountains. While climbing, though, Mt. Saddleback began to fall and I saved all my hiking companions' lives by catching the mountain with my face. Bismarck, who was yards ahead, heard me loudly yell, "Ouch!" but didn't think much of it until he saw me climb over the lip of the cliff. Blood covered my face. We cleaned off the blood and then continued down and up Mt Horn, and then down and up Mt. Saddleback Junior. All in all, a very tough day of steep ups and downs. I started to wonder if I would wake up with a black eye in the morning.

I saw a moose but couldn't get a picture; it ran away too fast. Who would think a moose could run so quickly through this rocky, mountainous terrain? And why was a moose on top of a mountain? It must be normal, though, because moose droppings appeared frequently in the higher elevations, far away from any water source that I could see.

We stopped at Poplar Ridge Lean to for the night at 2.00 p.m. and debated about hiking on. Rain is predicted for tonight and tomorrow, so we decided to stop for the day and stay in the shelter.

Nubbins was lagging behind. When she caught up to us, she decided to stay at the shelter, too. Once Nubbins summits Mt. Katahdin, she plans to catch a ride south and hike another six hundred miles through Virginia, North Carolina, Tennessee and Georgia in order to reach Springer Mountain and complete the Trail. Nubbins had started hiking northbound in Virginia and plans to hike southbound in October to avoid Maine's winter weather. At 69 years old, and weighing only 110 pounds, her pack is heavier than mine, and she can still hike the miles. What a strong woman! Nubbins has a doctorate in theology. All four of the people I'm now hiking with are devout Christians, yet we rarely speak of religion.

Three shelter maintenance workers from Maryland stopped by and talked a long time about their work. Their names are John, Jack and Henry. I think Maryland has the best shelters on the Trail. Our shelter is crowded tonight, and many more hikers are camped nearby. We all stopped early due to the threat of rain.

This shelter was the last known location of a 66-year-old section hiker named Geraldine Largay, AKA Inchworm. Inchworm had camped here on July 22, 2013. On that day, the weather had been wet and stormy. Afterwards, she disappeared and has never been found.

Violent crime on the Appalachian Trail is hard to track. Some murder victims weren't necessarily hikers. Occasionally, there is trail talk about death and murder, but death usually occurs from heart attacks, injuries, etc. Violent crime happens, but not often. The Trail is, in general, safer than most people's hometowns. Still, anywhere there are people, there's violence. My unreliable A.T. crime figure is eleven murdered hikers since 1974. In all cases except for one, the solved murders were committed by predatory opportunists from nearby roads, not fellow hikers.

DAY 178 SEPTEMBER 11: POPLAR RIDGE LEAN-TO TO SPAULDING MOUNTAIN LEAN-TO.
TODAY'S MILES: 8.0
TRIP MILES: 1,983.6

RW means Rain and Wind.

I woke up without a black eye from yesterday's encounter with the mountain. Today is the first day of my annual fall fishing trip back home with my fishing buddies. I'd be there if it weren't for being three weeks behind schedule.

It rained last night and was still raining when I left camp at 7:00 a.m. It looked like a miserable day to hike, gray and overcast with poor visibility, but the trail wasn't bad and I made great time. By 11:30 a.m. I had hiked eight miles and was calling it quits at Spaulding Mountain Lean-to. The rain was just too much, and I was cold and wet.

Hikers were already in the lean-to for the night. The wind was gusting at least 30 miles per hour. The rain came in waves all day. It would drizzle for a while, fooling me into thinking it was over. Then it would downpour. I was so glad to get out of rain and huddle in my sleeping bag.

I am just sitting out the rain. A short day again, and I am getting concerned about completing the hike. I will stop at Stratton tomorrow, only thirteen miles from here. I could have made it, but today's weather is miserable. Despite wearing rain gear, my clothes are soaked.

I had my second river ford today but was able to rock hop across without getting my feet wet. We have been lucky—the rivers are still low and easy to cross even with all this rain. The rivers have ropes attached from one side to the other for hikers to hang onto when the water is high. The forest is mostly spruce with some birch. Birch leaves are turning yellow, and the Trail is littered with their leaves.

Tonight's forecast is cold, maybe into the high thirties, with high winds and rain. We always know what the forecast will be because Bismarck carries a weather radio that never fails to pick up a signal. When cell phones don't work, his radio does. I didn't put up my tent like Nubbins, and I may regret it. The wind is blowing through every crack, and there's a strong breeze in the shelter. I will eat extra food this evening to lighten my pack and then head into Stratton for a zero day and resupply. I am so hungry.

DAY 179 SEPTEMBER 12: SPAULDING MOUNTAIN LEAN-TO TO STRATTON.
TODAY'S MILES: 13.6
TRIP MILES: 1,997.1

RW means a Restaurant named White Wolf. That's the place where I ate dinner tonight.

Last night was very cold. The shelter was located at 3,139 feet. It must have been in the thirties, and with the strong wind, the wind chill could have been below freezing. I am going to have to start sleeping with my water filter again so that it does not freeze at night. I got up this morning a bit chilly and put on my wet clothes. I made some hot coffee and hot oatmeal, which helped to warm me up. I am glad to have my stove back, even though I hate carrying the weight.

The weather was clear and we had a beautiful sunrise. The Trail was very wet, though, and I wore long pants, plus most of my clothing, for protection from the cold and damp. As usual, the morning started with a stiff uphill climb over Spaulding Mountain, rising from almost 900 feet to 4000 feet in only 0.8 miles. Then, over Sugar Loaf Mountain, and a 1,500-foot drop to the Carrabassett River. This was supposed to be a river ford, but to my great pleasure, there was a board across that part of the river, and I didn't get my feet wet.

Because I had an early start today, I had time to sit on a rock in the sun for over an hour and wait for Bismarck and Journeymen to arrive. It was beautiful, sitting there and looking at the trees and noticing the colors start to change in the Crocker Mountains. At the river was a posted sign asking for information about Inchworm, the missing hiker who disappeared in 2013. Bismarck thought she may have tried crossing this river during flood stage and was washed away. Nobody knows, but the search continues.

From there, we continued up a two-mile path rising 2,000 vertical feet up to Crocker Mountain, 4,228 feet above sea level. Even though it was only 2:00 p.m., I could see my breath at the top of the mountain. After climbing down, a woman parked on the road next to the trailhead offered to give us a ride into town, and we accepted. We were in our hotel by 6:00 p.m.

Hopper is here and ready to hike again. I hung out for a while with them, and then went to eat about 7:30 p.m. Hopper told us the FBI came to the hostel yesterday hoping to get some information about Inchworm's disappearance. It is good to know the search is still active more than a year after her disappearance.

While at dinner, Nubbins came in and we sat together. It was dark by the time she had gotten to the trailhead, and she was unsuccessful at hitchhiking into town. After hiking with her headlamp turned on so that passing cars could see her, she finally got her cell phone to work and called the motel. The owner of the motel rushed out to pick her up.

As we ate our dinner in the restaurant's bar room, I noticed a stuffed animal perched above the row of liquor bottles. And there it was, looking menacing—the strange, weasel-like animal I couldn't identify. I found Bismarck and showed him the stuffed animal. He confirmed that it was the same animal we had encountered on the trail a few days ago. The bartender told us it was a pine marten, and very rare.

DAY 180 SEPTEMBER 13: ZERO DAY.
TRIP MILES 1,997.1

RW means Rotten Waders. My feet keep getting wet in these new boots, and I wish I had waders or waterproof boots.

Zero day. We are now through the hardest part of Maine's mountains. Only a few more mountains ahead, and then we should start hitting the flat lands. I read that Achin' got off the Trail on September 8th and says he is done trying this year.

The weather forecast calls for cold temperatures all week, with lows in the thirties and highs in the fifties and sixties. This morning the fog is so thick, I can't see across the street.

We did our usual chores: laundry, grocery shopping, mapping out the next few days on the Trail, then eating, sleeping, and eating. Hopper, Bismarck and Journeymen went to a church service, but I passed today. I was tired and just wanted to nap. I called my wife and told her that if all goes well, I hoped to summit Mt. Katahdin on September 29th.

DAY 181 SEPTEMBER 14: STRATTON TO STAFFORD NOTCH CAMPSITE.
TODAY'S MILES: 10.4
TRIP MILES: 2,007.5

RW means Roaring Wind.

We left the restaurant after a nice breakfast and got to the Trail late, about 9:00 a.m. The day started cold, nearly forty degrees, and the wind was gusting. The wind in these mountains is never halfway. It is either very mild or very strong, and today it was very strong. The sky is steel gray and looks like November.

The five of us climbed three major mountains over 4,000 feet today. We began with a 2,400-foot climb up South Horn, then Bigalow Mountain, West Peak, and then Avery Peak. They were all above the tree line. The climbs were exhausting, made even harder by strong northwestern Canadian winds. At noon it was 40 degrees, not counting the wind chill.

The clouds hung low on the mountains all day, and we all wore rain gear to protect ourselves from the wind and cold. At one point, I was wearing all my clothes and gloves. Making matters worse, my nose dripped all day.

Early in the day I passed the 2000-mile mark and made a small sign out of sticks. I can hardly believe it. I am averaging just 11.1 miles a day, yet my body says it is more. It really is. Nearly every water source, town, hostel, shelter, and source of food is located off the Trail, adding additional miles every day. Compounding this are climbs that equal the same amount of effort for every thousand feet as walking two miles on flat ground. My body knows I have walked and expended far more than 2,000 miles of energy to get here. We are nearly out of the mountains, with only one smaller mountain to climb tomorrow. Then, we should be on easier terrain.

Tonight I am camped at Stafford Notch campsite. To get to this campsite, I walked by many boulders the size of apartment buildings. It felt like I was walking through part of Mahoosuc Notch. This campsite is situated below a high cliff. All of the huge boulders had fallen off the cliff wall over time.

It has been awhile since I slept in my tent. I am happy to be in it again, even though I am sleeping on a sharp angle between a boulder and a tree. This cold night should sting less inside my tent. The wind is still howling and the temperature is falling quickly. I have decided to sleep with my water filter in case it drops below freezing.

Camped next to me are two young thru-hikers. One is carrying a small sword, called a katana. He said it was given to him by another hiker in Damascus who had gotten tired of carrying it. After finishing a bowl of pot, he unrolled his sleeping bag and cowboy camped.

As we sat beside the campfire, I told Bismarck about a secret I'd carried around with me since returning to the Trail. We talked a long time, and he shared stories about his many thru-hikes. Journeymen and Nubbins finally came hiking in. Journeymen has been accompanying Nubbins most of the time now.

DAY 182 SEPTEMBER 15: STAFFORD NOTCH CAMPSITE TO WEST CARRY POND LEAN-TO.
TODAY'S MILES: 12.6
TRIP MILES: 2,020.1

RW means Richly Warm.

Last night was as cold as feared, but it didn't fall below freezing. I hit the Trail wearing most of my clothes. The day soon warmed up, though, and I hiked in my tee shirt for the rest of the day. The sun shone all day and the wind was calm, but the temperature was still in the fifties. We climbed the last mountain in the Bigalows and are now hiking on mostly flat lowlands. The pond is beautiful, and many houses and resorts are built along the lake. Loons are calling and the sound is so wonderful. I haven't heard many birds since early Vermont. It is nice to be low enough to hear birds again.

Today I ran into Mastermind sitting alone next to the Trail. As we filled our water bottles at a clear stream, he told me he was carrying the ashes of his late wife and spreading them along the Trail. He was still grieving, but said the hike was helping. He knew that when the last of her ashes were thrown to the wind on Mt. Katahdin, he would find peace and closure. I left him as he sat staring at the river.

Not many miles were covered today, but we were all very tired. I am wearing down and my energy level was low today. My Achilles tendon and knees hurt a lot. We stopped at West Carry Pond Lean-to, located at 1,345 feet. We are out of the mountains.

It is warmer here. I am sleeping in the shelter because we plan to hit the Trail very early tomorrow, and rain is forecast for tonight. Although I prefer sleeping in my tent, I don't want to take it down in the rain, and then carry a wet tent in my pack.

DAY 183 SEPTEMBER 16: WEST CARRY POND LEAN-TO TO CARATUNK.
TODAY'S MILES: 14.0
TRIP MILES: 2,034.1

RW means River Wading.

Last night was warmer than the past few days, mostly because of the lower elevation. Nubbins and I hit the Trail at daybreak, 6:20 a.m., in our rain gear. It had started to drizzle earlier about 4:45 a.m. and didn't stop until eleven o'clock. We made good progress, and many parts of the Trail were pleasant despite the rain. The temperature stayed in the fifties. This forest is young and looks like it was clear cut for logging in the past ten to twenty years.

Hopper told me yesterday how lucky we are to avoid the logging. When she first hiked this section of the A.T. years ago, huge log piles covered the Trail. As they hiked through the logging work zones, felled trees crashed to the ground all around them, and she despaired at seeing the carnage.

We stopped for lunch at Pierce Pond Lean-to, and Bismarck told me the story of a thru-hiker who drowned in Pierce Pond in June 2012. A thru-hiker named Paul Bernhardt, twenty years old, stopped at the shelter after a long day of hiking and took a swim in the pond. His legs cramped too far from shore, and he drowned.

At 2:00 p.m. we arrived at the Kennebec River, where we canoe ferried across the river. The river is wide and dangerous, and the many dams on the river release water at unpredictable times. While waiting for my turn to cross, one of the dams must have released water, because the river rose about a foot during the short time I waited. There were ten hikers waiting for the two-person canoe, so I waited forty minutes for my turn.

After crossing, we hiked to the post office in the little town of Caratunk, where we called the Sterling Inn, a bed and breakfast place. I recommend it. The owner drove the five of us, plus Loon, a young Japanese hiker who recently moved to the United States, to a good restaurant down the road. The hostel had a nicely provisioned backpacker grocery store, so I loaded up with food for the hike to Monson. Tomorrow I start for Monson and plan to be there on Friday.

DAY 184 SEPTEMBER 17: CARATUNK TO BALD MOUNTAIN BROOK SHELTER.
TODAY'S MILES: 14.7
TRIP MILES: 2,048.8

RW means Rusty Wonder, a name given today by Walkintree, a formerly deaf, three-time thru-hiker who recently had a cochlear implant and can now hear.

Walkintree loved listening to the loons and talked at length about how wonderful it was to hear the sound of the birds. After breakfast, we hit the Trail. Nubbins stayed back and decided to leave several hours later. Journeymen decided to hike alone, so he also left later. Loon left with us, but is very fast and quickly disappeared.

I walked ahead and alone most of the morning. It was cool, but the light through the trees and fog was stunning. I took lots of pictures of the light-rays through the trees. The Trail was a mixed bag today. I had to high-step for hours because of the roots that pulled, tugged, twisted and grabbed, all intent on tripping me.

There were also nice, flat sections on the Trail, covered in spruce needles as soft and smooth as a carpet. That was wonderful. The rocks are changing from granite to a black slate that is slippery even when dry. The trees remain mostly spruce, with birch and maple mixed in. Hardwoods are getting more colorful every day. I'm looking forward to seeing the changing fall colors of New England.

I ran into Gray Ghost today, who is flip-flopping due to injuries. He was hiking with Rob, the guy I hiked with after Hot Springs. When Gray Ghost got injured, he was forced off the trail for five weeks. The three of us hiked together and walked by several beaver ponds. After the cool morning, the day turned into an excellent hiking day under a beautiful blue sky.

Now that we are temporarily out of the mountains, and at a lower elevation, hiking is so much easier. We climbed only one mountain today, Pleasant Pond Mountain, at 2,470 feet—which isn't very high compared to our recent mountain climbs. Still, it was quite a climb since Curutunk is situated at 520 feet above sea level, lower than the elevation of my house in Illinois.

I am not doing high miles because of the tough mountains. These past few weeks have taken a lot out of me. I am tired and sore and using these easy days to try to heal before entering the Hundred Mile Wilderness. Even if I did hike faster, I would save only a few days. Why push myself for so little gain? There are only 136.5 miles to go. A section hiker named Indy from Kokomo, Indiana, is here with the three of us.

I disturbed Hopper quite a bit today. I kept trying to strike up a conversation with her, but she wouldn't respond. Later, she told me I had interrupted her silent prayer chain. Apparently I had done this before, and she was getting tired of it. In my defense, I didn't know she was praying or meditating every day, especially in the afternoon.

DAY 185 SEPTEMBER 18: BALD MOUNTAIN BROOK SHELTER TO HORSESHOE CANYON LEAN-TO.
TODAY'S MILES: 13.0
TRIP MILES: 2,061.8

RW means Reeling Wind. It's very windy today.

This is the first day of my seventh month on the Trail (six months and one day). Last night was pleasant and I slept with my sleeping bag open most of the night. Again I decided to leave early, and I hiked for an hour alone before Hopper and Bismarck caught up to me. By then I was well on the way to climbing the 1,300-foot rise to the top of Moxie Bald Mountain, which stands at 2,629 feet above sea level.

The climb was long and as we neared the top, clouds moved in and the wind started to blow hard. It was cold and windy, and we had no views. After spending a few minutes on top, we hurried down the mountain. When we came down a thousand feet, the weather warmed up and the sky cleared. I was able to hike in a tee-shirt but still wore long pants.

The Trail was again a mix of rocks, roots, and spruce needles, and there was evidence that the Trail had recently been relocated. It is easy to recognize recently moved sections of the Trail. There aren't many roots and rocks, and the Trail isn't eroded into a shallow ditch. Around noon we came to our first ford of the day and were able to rock hop across without getting our feet wet. It seemed like we kept passing many beautiful ponds, each one even more stunning than the last. Such a beautiful area! All along the way, I took pictures. The fall colors are really coming on strong now.

We hiked along the banks of the West Branch of the wonderful Piscataquis River for miles. Late in the afternoon we had to wade across the river, and this time my luck ran out. I carried a cheap pair of hard plastic camp shoes for situations like this, but they would slip off my feet in the water. To remedy this, I purchased a pair of shoe strings in Stratton and used them to secure the camp shoes to my feet during river crossings.

I took off my boots, tied the camp shoes to my feet, and waded across. It was slow and shallow, but my homemade shoe straps worked. Surprisingly, the water wasn't too cold. It gave me a chance to wash up. Still, the river must be dangerous in high water. A rope was stretched across the river for hikers to hang onto.

Soon after the river crossing, we arrived at Horseshoe Canyon Lean-to. I was ahead of everyone and sat by the river soaking my feet and taking pictures of a small waterfall. The others passed me, but I stayed for another fifteen minutes just enjoying the colors.

My feet hurt a lot and I needed to pace myself. I was breaking down and in pain all the time now. My anxiety was growing. It had shifted from worrying about running out of time, to whether my body would break down before the end. I had the time, so I rested as much as possible and enjoyed the views.

When I arrived at the shelter, to my surprise, Journeymen was already there. Apparently he'd left very early in the morning from his campsite and passed us before we even started hiking for the day. Loon was there, and Indy, Karate Kid, and Heike. Karate Kid is a superfast hiker doing high-mileage days.

Heike is a middle-aged veterinarian from Germany, hiking the Trail alone. She is very interesting. While talking about food with her, she was amazed at how much weight she had lost, yet how much she ate. She said before the hike, a six-inch pizza was too much for her to eat, but now she was eating a twelve-inch pizza and leaving the table hungry.

The temperature started to get cold fast, and by 7:30 p.m., everybody was huddled in their sleeping bags. Our breath was heavy, and even the fire we built didn't generate much heat. We had hung our food far away from the shelter because mice were already active at 6:30 p.m. The mice knew how to get inside food bags hung in the shelter. Now we hang our food out in the woods and hope the mice won't travel that far to find it.

Journeymen told us he barely slept the night before. He made the unfortunate decision to keep his food bag with him inside the tent. Mice crawled all night long on his tent. He stayed awake chasing them off, fearing they would chew holes if he slept. He swore never to do that again. Besides being tired, his stomach was now upset. He had run out of water purification tablets a few days ago. Even though we filtered water for him whenever we saw him, he often hiked alone and followed behind. As a result, when Journeymen ran out of water, he drank directly out of ponds. We feared he had Giardia.

DAY 186 SEPTEMBER 19: HORSESHOE CANYON LEAN-TO TO MONSON.
TODAY'S MILES: 9.0
TRIP MILES: 2,070.8

RW means Ready for the Wilderness. Only 114.5 miles to go!

We all shivered inside the shelter last night instead of tenting, because the campsites were so steeply pitched. Karate Kid's fancy watch said it was still summer and twenty degrees outside. We thought his watch might be broken, since nothing appeared to be frozen. Last night had been extremely cold, though. We learned later on that there had been a heavy killing frost in Monson, and the temperature had fallen to 28 degrees. A near-record cold, even for up here!

We all got up at pre-dawn and packed. I ate the last bagel and used up all of my fuel to make coffee. I was cold and stiff, even with a winter-weight sleeping bag. During the middle of the night, frigid air forced me to get up and put on a shirt and pair of socks. Usually I only slept in underwear for comfort, which is fine inside my tent, but caused problems in the shelters. Shelter stays required putting on clothes while still inside my sleeping bag every morning, and whenever I needed to get up and relieve myself during the night.

At daybreak, we all hit the Trail with empty or nearly-empty food bags and no fuel. We traveled very light, certain we would make Monson by lunchtime. I left before the others because I was so cold. Wearing most of my clothes, I hiked alone for over an hour and stumbled along the rooty trail until my legs warmed up. The forest was very quiet. When the sun finally shone through the trees, it lifted my spirits and brought warmth to the day.

After a while I came to the East Branch of the Piscataquis River and faced another ford. I studied the river and found a place downstream where, with care, I was able to cross over on a couple of rocks and fallen tree. Then I waited for the rest to show up. Loon and Bismarck followed my path and had no trouble. Journeymen partly fell in, and Hopper just put on her camp shoes and waded across. The fun started when Karate Kid came by and tried to follow in my footsteps without trekking poles. He started to lose his balance in the middle of the river, so Journeymen threw Karate Kid his trekking poles.

You can guess the rest—the first pole landed eight feet short and got stuck like a javelin. The other pole went wide of the mark in deep water and sank to the bottom. Journeymen had purposely thrown the poles upriver because he thought they would float down to Karate Kid. Trekking poles don't float, in case you are interested. After several hilarious attempts to recover the trekking poles, Hopper simply waded back into the river, retrieved them, and then helped Karate Kid cross the river.

We kept on hiking and made it to our shuttle pickup point by 11:30 a.m. We drove to Shaw's in Monson for the night. For days we had been talking about barbeque, and planned to go to the only barbeque joint in town that night. Unfortunately, the owners were on vacation and the place was closed. We were crushed and went to a local restaurant for hamburgers.

Shaw's is a nice place, and Heike, Karate Kid, and Loon are staying here with us, along with other hikers. I have a nice room to myself here, and I am thoroughly enjoying the decadent luxury of a hot shower, heated room, comfortable bed, and good company.

Journeymen was seriously ill today with an upset stomach. It was also his birthday. He is 65 today. We planned to zero here tomorrow and start the Hundred Mile Wilderness on Sunday. Luckily, I have already mailed the food drop for the Hundred Mile Wilderness to this location. There isn't much as far as grocery shopping goes in this town.

DAY 187 SEPTEMBER 20: ZERO DAY.
TRIP MILES: 2,070.8

RW means Rope Warrior, because of the ropes used at the ford crossings.

Today is a zero day and I am resting and eating a lot of food. My feet, knees, and Achilles tendon are very sore, and I am now taking about 1500 mg. of ibuprofen daily just to walk. In the mornings, I hobble around for fifteen minutes before I can walk normally. New pains started yesterday in my left hip and tibialis anterior tendon. I iced my ankles and knees and stayed off them as much as possible. I am concerned about tackling the Hundred Mile Wilderness with so many injuries.

Tomorrow I enter the Hundred Mile Wilderness with Hopper and Bismarck. Heike and Loon will probably leave with us. Journeymen is still feeling poorly and will decide tomorrow if he can hike. Nubbins arrived today and is still considering a zero tomorrow. All I know for sure is that three to five of us are heading out to cross the Wilderness in seven hard days. Day one will be full of many short, but steep, ridges that will be exhausting and slow us down.

The following three days of mountain hiking will also be low mileage. Afterwards, we head down to the lowlands. Hopefully the rain holds off and the lowlands won't turn into marshes. It is almost the end of summer, and the blackfly season is over. The recent spell of dry weather might help us to make up time and do high miles in the lowlands. There will be several river fords. According to the weather forecast, there is a 60 percent chance of rain on Sunday, but the temperature is forecasted to warm up to normal.

Bismarck and Hopper are veteran A.T. hikers. They have both thru-hiked before, and have completed sections of the A.T. as well. Between the two of them, they have hiked the Trail at least six times. I am following their lead through the Wilderness and feel lucky to have met such experienced hikers. I am not sure if I will make it.

We arranged for a food cache to be dropped off four days out. I will carry four days' worth of provisions, and then locate the cache. When I was staying at The Cabin, I had purchased enough food for nine days and had it mailed here. Since then I changed my mind and will only carry eight days' worth of food on the seven-day trip, with the extra ration carried in case of emergency. The remaining ninth days' worth of food was donated to a hiker box. Carrying less food should help increase my mileage and improve my chances for making it through to the other side. If all goes as planned, I will be in Millinocket next Saturday. On Sunday, I'll hike ten miles into Baxter State Park, and then summit Mt. Katahdin on Monday, September 29th.

Cat arrived today and confided that he was broke. As a result, he has to rummage and scavenge for food during his last push to Mt. Katahdin. Cat is planning to cross the Wilderness and climb Mt. Katahdin in less time than me, because he doesn't have enough food to hike for another day.

Monson is a small and friendly town. Shaw's is an excellent hostel and serves a good breakfast. It's the only meal they offer, and it costs extra. This hostel is for sale at the moment. The other hostel in town is called the Lake Shore. It has a restaurant that is only open for lunch and dinner. Their food is good—a little expensive, as all the food seems to be up here—but the places are always crowded.

DAY 188 SEPTEMBER 21: MONSON TO LONG POND STREAM LEAN-TO.
TODAY'S MILES: 15.1
TRIP MILES: 2,085.9

RW means Rain in Wilderness.

Only 99.4 miles to Katahdin! Today is the first day of autumn. I started hiking on March 18th, just a few days before winter's end. I have hiked in all four seasons on this adventure!

The months on the Trail are taking a toll on my camera phone. It worked randomly today. Just like my body, the camera phone is breaking down. I hoped to take a lot of pictures of the Wilderness, but it looks like I may end up with nothing, given the failing condition of my camera.

Hopper, Bismarck, Loon, and I finally started the Trail about 8:40 a.m. after a great breakfast. Journeymen and Nubbins both planned to head out later in the day, so we left without them. The day's hiking was not difficult, but the constant little ups and downs added up to a fair amount of elevation changes.

The forest is magnificent and getting more beautiful every day. The colors of the trees and plants are really coming on strong. I hiked along ponds, lakes and streams filled with water that is deep blue and clear. Waterfalls cascaded into streams. The sound of rushing water fills the air. I hiked faster than the rest and spent most of the day alone on the Trail.

It started drizzling around 1:30 p.m. with occasional rain, but no downpours. Just enough rain to make sure everything got good and wet and slippery all afternoon. Black slate rocks glistened, warning me not to trust their foothold or risk a muddy and painful fall. I fell twice before arriving at the Wilson Valley Lean-to about 2:30 p.m., where I waited for the others to show up.

About 3:00 p.m., Bismarck, Hopper and Heike arrived and got inside the lean-to. We sat and waited for half an hour to see if the rain would stop. It didn't. Bismarck ribbed me about the secret I had told him a few days earlier and I got peeved, so I decided to leave and hike to the next shelter.

The rain was light and it was too early to stop anyway, so I put on my new chartreuse poncho and hiked another 4.7 miles to the next shelter, Long Pond Stream Lean-to. The hike was wet, but not bad, and I hiked alongside a scenic stream with many waterfalls. I often thought about setting up camp next to the stream, where there were many nice camping spots.

I forded three streams. The first was an easy rock hop. The second required wading. While wading, my foot slipped and wedged itself into the rocks. As I write this entry, my foot and toes hurt a lot, and I wonder how they will feel in the morning. The third ford was another rock hop, but the rocks were slippery, and my left leg sunk up to the knee in the water. In soaking boots, I walked to the next shelter. Upon arrival, I immediately hung out my boots and socks to dry.

Cat was already in the shelter, and soon Indy and Heike arrived. We were cozy and dry. Heike said that Bismarck and Hopper were staying where they were, and Journeymen and Nubbins joined up with them and called it quits due to the rain. We ate and talked about the Wilderness and our final day, when we planned to climb Mt. Katahdin. We were all excited to be nearing the end.

DAY 189 SEPTEMBER 22: LONG POND STREAM LEAN-TO TO CHAIRBACK GAP LEAN-TO.
TODAY'S MILES: 10.9
TRIP MILES 2,096.8

RW means Reaching Wonderful.

The countdown continues—only 88.5 miles left. Last night was warm and rainy. The rain started to downpour at 5:30 a.m., so everybody in the shelter decided to sleep in. The morning was incredibly dark and I wanted to wait until I could see some daylight before hiking. The rain stopped about 6:30 a.m., but the forest was soaked and the dripping water from the trees felt just like rain.

We packed up slowly, and by 8:15 a.m., I was hiking in my chartreuse poncho. I wore the poncho now because the rain suit is just too hot. The poncho provides plenty of ventilation and still keeps me dry. I used the rain jacket now as a camp jacket on cold nights. Besides, wearing this bright color, hunters will know I am not a moose. It's moose hunting season, and several hunters have already been sighted walking on the Trail on their way to a hunting spot.

The Trail was wet, and large mud puddles slowed me down. I leaped and walked around them whenever possible, but my feet were still soaked. I could hear the all-too-familiar sound of squishy socks with every step. I began an all-day routine of climbing and descending steep, slippery black slate rocks, and fell several times. There were many small cliffs, six to ten feet in height—very tiring.

I climbed Barren Mountain, Fourth Mountain, Mt. Three-and-a-Half, Third Mountain, and Columbus Mountain. I never did find out why the mountains are numbered this way. In the afternoon, a strong, cold north wind gusted and the clouds closed in, dark and threatening. The forecasted cold front was announcing its arrival in a dramatic way.

When we put together our trail plan for the Hundred Mile Wilderness, Chairback Gap Lean-to was our proposed second-day stopping point. So when I arrived at 3:00 p.m. I decided to wait for Hopper and Bismarck, hoping they would hike the extra miles to catch up. The cold wind was blowing directly into the shelter, so I found a nice, protected flat spot to set up my tent. Heike and Cat passed by without stopping. They planned to hike at least another five miles and reach their food cache. They needed to make it through the Hundred Mile Wilderness in six days.

Around five o'clock, Mad Jack showed up with his wife. Mad Jack started the A.T. one day before me, on March 17th. We had bumped into each other many times on the Trail. A week ago, Mad Jack fell while climbing Little Bigalow Mountain and hit his head so hard that he knocked himself out. Other hikers found him lying on the ground and gave him assistance. He went to a hospital, where he received half a dozen stitches, and then got right back on the Trail. He is my age, I think, and likeable. Mad Jack and his wife set up for the night in the shelter.

About dusk, Hopper and Bismarck arrived exhausted and set up in the shelter, too. Indy hiked in later and rigged up his ground cloth as a tarp near the shelter. He had stopped carrying his tent to save weight and was counting on fewer hikers to fill up the shelters at this late date. The sun set early and winds howled when I crawled into my sleeping bag at 7:00 p.m. I was very preoccupied with the condition of my phone/camera, since it hadn't worked most of the day. I tried my best to keep it dry. My camping spot is perfect—level and out of the wind, with a thick mound of pine needles as soft as a mattress.

DAY 190 SEPTEMBER 23: CHAIRBACK GAP LEAN-TO TO LOGAN BROOK LEAN-TO.
TODAY'S MILES: 17.1
TRIP MILES: 2,113.9

RW means Risky Window.

Only 71.4 miles to go! Last night turned out well enough for me in my protected tent location, but the others complained of a miserably cold, windy night. Even though the ground was wet, I stayed dry. I love my Big Agnes UL2 tent.

I got up very early, intent on making it a long day. I told Hopper and Bismarck about my plans, and they said it was unlikely they would hike that far because of the mountainous terrain. I felt strong though, and rested, ready to tackle the Trail today. I was going to prove I was still capable of finishing the hike, despite all my pain.

The Trail accepted my challenge. Yesterday, it had been a battle between me and the Trail, and the Trail got the better of me several times. Today I was determined to get my advantage back. I left before daybreak with my headlamp beaming and watched a beautiful sunrise as I headed down the morning shadow of the mountain. Thick clouds filled the Trail, making the mountain shadow even darker and more foreboding. I used my headlamp far longer than any other morning hike on the Trail. After a few miles I passed another milestone, the 2100-mile mark. Someone had written the mileage on a rock near the Trail.

I took a picture of it and felt buoyed by the sign. It was the only photo taken today. After that, the cell phone shut down completely. The Trail was retaliating by denying me any more photos for the rest of the day.

The water was cold and swift at the West Branch of the Pleasant River ford and my feet froze in the crossing, but I waded in and over without incident. The battle between the Trail and me was still even at this point. The Trail smoothed out for several miles, and I knew that I had made the correct decision to push for a high-mileage day. Score another point for me.

I scratched a message in the dirt for Hopper and Bismarck and left another one for them at a lean-to, letting them know how far ahead I was if they decided to push for a high-mileage day. I made great time initially.

Shortly after lunch, I began a rigorous series of mountain climbs, rising from 718 feet to 2,406 feet. I crossed over Gulf Hagas Mountain, West Peak, Hay Mountain, and finally White Cap Mountain. Several climbs were steep and tiring, but I felt strong and charged up the slopes. Score one point for me. The ibuprofen was working extra well today. When I climbed back above the tree line, the wind howled, and it was cold and cloudy.

My first official view of Mt. Katahdin could have been seen from White Cap Mountain, but the Trail denied me the view by burying me inside clouds. Score a point for the Trail. Even if I had been able to see it, the Trail had already jinxed my camera phone. The fall colors were intensifying. I wish I had a picture. Points for the Trail!

I climbed down the mountain and made it to Logan Brook Lean-to at 4:30 p.m., still feeling strong. Score a point for me. I thought about going on but didn't want to strain my Achilles tendon, which felt good today. Loon and Tomo were at the shelter. They were the two Japanese men who had left Monson a day before me. We were all surprised that I had caught up to them. Everything was still wet from the rain two days ago, so we quickly gave up our attempt to start a campfire. Score a point for the Trail. Still, we had fun, and soon Indy arrived.

Other hikers I had never met before showed up with a message from Hopper and Bismarck. They weren't going to make it this far today. They'd stopped five miles behind for the night.

Loon carried a small set of tools for his camera gear, so we took apart my phone and cleaned the parts with camera cleaner. It worked! Score ten points for me!

I thought about pitching my tent, but sharing the evening's conversation with Loon, Tomo, and Indy in the shelter seemed more important than sleeping outside my tent. We all went to sleep early, because darkness fell quickly and completely in the box canyon. Trees obscured our view of the night sky. Score one last point for the Trail. Maybe the stars were hidden from sight, but I still won the day.

DAY 191 SEPTEMBER 24: LOGAN BROOK LEAN-TO TO COOPER BROOK FALLS LEAN-TO.
TODAY'S MILES: 11.7
TRIP MILES: 2,125.6

RW means Resting in Wilderness.

Only 59.7 more miles to go! It was a rather chilly night in the low forties, but not nearly as cold as a few days ago. We all got up early and Loon knocked over his stove while cooking breakfast. The flaming alcohol spilled and spread onto the shelter floor, causing a considerable fire. Loon tried to blow out the fire, but this just spread the alcohol flames farther into the shelter—where Indy continued to sleep, oblivious to the commotion.

Loon kept his cool and used the pot lid to douse the fire, one pot lid at a time. Soon the fire was out, nobody was hurt, and the shelter hadn't suffered any real damage. Indy never stirred. It reminded me of a similar incident told to me by a thru-hiker I had met while still training for the hike.

I hit the Trail at 7:20 a.m. and immediately made good time. It was all downhill with a minimum of roots and rocks. It was practically a racetrack! One easy rock-hop ford across shallow water didn't even slow me down today.

I ran into Gus on the Trail. I thought he was an old man, but found out he was actually my age. Gus walked slowly, carried a heavy pack, and wore lots of warm clothing. As we talked, I learned that this was his eighth day in the Wilderness and he was worried about his food supply. He had thru-hiked the Trail once before. He told me that he'd recently purchased his first home in a very rural part of Maine for $13,000 and was celebrating becoming a homeowner with this hike.

My phone worked this morning and I took several marvelous pictures, but it died again before lunch and wouldn't work again until evening. I enjoyed hiking today. Besides being a great Trail, the fall colors continued to grow in splendor. At times, the leaves appeared iridescent. Warm sunshine and a clear sky added to my pleasure, making it a great day to be hiking in the woods.

By 2:00 p.m. I had reached our rendezvous location. No one was there yet, so I chose the best campsite, washed clothes, waded and bathed in the stream, and then basked in the sun for a few hours. I ate my last protein bar and last cheese cube. In the process, some crumbs dropped into the waterfall pool, and little fish nibbled at them. They reminded me that I had missed both my spring and fall annual fishing trips this year. I just kept dropping crumbs into the water, wondering if I could catch a fish and eat it. I decided against it. I would let them live.

By now I was drinking massive amounts of water to stave off hunger. It worked, but I was peeing all the time. My Achilles tendon, knees, and hips were hurting, so I continued to rest and soak in the cold water for nearly an hour. I needed to slow down or I wasn't going to make it. I laid the camera/phone in the sun, hoping it would dry and fix itself. It did, but not until the evening.

About 5:30 p.m., Hopper and Bismarck arrived and told me they saw a magnificent view of Katahdin on White Cap Mountain this morning. Darn Trail! Yesterday, it refused to let me see that view. Gus hiked in after dark and set up in the shelter. He said he had about three days of food left and was worried that his food supply would run out before he was able to walk out of the Wilderness. It had taken him eight days to hike what we hiked in four days. Hopper and Bismarck gave him their two emergency candy bars.

I had one pack of ramen noodles that I carried for an emergency, but I didn't share it. I should have given it to him; that's what it was for. It was wrong not to give Gus the food. I had a food cache waiting for me the next morning.

DAY 192 SEPTEMBER 25: COOPER BROOK FALLS LEAN-TO TO NAHMAKANTA STREAM CAMPSITE.
TODAY'S MILES: 15.7
TRIP MILES: 2,141.3

RW means Ramen Weight. I was still carrying my emergency ramen noodles.

Forty-four miles to go! The night was calm and fairly warm. We got up early, and the three of us left before 7:00 a.m. Gus was sleeping soundly when we left. We hiked 3.7 miles in just over an hour and got to our food cache. We each had a bucket of food waiting for us that we'd paid a hostel to cache in the woods. I also had Nubbins' food drop, so I resealed the bucket and left it hidden in the woods. We discovered other buckets already open that had a few candy bars left behind. We grabbed them and left a note at the bridge for Gus to take the candy bars. Then we packed up our food and headed out.

The Trail was generally smooth but still had plenty of rocks and roots. We walked by lakes, ponds, and streams all day. I saw Katahdin for the first time at Pemadumcook Lake, looming up over the horizon, huge and imposing. The gray brown of Mt. Katahdin provided a perfect backdrop for the cherry red maples and golden yellow birch trees set in the foreground of a deep blue lake and cloudless sky. Awesome and inspiring, we just stood looking at Katahdin for a long time. Knowing that I had to hike another forty miles just to get to its base drove home the massive height of this mountain, compared to everything around it.

I am so lucky. This part of the Trail is low ground, and if it had been raining, I would be trudging through bogs. The long bog-log bridges are frequently under water after a rain in this section of the Trail. The trees are larger here, and many are cedar. I haven't noticed such large numbers of cedar trees before on the Trail. The lakes were lovely and we ate lunch on the beach at Jo Mary Lake. In the afternoon there was one river ford, but again, low water made it a simple rock hop.

That night, Loon told me Tomo is a well-known international outdoorsman in Japan, famous for bringing the sport of ultra-light backpacking to his country. Tomo owns his own outfitter store in Tokyo, called Gear Depot, and creates his own designs for hammocks and accessories. He was wearing one of his personally-designed down jackets.

DAY 193 SEPTEMBER 26: NAHMAKANTA STREAM CAMPSITE TO RAINBOW LAKE CAMPSITE.
TODAY'S MILES: 17.7
TRIP MILES: 2,159.0

RW means Rainbows in the Wilderness.

Twenty-six more miles! Last night, my winter gear proved to be too insulating, so I just used the sleeping bag as a blanket. We got up early and left camp before 7:00 a.m., intent on making it a big mile day. The Trail was generally smooth, but there were some slight ups and downs with many roots and rocks to trip over. We enjoyed the warm weather and fantastic fall colors that just keep intensifying every day. I took some pictures, but my camera/phone continued to work intermittently, not on demand. Not knowing whether the camera would work whenever I wanted to take a picture was driving me crazy.

As the day progressed we climbed 700 feet to the top of Mt. Nesuntabunt, and once again got a view of Mt. Katahdin. The Guide said it was a 16-mile line-of-sight view from this vantage point, but it looked so close and big. As we hiked, we enjoyed the fall colors and climbing up a gorge full of waterfalls. We ate on a lakeside beach and enjoyed the wonderful day.

Hopper frequently was in the lead today, which is unusual because she generally lags behind in order to be discrete when nature calls. This is surprisingly hard to do, even in the Wilderness. I now have a survival plan if I ever get lost anywhere in the wilderness. I'll just drop my pants! It is a near guarantee that someone will walk by.

Now that Hopper was ahead of us, she used her trekking pole to draw hearts in the dirt so Bismarck could track her location. Since I was hiking between them, I would spot the valentines before Bismarck. I thought it would be amusing to scratch my trail initials, RW, inside the hearts.

When Bismarck told her about the embellished hearts at their next break, Hopper was not amused. So, for the rest of the day I hung back and hiked with Bismarck. We discussed the

2,000 Miler award, and once again, he ribbed me about my secret. He told me neither one of them had ever applied for the award. Hopper and Bismarck didn't mind being excluded from the statistics.

He said they skim through the 2,000 Miler Award list every year, and based on the hikers they met, can pretty much pick out the ones who weren't entirely truthful. He thinks roughly 25 percent of all 2000 Milers didn't thru-hike the entire trail. I doubt the numbers are this high, but I had met plenty of aqua-blazers, blue-blazers, and yellow-blazers who believed they deserve the award.

Hopper arrived at the Rainbow Lake Campsite first, then me, and later Bismarck. Since I have a small two-person tent, I quickly found a nice campsite next to the lake. Bismarck and Hopper, however, had a very large two-person tent and couldn't find a level place to set it up. After a brief discussion, they decided to hike ahead and find a place to camp on the Trail. I decided to stay put and said I would catch up to them tomorrow. Soon, Loon and Tomo arrived and pitched their tarp and hammock near me.

As evening fell, I went to clean up at the lake with Loon. I took off my shirt, and he exclaimed, "You are so skinny!" I looked down. I hadn't been this skinny since I recovered from a near-fatal attack of pancreatitis 16 years ago. I must have been down at least twenty pounds, roughly ten pounds underweight for my build. With all the lean muscle, I was looking more like a teenager, and I liked the way I looked. It made me feel young again.

I ate most of my remaining food and sat by Rainbow Lake, listening to the loons and enjoying the sunset. The campsite was full of thru-hikers, many I knew. We all appreciated the warm night and great campsite. After sunset, a group of six thru-hikers arrived with their headlamps on. Since there were no other places for them to set up for the night, they laid their sleeping bags on the Trail and cowboy camped. Tomo, Loon, and I built a nice fire and chatted until the embers died. Night came early, and by 9:00 p.m. we were all inside our sleeping bags.

In the middle of the night I got up and walked to the lake. The night was crystal clear and stars crowded the sky. The Milky Way shimmered across the heavens in wisps of white vapor, while stars studded the foreground. A falling star streaked across the sky. I just looked up for a long time. This was my last night camping on the Trail.

DAY 194 SEPTEMBER 27: RAINBOW LAKE CAMPSITE TO ABOL BRIDGE.
TODAY'S MILES: 11.2
TRIP MILES: 2,170.2

RW means Really about the Wife.

Only 15.1 miles to go! Last night was very warm, but it wasn't the weather that kept me from sleeping well. It was my last night in the Wilderness, and the last night in a tent, and the first end of several more endings over the next few days. My time in the woods and on the Trail was ending. I got up about 4:45 a.m. and began to pack. Loon and Tomo got up, too. I was on the Trail by 5:50 a.m. and turned on my headlamp to see. Only protein bars left to eat. The morning was very quiet. I had to be careful leaving the campsite in order to avoid stepping on the hikers sleeping on the Trail.

I hiked quickly with my lightened pack and looked for Hopper and Bismarck along Rainbow Lake. This large and lovely lake's reflection of fall colors looked more like a mirror. I kept staring at it, knowing that as soon as I climbed the next mountain, I would never see it again.

I hoped Bismarck and Hopper hadn't hiked very far ahead yesterday. I didn't find them anywhere and called out their names at various places, but never got a reply. I hiked on and came to a picture-postcard view of Mt. Katahdin, and my camera/phone worked fine. I sat on the rock bluff, just staring at it. "The day after tomorrow, I climb you!"

Earlier in the week, Bismarck and I talked about climbing Mt. Katahdin together and then hiking down the Knife-Edge Trail afterwards. It's spectacular, but too dangerous to hike in anything but good weather. With the day of the climb approaching, the weather forecast was calling for rain. We both agreed not to take the Knife-Edge if it was raining.

I talked about leapfrogging ahead and climbing tomorrow on a good day, and then hiking south from the base of the mountain the next day to Abol Bridge. I didn't want to get held up by bad weather, and thought it would be best to climb Katahdin on a clear day. Bismarck said he wasn't going to do that. He only hiked north and preferred to wait for a good weather day, no matter how long it took.

I hiked on, hurrying and thinking Hopper and Bismarck must have left early or hiked farther than I expected. I was sure that I would catch up to them before the Hurd Brook Lean-to. The Trail was fast and easy, and in many places, the forest floor was totally blanketed with moss.

I didn't find them at the Hurd Brook Lean-to, and they hadn't signed the trail log yet. I WAS AHEAD OF THEM! It was the same situation as Rob all over again, but this time I knew I was ahead. I needed to slow down, not speed up.

I left a message in the logbook for them and headed out. I crossed a long bog-log bridge over a dried-up bog and skipped out of the Wilderness onto the Golden Road. A short walk later, I was asking for a table at the Abol Bridge Restaurant. While I was shown to a table, my wife pulled up in our truck. What great timing—and what a sight, to see her again after so many months!

There was another thru-hiker in the restaurant called Bikini. He had started out from Springer Mt. on March 18th, the same day as me. Yet, as unbelievable as it sounds, this was the first time we had ever run into each other on the Trail. Amazing!

Soon Hopper and Bismarck arrived, then Loon and Tomo. Bismarck and Hopper had hiked a little further last night and found a nice beach to camp on at Rainbow Lake. I introduced everybody to my wife, and we all enjoyed a wonderful lunch.

While there, we learned that the restaurant would be open for only one more day, and then would permanently close for the season. We worried that Nubbins and Journeymen wouldn't make it to the restaurant before it was shut down, and we didn't know how far behind they were. While at the restaurant, we learned that Gus was only one day behind us and had enough food to make it out of the Wilderness. A bucket full of good news!

Loon and Tomo were hiking on to the base of Mt. Katahdin and would camp there for the night. They were going to summit tomorrow. My wife drove Bismarck, Hopper, and me to Millinocket, where she had made reservations at a motel.

I decided to sleep on the decision about climbing Mt. Katahdin tomorrow or the day after. Tomorrow looked to be a gorgeous day, but the day after that was expected to be overcast, with rain in the early afternoon.

DAY 195 SEPTEMBER 28: ABOL BRIDGE TO KATAHDIN STREAM CAMPGROUND.
TODAY'S MILES: 9.9
TRIP MILES: 2,180.1

RW means Rosy Weather. We had fantastic weather today.

Hopper, Bismarck, Cathy, and I went to church in the morning. While sitting in the pew, I decided I would hike to the base of Mt. Katahdin today and just pray for a weather window tomorrow.

My wife drove us back to the Trail, and we hiked the last few miles to the base of Mt. Katahdin. We took our time and slackpacked under a warm and cloudless sky. We started about 10:00 a.m. The Trail was smooth and fast, and I used the new digital camera my wife bought for me, since my phone/camera was still unreliable. The fall colors were unlike anything I can remember seeing in Illinois. The trees radiated vibrant colors of eye-popping yellows and brilliant reds. I started to wish that I was climbing Mt. Katahdin today. Did I make the wrong decision? I may have to delay my climb until Wednesday, but only if the weather is really dangerous. Bismarck and Hopper are adamant about not climbing tomorrow.

We hiked along the Penobscot River for hours. The fall colors of the trees reflected on the flowing waters, and the pleasant rippling sounds of the river provided a musical accompaniment for this beautiful day. It really was a walk in the park: Baxter State Park! Were thru-hikers treated to this quick, easy trail by design before reaching the last few grueling miles up Mt. Katahdin? We stopped often to take pictures and enjoy the numerous waterfalls. There were two river fords, but just like last week, the water was low, turning the crossings into easy rock hops.

Just before the Katahdin Stream Campground, I got my final taste of trail magic. There in the woods, only 0.1 miles from the campground, a twelve-pack of root beer and several bags of donuts were lying by the side of the Trail. Ending with trail magic is so special! There wasn't much trail magic during the last three hundred miles.

When we reached the campground, we saw Indy, Tomo, Loon, Heike, and Cat, just as they were finishing their last few steps coming down from Mt. Katahdin. They had a fabulous day to summit with unforgettable views. We all celebrated and congratulated them. They wore the happiest, broadest smiles on their faces, and then we all started to say goodbye. Everyone was heading home as soon as possible.

My wife picked us up and drove us back to Millinocket, where the four of us enjoyed a dinner together at a nice restaurant. I went to bed early, determined to summit the next day. The latest weather forecast called for clouds in the morning with rain in the early afternoon. I can make it if I leave early enough! I told my wife about my secret; she was surprised, but agreed with my plan.

DAY 196 SEPTEMBER 29: KATAHDIN STREAM CAMPGROUND TO MT. KATAHDIN.
TODAY'S MILES: 5.2
TRIP MILES: 2,185.3

RW means Retired Walker.

The Appalachian Trail ends at the top of this mountain. The climb up Mt. Katahdin is 5.2 miles up and 5.2 miles back down. Of course, the return miles back down don't count as official Trail miles. Native Americans called this mountain "Kette-Adene," which means The Great Mountain. I would have to climb 4,162 feet, or 79 percent of its nearly mile-high summit, to 5,268 feet. It was the longest single climb on the entire Appalachian Trail, and the last great challenge, but one the Trail had prepared me for with 2,180 tough practice miles.

I decided to climb alone. It didn't matter if there weren't going to be great views today. I was completing the adventure of a lifetime, and weather, good and bad, is part of the adventure. I didn't mind bad weather, although I do get tired of it. Frequently, bad weather can be more interesting than good weather. Today was no exception. Besides, I am the guy who trudges into the shelter after the rain has been pouring for ten minutes, instead of the guy who skates in just before the first raindrop. Climbing Mt. Katahdin in bad weather must be my karma.

This was it, the end of my pilgrimage, and I was facing it alone. It was something I had to do on my own. Everyone I started with in the beginning had succumbed to the Trail. The A.T. was harsh, and it controlled the life of every thru-hiker. Now I was climbing on hallowed ground, headed for its most sacred summit. When I started out on this journey last March from Springer Mountain, I wondered what I would find on the Trail. What I found was adventure, challenge, and friendship.

I suffered and enjoyed, hungered and feasted. I traveled outwardly more than 2,000 miles, while inwardly, my soul walked the universe. I witnessed many of His most beautiful creations and felt the Hand of God. At the end, I joined up with a group of pilgrims who brought me through the Wilderness to a sacred mountain. Now, after 196 days of hiking, I was finally going to reach the end of my journey.

I left the motel at 5:00 a.m., grabbed a drive-thru breakfast and headed for the base of the mountain. By 6:00 a.m. I was waiting for the gates to open at Baxter State Park, and by 6:30 a.m. I was standing at the point where I had stopped hiking the day before in the Katahdin Stream Campground.

An official warning sign greeted me at the start of the climb. It said: "You are entering Maine's Largest Wilderness. Your safety is your responsibility. Set a turnaround time and stick to it. Your destination is your safe return to the trailhead. Rescue can be many hours in arriving." I told my wife to expect me back by 2:30 p.m.

With adrenaline pumping and fortified with ibuprofen, I nearly ran from the campground. I felt as if I was going to talk to the all-knowing Wise Man at the top of the mountain. What revelations awaited me at the summit?

I only carried essentials in a light daypack. Trees dazzled with fall colors, and birds sang in the lower elevations. I passed a roaring waterfall. They were all celebrating and announcing to the world the end of my journey. It had been a four-season hike! In the beginning, new life was barely stirring from winter's slumber. And now, at the end of the journey, New England's display of fall colors heralded the final pageant.

The Trail steepened. I was above the tree line and in the clouds. I couldn't see the summit, or much of anything else, because of the impenetrable clouds. I was excited, yet I wondered what it must feel like for flip-floppers. Their journey doesn't end here, but at some nondescript place on the Trail. Would they experience the same exhilaration that I now felt?

By 9:00 a.m. the temperature was noticeably colder as I continued to climb. Clouds thickened and filled the air with mist. The ground was wetter, the rocks more slippery, and visibility shrank to two hundred yards. I continued to climb. The Trail rose even higher, becoming a hand-over-hand boulder climb on a narrow rock spine looking down on sheer cliffs on both sides. Iron handholds drilled into the rock were necessary for climbing up and over large boulders. This section was 40 percent of the elevation change, 1,668 feet in only one mile.

I didn't look back, only forward, but I began to wonder what climbing back down that dangerous section would be like with bad weather moving in. Had I made the wrong decision to climb in questionable weather? No, I could do this! The Trail had prepared and tested me for this very moment.

At the top of this section, I reached a part of the mountain known as the Tableland, a half-mile of fairly flat land marked by cairns. I hiked from cairn to cairn, barely able to pick out the next in the thick clouds. I begrudgingly stopped to put on rain gear. I was soaked in the mist and shivering. Everything became strangely silent and still. The familiar sound of the wind was absent, and no creatures could be heard—only my labored breathing.

Then suddenly out of the mist and clouds, two young thru-hikers appeared from behind: Skippy and Nora-V. I had met Skippy in Massachusetts, and Nora-V somewhere on the Trail. Skippy got his name because he was perpetually happy and never seemed to get tired. He is 24 and looks 18. Nora-V was a striking 25-year-old redhead who had gotten very sick with Norovirus in Damascus. They both passed me by quickly and disappeared into the mists ahead.

At 9:45 a.m., as I completed the last steep hill climb, I finally spotted a large, weather-beaten wooden sign about a hundred yards ahead. It was perched on top of a pile of wet, reddish rocks and it announced the summit of Mt. Katahdin. I scrambled on top of the summit sign and Skippy took my picture, then I took his picture, and Nora-V's picture. Skippy pulled out a bottle of champagne. We all had a drink, toasted each other, and laughed as the weather worsened and a light rain started to fall. Clouds gathered around us, heavy and wet, and visibility fell to yards. We ignored the weather and had a group hug. We had achieved the goal.

I asked Skippy what happened to his two hiking companions, the pink blazers. He said the guy fell three weeks ago and broke an arm while going through Mahoosuc Notch. His girlfriend stayed with him. Skippy wasn't sure if they would finish. After a quick calculation, I determined they had been ahead of me when they attempted the Notch.

Skippy and Nora-V left quickly, and I had the summit to myself for a while. After about fifteen minutes of alone time, I started back down—cold, wet, but energized. The summit had delivered everything, and more. It wasn't about the view. A mountain top view in good weather, shared with a large party of hikers at the top, would have been nice, but I didn't miss it.

Covered in clouds, I didn't even notice the climb down over the wet, slippery boulders. Suddenly I was back in the lower elevations, surrounded by the warm, lively beauty of the forest colors. It was dry here. The rain had stayed at the top. On the way down, I passed a dozen or so thru-hikers, including the hiker with the katana sword. Like me, they were all feverish to finish, hardened by their journey, and ready for anything.

Once back in the trees, I realized I was hungry and ate my lunch under a towering pine tree overlooking the Katahdin Stream Falls. By 1:30 p.m. I was back at the campground, registered, and officially logged in as the 694th thru-hiker to climb Mt. Katahdin this year. This number also represents northbounders, flip-floppers, and southbounders.

In the campground I ran into Journeymen and Nubbins, who were setting up camp just as it started to rain. They planned to summit tomorrow, or the next day, depending on the weather. Tomorrow's weather forecast was awful.

Cathy picked me up with the truck. Just before pulling out of the parking lot, we offered a ride to a couple of young thru-hikers who had just hiked in to the campground and hoped to summit Katahdin tomorrow. They were a couple. He was called Sparklefeet because his shoes had once been covered in mica, and she was called Gary, short for Gary Busey. Gary was still recovering from Bell's palsy caused by Lyme disease. She was taking antibiotics. Bell's palsy or Lyme disease wasn't going to stop her from completing the hike. After Sparklefeet and Gary finished the climb tomorrow, they planned to drive nonstop all the way to Oregon and get back in time to start their senior year of college.

Bismarck, Hopper, Cathy and I went to the Appalachian Trail Café in Millinocket, where I signed one of the ceiling tiles. Now considered a thru-hike tradition, successful thru-hikers visit the A.T. Café after summiting Mt. Katahdin and sign their trail name on the ceiling. We eagerly scanned the ceiling tiles, hoping to find trail names of fellow thru-hikers. I found the names of Left-Turn, Isn't Black, Bear Bag, Loon, Surefoot, Rob, Murphy, Guy-on-a-Buffalo, Cat, Cowboy, Gargamel, Cornwall, Bree, BlueJay, and Racewalker. I saw Loon and Tomo eating in the café, and we said our goodbyes for the very last time. Bismarck and Hopper's names were already on ceiling tiles from earlier thru-hikes. I got my Appalachian Trail Passport stamped for the 44th, nearly completing the book, which holds a maximum of 48 stamps. Later that night, I said goodbye to Bismarck and Hopper. My wife and I were leaving in the morning and heading home.

THE SECRET

RW means Redemptive Winner.

A close reading of this journal will reveal that on Day 93, June 17th, my daily miles are zero (0), but the total miles are higher than the prior day. I didn't go back and hike the leapfrogged miles after hitching a ride into Duncannon. I was left in a bad situation when the unconfirmed shuttle driver didn't show up at the appointed road crossing, and I was too injured to hike the 9.1 miles to Duncannon.

On June 17th, I couldn't get a ride out of Duncannon to the spot where I left the Trail, so I took a much-needed zero day. The next day, I headed north on the Trail from Duncannon.

I knew that even with all the great things I'd discovered and experienced on the hike, missing those few miles would haunt me and whisper, "You did not hike it all, like you said!" I would be a liar if I didn't go back and walk those last 9.1 miles.

After Mt. Katahdin, my wife and I drove down the Eastern seaboard, dined on Maine lobster, and toured historic sites along the way toward Duncannon. During the drive, I learned that Bismarck, Hopper, Journeymen, Nubbins, Mad Jack, and Hey Everybody had all summited Mt. Katahdin.

My wife dropped me off on the Trail outside of Duncannon at 1:30 p.m., and I hiked the last 9.1 miles into town. She planned to wait for me at the Doyle Hotel bar. In an unexpected twist of fate, the Doyle Hotel became the official end of my 2014 Appalachian Trail thru-hike.

Walking into the bar, I was greeted with the sound of applause, a round of handshakes, and several celebration toasts. Miss Vicky and I posed together at the bar and formally marked the end of the trail with one final photograph.

Maybe finishing at the Doyle Hotel wasn't a mountain top experience like Mt. Katahdin, but it was uplifting. The weight of an invisible backpack slipped off my shoulders. I really was a thru-hiker.

BISMARCK'S SECRET

Bismarck held the greatest secret of anyone I met on the Trail. About seven months after I completed the Trail, Bismarck, whose real name is James T. Hammes, was captured by the FBI on May 16, 2015, at the Trail Days festival in Damascus, Virginia. He had approximately $11,000 in cash and $4,000 of gift cards in his backpack. Over an 11-year period Bismarck had embezzled roughly $8.7 million from the Cincinnati-based company G&J Pepsi-Cola bottlers. He fled in 2009 when his crime was discovered and lived most of the time on the Appalachian Trail as a fugitive. He was charged with 75 counts, including money laundering and wire fraud. On October 23, 2015, he pleaded guilty to one count of wire fraud. The other charges were dropped provided he return the mostly-unspent money and explain to the FBI how he had hid the money for so long. At the time of this writing, he was still awaiting sentencing.

I often wrote about Bismarck during the last month of my hike, and looking back, the only time he didn't tell the truth was when he talked about his source of funds and former profession. He told me he owned a company that installed computer peripherals, printers, scanners, etc. to complicated computer networks in Bismarck, North Dakota. This wasn't true and I never learned the reason why he chose the name Bismarck.

AFTERWORD

RW means Really Worth it.

The first question many ask is: "Would you do it again?" There are sections of the Trail I hope to hike again, someday, but no thru-hike. I accomplished far more than I planned for or thought was possible. The Trail is like entering the Land of Oz, and I traveled along the Yellow Brick Road.

My adventure was wonderful, and I met many people who I could easily say are "friends for life." I miss several of them already, and have remained in contact with a few through social media and the exchange of cards and letters. Some I have even seen again.

The Trail forced me to do new things, like stay in hostels, hitchhike, confront rattlesnakes, live in the woods, befriend the homeless, rely on the generosity of strangers, and become involved in a trail culture that I never knew existed. The Trail changed me and brought me closer to God.

All cultures have their own jargon, and the A.T. is no exception. The many different ways to hike the Trail are coded for easy reference. When hiking your own hike, or HYOH, the Trail offers different paths to follow, each blazed with their own descriptive color: white, blue, yellow, brown, pink, and aqua. Each of the blaze colors denotes a hue of purity. The devoted hiker must white blaze continually in one direction and carry a full pack. The executive hiker's only objective is to walk from one end to the other, without any other restrictions. Hikers are further subdivided into groups: SOBOs, NOBOs, flip-floppers, skippers, and grazers. Additional titles that may be bestowed on a hiker are: thru-hiker, section-hiker, LASH, day-hiker, long-distance hiker, and executive hiker. There were night hikes and day hikes, and PUDs. I stayed in huts, shelters, lean-tos, hostels, hiker-motels, and of course, my tent. I experienced hiker perfume, hiker bubbles, and AYCE. I discovered trail magic, trail angels, 2,000 Milers, and triple crowners. I am sure there is plenty more trail lingo that I have forgotten already.

Torn pages from two guidebooks, the AWOL and Companion, travelled with me at all times and became my compass and Northern Star. For a NOBO like me, I learned that no matter what direction I faced, east is always right, west is always left, south is always behind, and north is always ahead of me. This, of course, is completely opposite for SOBOs.

Before I started, I thought I would spend my days involved in a great physical test of endurance, alone with my thoughts. It was a test of endurance, and I had plenty of alone time, but the Trail also provided a richness of experiences that I didn't expect. I understand why many choose to hike the Trail repeatedly. Trail life is infectious and a good alternative to the daily grind.

Once I climbed Mt. Katahdin, I felt like Dorothy after she clicked her heels and suddenly found herself back in Kansas. "There's no place like home!" The A.T. ended just that quickly for me.

Before I started the hike, my doctor performed a thorough examination After my return, he repeated the tests. Despite losing seventeen pounds, walking 2,185 miles, living in the woods for nearly seven months, and eating poorly, my test results hadn't changed significantly. I was in good health before I started, and remain in good health today. I was tested for Lyme disease. I never got it, even though I was bitten by many ticks.

Toward the end, I was taking 1600 mg of ibuprofen a day, and went cold turkey after climbing Mt. Katahdin without any side effects, other than experiencing pain in my knees and Achilles tendond. My knees hurt for about three weeks after the hike. The Achilles tendons are still sore, but my feet are fine.

I quickly gained back five pounds, and by the end of December had gained ten more pounds. I lost upper body strength. My dentist was concerned about my wisdom teeth and a bone infection in my jaw. In the end, I had all my wisdom teeth removed and underwent four periodontal surgeries to save the rest of my teeth.

The hike was far more expensive than expected. The medical bills, travel expenses, cost of hostels and motels, food, shuttles, and replacement of clothes, shoes, and equipment were all under-estimated. I don't know what it cost in total, but it was significantly more than the guidebooks had estimated.

The second question I hear is: "What would I do differently?" Experience is a wonderful teacher. I wouldn't worry so much about resupplying and hitchhiking, and I wouldn't spend as much time in hostels. I would monitor weekly mileage and not worry about keeping a daily hiking plan.

Finally, people ask me how many of the hikers I met completed the hike. I don't really know, but most of the hikers I mention in this book did successfully complete their thru-hike. Some of the names and places have been changed to protect the identity of the people involved.

Good luck, and thanks for all the well wishes. Keep in touch and contact me if you plan to thru-hike. I would like to follow your progress and provide encouragement. See you on the Trail!

PHOTOGRAPHS

Trail gear at start of hike

Tree of Lost Soles at Neel Gap, Day 3

Bear bagging at Tray Mountain Shelter, Day 5

Miss Janet's Van, Erwin, TN, Day 29

Leaving Silers Bald Shelter in Great Smoky Mountains National Park, Day 17

Filtering water at Paint Branch campsite, NC, Day 21

Mark and RW camping near Mile 524, Day 50

Isn't Black, Bear Bag, and Curious George near Audie Murphy's grave, VA. Day 61

Rhododendron Wonderland near Dragon's Tooth, Day 62

McAfee Knob, VA., Day 63

Little Stony Man Cliffs in Shenandoah National Park, Day 77

Hiking in thunderstorm, Day 71

Snowstorm at Beauty Spot Gap, Erwin, TN, Day 30

*RW, Steve, and Denise at Big Meadows Wayside in Shenandoah
National Park, Day 76*

1500 miles near Bear Mountain, CT, Day 136

Climbing iron rungs in Lambert Ridge, NH, Day 156

Climbing to Superfund site near Palmerton, PA, Day 121

Fording Piscataquis River, Maine, day 185

Mt. Washington, Day 164

RW in Hundred Mile Wilderness, Maine, Day 190

Mt. Katahdin summit, Day 196

EQUIPMENT RECOMMENDATIONS

Based on my 2014 Appalachian Trail thru-hike experience, here are certain equipment revisions and recommendations that I would suggest for anyone considering or planning an A.T. hike in the near future.

- Mouse and insect deterrent: Other than Deet for mosquitos, I didn't personally use any insect deterrents. However, Penguinman used the following homemade remedy and swears it works: 4 oz. of Aloe gel, 2 oz. of Tea Tree oil, and 10 drops of Peppermint oil. He found it deterred mice and doubled as a hand sanitizer. For ticks and other biting insects, many hikers used Permethrin Insect Repellent made by Sawyer International.

- Trekking Poles: I used Black Diamond poles. They worked fine, but I wore out the bottom point on one pole, and twice on the other pole. I would prefer to hike with Leke poles instead, because replacement parts are abundant, and Black Diamond parts are hard to find. I don't recommend attempting the Trail without trekking poles.

- Tent: I love my Big Agnes Fly Creek UL2. It worked well, never leaked, and the two-person tent is ideal. I would try using a hammock if I did it again. The Trail is much more suited to a hammock than a tent.

- Water Filter: Forget the Sawyer Mini, use the full size Sawyer.

- Backpack: I used two packs: a Granite Gear 60L and a Gossamer Gear Mariposa. Both worked well, but each had flaws. The Granite Gear is tough, but is just a big sack on your back. There were no condition issues with the pack, and I hiked 1240 miles with it. The Gossamer Gear pack is lighter and more organized, but far less durable. Gossamer Gear agreed to replace the hip belt because the pockets blew out, but wouldn't do anything about the holes in the pack. I hiked with the Gossamer Gear pack 945 miles and owned it for only two months.

- Sleeping Bag: I liked my Sierra Design 12-degree bag and will continue to use it. It was perfect for the cold days at the start and end of the Trail. My REI 45-degree bag proved to be inadequate and I would prefer a warmer summer bag, or to supplement it with clothing. I used a silk bag liner and recommend its use to everybody. It keeps the bag clean and adds comfort.

- Sleeping Pad: I used two. My favorite is the self-inflating Therma-rest. I didn't like the Gossamer Gear sponge 3/4 length pad. It was light, but grossly inadequate.

- Stove: I used the Esbit alcohol stove and found it worked well for me. Fuel is easy to get, and the yellow bottle of Heet works great. A canister stove is also good, and its fuel is easy to obtain. I am considering a chimney alcohol stove set-up for future hikes because it appears to be more efficient.

- Cook Set: I had a 30 oz. pot and a cup, but a 20 oz. pot with a lid would have been more efficient.

- Headlamp: I suggest getting a headlamp with a strong red spotlight. My current headlamp only has a wide-angled red light, but otherwise is rechargeable and works fine.

- Shoes: Get what works for you, but I recommend getting a size at least 1/2 size larger and wider. Your feet will swell. I used trail shoes and waterproof Gortex boots. Gortex boots were desirable for the first month, and later, from Massachusetts north. Those are the wet sections of the Trail, and wet feet and wet socks took a terrible toll on my feet and were the major cause of blisters. The idea that trail shoes help keep your feet dry is only partly true. They only work in dry weather. Otherwise your feet stay wet as long as the Trail stays wet, which is frequently for days.

- Socks: Darn Tough, the best there is.

- Trailjournals.com: This is a great site and I highly recommend it. Use it to write your journal daily and post to it when you can. You can register and set up an online account at www:trailjournals.com.

- Phone Service: Verizon is it. AT&T did not work well south of mid-Virginia, and worked poorly in Vermont, New Hampshire, and Maine. The other carriers are worse. Hikers with Verizon seemed to have much better luck getting a signal.

CPSIA information can be obtained
at www.ICGtesting.com
Printed in the USA
LVOW05s1928110416

482845LV00041B/134/P